Fashion in Fiction

Fashion in Fiction

Text and Clothing in Literature, Film, and Television

Edited by
Peter McNeil, Vicki Karaminas,
and Catherine Cole

LEARNING
RESOURCES
CENTRE

HAVERING
COLLEGE

Oxford • New York

English edition
First published in 2009 by
Berg
Editorial offices:
First Floor, Angel Court, 81 St Clements Street, Oxford OX4 1AW, UK
175 Fifth Avenue, New York, NY 10010, USA

© Peter McNeil, Vicki Karaminas, and Catherine Cole 2009

All rights reserved.
No part of this publication may be reproduced in any form
or by any means without the written permission of Berg.

Berg is the imprint of Oxford International Publishers Ltd.

Library of Congress Cataloging-in-Publication Data

Fashion in fiction : text and clothing in literature, film and television / edited by
Peter McNeil, Vicki Karaminas and Catherine Cole.
p. cm.
ISBN 978-1-84788-357-5 (pbk.) — ISBN 978-1-84788-359-9 (cloth)
1. Clothing and dress in literature.   2. Clothing and dress in motion pictures.
3. Clothing and dress on television.   4. Fashion in literature.   5. Fashion in motion
pictures.   I. McNeil, Peter, 1966–   II. Karaminas, Vicki.   III. Cole, Cathy, 1950–
PN56.C684F38 2009
809'.93355—dc22
2009000917

British Library Cataloguing-in-Publication Data

A catalogue record for this book is available from the British Library.

ISBN 978 1 84788 359 9 (Cloth)
978 1 84788 357 5 (Paper)

Typeset by Apex CoVantage, LLC, Madison, WI, USA
Printed in the UK by the MPG Books Group

www.bergpublishers.com

Contents

List of Illustrations

Plates

Figures   Page

Acknowledgments

This volume began life in the setting of an international conference, *Fashion in Fiction,* conducted jointly between the Faculties of Design, Architecture and Building; and Humanities and Social Sciences at the University of Technology, Sydney (UTS), in May 2007. UTS supports the interrelationship of scholarship and the creative industries and the participation of writers, filmmakers, journalists, designers, dressmakers, and curators in the conference attested to this nexus. Participants journeyed to Sydney from Stockholm, Great Britain, New Zealand, and the United States from universities and other organizations to participate in the conference, and this marked the beginning of long-distance scholarly relationships. The editors would like to thank professors Andrew Benjamin, Desley Luscombe, and Theo van Leeuwen for their encouragement and support.

Images are key to the way in which our authors argue in this volume, and for the opportunity to publish in high-quality color we thank both Dr. Louise Wallenberg of the Centre for Fashion Studies at Stockholm University and Professor P. J. Smith, the School of Creative Media, RMIT University. We also are indebted to Eric Hagan of the School of Design, UTS, for creating the striking fashion cover illustration. We also thank Bronwyn Clark-Coolee, Dr. Ian Henderson, Emily Howes, and Susan Osmond for their assistance. Marking as it did the retirement presentation of one of Australia's significant art and dress historians, Associate Professor Margaret Maynard of the University of Queensland, the conference and this volume attest to the growth of fashion studies in Australia in the past twenty-five years. We dedicate this publication to Sydney writer and editor Pat Skinner, who passed away suddenly during the completion of the manuscript.

List of Contributors

Rosy Aindow's current research is concerned with the representation of clothing in late nineteenth-century literature. She is interested in whether clothing as subject matter actually constitutes a literary convention in its own right.

Denise Amy Baxter is assistant professor of art history at the University of North Texas. Her research focuses on the relationships between material culture and the constitution of the self. A co-edited book, *Architectural Space in Eighteenth-Century Europe: Constructing Identities and Interiors,* is forthcoming.

Marilyn Casto is Associate Professor of Interior Design in the School of Architecture and Design at Virginia Tech University, where she teaches design history. Her book, *Historic Theaters of Kentucky,* won the Southeast Society of Architectural Historians Annual Book Award in 2000.

Catherine Cole is Professor of Creative Writing at RMIT University (Royal Melbourne Institute of Technology), Australia. She is the author of *The Poet Who Forgot; The Grave at Thu Le; Dry Dock; Skin Deep;* and *Private Dicks and Fiesty Chicks: An Interrogation of Crime Fiction.*

Sophia Errey combines the roles of artist and art historian and lectures at RMIT University, Melbourne. Her current research is focused on the historical and ethnic influences on contemporary fashion and the relationship of fashion and identity.

Gabrielle Finnane is a filmmaker, media artist, and writer on film and art. Her works include the video trilogy *On a Dark Night* and the film *I, Eugenia,* which won the Dendy Award for Australian Film (General) in 1998. She lectures in the School of Media Arts, College of Fine Arts, University of New South Wales.

Sarah Gilligan is a Lecturer in Media, Film, and Photography at Hartlepool College of Further Education (United Kingdom). She is the author of *Teaching Women and Film* (British Film Institue, 2003). Her research interests include work on Gwyneth Paltrow as a fashion icon, postheritage cinema, teen films, and sci-fi/action cinema.

Maja Gunn is a Swedish designer based in Stockholm and New York. She has worked for companies including H&M, Marc Jacobs, and the Royal Dramatic Theatre, Sweden. Parallel with her work as a designer, Gunn is guest lecturer at Stockholm University and HDK-Steneby Gothenburg University.

Joseph Henry Hancock II (PhD) is an Assistant Professor at Drexel University in the Department of Fashion and Design & Merchandising. His work is focused in the areas of retail branding, popular culture, and men's style. He serves on the boards of Popular/American Culture Associations of America, Fashion Group International, and *Journal of American Culture.*

Catherine Harper is Head of the School of Architecture and Design, University of Brighton. She published *Intersex* (Berg) in 2007 and is writing a second book, *Fabrics of Desire* (Berg). Catherine is U.K. Editor of *Textile: The Journal of Cloth and Culture,* Contributing Editor for *Selvedge,* and a board member of *International Journal of Fashion Design, Technology and Education.*

Clair Hughes held the position of Professor of English and American Literature at International Christian University of Tokyo. Recently retired, Professor Hughes has written several books on British art and various articles on Henry James and Anita Brookner, including *Henry James and the Art of Dress* in 2001 (Palgrave) and *Dressed in Fiction* in 2005 (Berg).

Vicki Karaminas is Senior Lecturer in Fashion Theory and Design Studies at the School of Design, The University of Technology, Sydney. She is a critical theory and cultural studies scholar with a background in gender studies and visual culture. Forthcoming titles include *Queer Style* (Berg), *Designer Kids: Children's Fashion* (Berg, co-author with Michelle Bakar), and *The Men's Fashion Reader* (Berg, co-editor with Peter McNeil).

Tim Laurence is General Manager Education at UTS: Insearch and Adjunct Professor in Design at the University of Technology, Sydney. His area of research is the interrelationship of art and design, specifically hybrid practices that obscure the discipline boundaries of both art and design.

Peter McNeil is Professor of Design History at The University of Technology, Sydney, and Foundation Chair of Fashion Studies at Stockholm University. He is the co-editor of *Shoes: A History from Sandals to Sneakers* (Berg, with Giorgio Riello). Forthcoming titles include *Fashion: Critical and Primary Sources* (4 volumes, Berg); and *The Fashion History Reader: Global Perspectives* (Routledge, with Giorgio Riello).

Margaret Maynard is Associate Professor and an Honorary Research Consultant in the School of English, Media Studies and Art History, The University of Queensland. Her most recent book is *Dress and Globalisation* (2004, Manchester University Press). She is Editor of the forthcoming "Volume Seven: Australia, New Zealand, and the Pacific," of *The Berg Encyclopaedia of World Dress and Fashion.*

Toby Slade lectures at the University of Tokyo. His research explores Asian modernity, the social life of things, and the history and theory of fashion. He is the author of the forthcoming *Japanese Fashion* (Berg).

Dagmar Venohr is a dressmaker, textile artist, fashion journalist, and cultural scientist. She is a doctoral candidate in the department of Arts and Media at the University of Potsdam and scholarship holder of the Hans-Böckler-Foundation, Düsseldorf.

Louise Wallenberg holds a doctorate in Cinema Studies from Stockholm University (2002). Since 2006 she has been involved with the establishment and development of the Centre for Fashion Studies at Stockholm University, where she currently works as its Director. She has published on queer and mainstream films, fashion and film and feminist and queer philosophies.

Foreword

Fashion has its own set of reliable companions such that, if they disappeared, fashion could not be. They inspire, support, and vitalize each other in a crossing relationship that is symbiotic, flexible, and constantly changing. These companions are our dreams, desires, and idealizations. Like fashion, they are nebulous, abstract, and elusive phenomena, always aspiring for something more and something better, constantly evading any clear-cut definition. Perhaps they can be described and defined only by their opposites, which must be seen as tangible, concrete, material, and "real." Fashion's most obvious counterpart is, of course, dress: the very material we put on our bodies, that which we wear next to our skin, and hence, that which gets soiled and worn out through an encounter with and through time. Fashion is the "idea," the non-real. With desires, dreams, and idealizations as its counterparts and companions, and as its main driving force—fashion is also *fictive*. Fashion, then, is a species of fiction.

It is the fictive essence of fashion, its constant aspiration, that makes any kind of fashion-tangibility impossible. Fashion always sits on the brink of becoming passé: no matter how new it is, it is always about to cease to be "fashion." It is the idea, the dream, the ideal construction that we might aspire to incorporate, but once it is *on* the body—as dress and clothes—it no longer is, it can no longer be. Fashion has to do with *becoming,* and not with being, and hence it is a process that cannot be fixed or frozen.

Yet, as Elizabeth Wilson has argued, clothes (and dress) are also images, communicating "more subtly than most objects and commodities, precisely because of that intimate relationship to our bodies and our selves" (Wilson 1985a: vii). Following Wilson, we can argue that like fashion, dress can also be understood as a fiction, since it functions as narration and expression of self. If fashion is about idealization, striving for a perfection that can never be, then dress is about the actual presenting of the self, which is always a type of constructing the self. This is done in relation to fashion, whether one tries to follow the rules of fashion or not. Fashion dictates rules for being fashionable (which is a project doomed to failure), and dress is the expression of and the negotiation with this "chimera," fashion.

But fashion not only dictates rules for how to be "in" fashion: it also dictates rigid rules for the management of gender, sex, and sexuality. Dress is the primary object we use in our masquerading as sexually different individuals—and this masquerade is crucial for our passing, passing as bodies that matter. Most fashion is the idea of a perfect dualist sexual difference, dress being the concrete manifestation of this difference. In a not totally erroneous gesture, fashion has been the target for harsh criticism from sociologists and feminists alike. It has always been women's fashion that has occupied the center of judgmental attention. Fashion dictates rigid rules both for femininity and for masculinity, hence reinforcing the idea of gender difference and (hetero-)sexual difference as "real" and as natural. As a form of fiction, fashion—and dress—can therefore be said to constitute a "gender technology." It works in ways similar to those of film, television, advertising, and other powerful frameworks and mechanisms that strive to form and mould individuals into gendered beings (de Lauretis 1987). Like other fictions, fashion can also be understood as a counterpoint to dominant discourses of gender, sex, and sexuality. In its fictionality and its playfulness, fashion can also serve to question sexual differences as natural and "real." Fashion holds within itself—together with its companions, those dreams, desires, and idealizations—a powerful will to transgression and denaturalization. Even when seen to reinforce these dualist differences, it actually transgresses them by laying bare their constructed nature. It exposes differences of gender, sex, and sexuality as social forms. Furthermore, fashion has the will and the power to mix and to mingle: to steal paraphernalia belonging to one gender and present it to the other.

Fashion moves, like most cultural expressions, in a pendulous manner, from one extreme to another. It is always situational, always closely connected to political, economic, cultural, and social discourses. Let me give an example: in studying women's fashion during the past 200 years, we can see a marked swinging movement between those fashions that were characterized by physical freedom and those fashions characterized by physical restraint, between outspoken wishes for androgyny and outspoken desires for a marked sexual difference, which have often been of a rather sexualized kind. By looking at how fashion has moved between these two positions, we learn a great deal about gender relations, about male dominance and female subordination—about the longing for a gendered and sexual freedom that refuses any dualism. Studying this movement, we can also see how heterosexuality and heteronormativity alike have exerted power and how closely related they are to the idea of a natural sexual difference. By emphasizing this difference as normal, desirable, and natural—always in line with homophobic and misogynist discourses—desire for the other has been forwarded as natural, whereas all other sexual desires have been rendered deviant. When studying this movement, we can also see how the focus on sexual difference, heterosexuality, and heteronormativity has been challenged by fashion from time to time.

In times of greater acceptance and openness, all of which seem to be tainted by pro-feminist powers, fashion can work as a vehicle for pluralism and transgression. Fashion as powerful fiction—with help from desires and dreams, but also with the support of idealizations—may contribute to a deconstruction of the rigid models upon which the dualist sexes, genders, and sexualities are based. I imagine—and think it possible—that fashion can initiate a move from dualism to pluralism that not only is for the interim, between longer periods of torpor, but will also be of a more permanent status. To critics of poststructurally informed feminist and queer theory, this belief may appear wishful, utopian thinking, maybe another form of imaginative desire.

But to dream the utopian is not to dream the impossible, for, as Jacques Derrida writes, there must be something that precedes that dream, something that nurtures its existence: "But where would the 'dream' of the innumerable come from, if it is indeed a dream? Does the dream itself not prove that what is dreamt of must be there in order for it to provide the dream?" (Derrida, 1995: 108).

Louise Wallenberg
Director, The Centre for Fashion Studies,
Stockholm University, Sweden

Introduction

Fashion in Fiction: Text and Clothing in Literature, Film, and Television

Peter McNeil, Vicki Karaminas,
and Catherine Cole

Any story must say a lot about the human body; if not, it must talk about its clothes ... The fabric of clothes indicates the hidden secret of his characters.

> Manoly Lascaris on the writing of Patrick White, Australian
> Nobel Laureate 1973; recollection of Vrasidas Karalis

The literary theorist Roland Barthes (1915–1980) proposed that "real" or "actual Fashion" was less able to produce a deep understanding of the mechanism of clothing than a focus upon "written" or, as he put it, "described" fashion. In so doing, Barthes did not wish to ignore the object-based or economic function of fashion; rather, this dimension did not serve the method that he was proposing. Nor was Barthes suggesting that fashion was a type of cultural mirage or illusion. Far from it; Barthes was concerned with the significance and weightiness of fashion in the practice and discourse of everyday life. Barthes' strategy was to underline fashion's communicative and mythic dimension, fashion as "described," in order to argue that fashion could be explained through the techniques of structural linguistics applied to a nonlinguistic object, fashion-clothing. To Barthes, fashion was a language that was authorless; hence very significantly within his system it was not the story of designers or makers. Barthes' structural method encouraged a greater comparative method across different genres and forms. As he noted, "Even if the garment of fashion remained purely imaginary (without affecting real clothing), it would constitute an incontestable element of mass culture, like pulp fiction, comics, and movies" (Barthes 1985: 9). Barthes identified in fashion a grammar that created the magic illusion of individual choice. Like the speaking of a language, fashion proceeded within a structure that appeared to be agreed upon by those who "spoke" and wore it, but was arbitrary and evolving, the whole and the parts existing only in relationship to each other. Barthes' theory of fashion, as Andy Stafford notes in his recent critical commentary, has come to "percolate" throughout the academic study of fashion, frequently with little recognition of Barthes' achievement in creating a wide-ranging body of influential writing (Andy Stafford, "Afterword," in Stafford and Carter: 120).[1]

In a more pessimistic turn characteristic of post-1968 politics, the poststructural approach would permit Jean Baudrillard to argue that "modernity defines itself by the rate of change tolerated by the system without really changing anything in the essential order ... Modernity is a code and fashion is its emblem" (Slade 2006: 249). Such ahistorical (and atemporal) views are now generally adjusted by scholars who have returned to differently grounded studies. Nonetheless, the impact of Barthes' semiology, his questioning of authorial intent as the principal structuring question, and his demand for the connectedness of written and "image" texts is evident throughout the academy, and very present in this volume. In rejecting the decorative, psychological, or functional aspects of fashion as their primary originating force and locus of meaning, Barthes was able to move beyond the problem that past fashions were simply "out of date," neither elevated nor sublime like art, and therefore immune to analysis within any philosophical system. Ironically for the purposes of our volume, Barthes avoided the analysis of fashion within the domain of literature. As Ulrich Lehmann notes, Barthes felt that the literary forms crafted by famous authors were too personal, too "fragmentary" and variable to be of use to his project (Lehmann 2000: 288). Nonetheless, Barthes was attracted to the strategies of the prose of nineteenth-century Symbolist poet and fashion journalist Stéphane Mallarmé. Barthes praised the "next-to-nothings in which Mallarmé could then enclose a whole metaphysics of the new power of Man to make the tiniest of things have meaning" (Barthes, "From Gemstone to Jewellery [1961], in Stafford and Carter: 64). As Andy Stafford notes, Barthes might also have been attracted to Mallarmé's ability to conjure up the paradox of the weighty "void" of emptiness of modern consumer society.[2]

This edited volume brings together critical essays written by dress, literary, and art historians; writers; filmmakers; designers; and cultural theorists exploring a wide range of genres and cultures covering the period from the late eighteenth century to the present day. The anthology does not primarily aim to extract the fashion trace in literature and literary sources, although necessarily many of the anthology's authors consider that aspect. Rather, it is concerned with the imaginative capacity of fashion to perform several of these functions simultaneously. Topics range from the fictional characters, the fashion-addicted grisettes and cocottes of mid-nineteenth-century Paris, to the role of the novel *Naomi* (1924) in shaping Japanese sartorial modernity.

Our contributors share particular themes. How are fashion's mythologies constructed and disseminated through fictional texts? What are the roles of word and image in a fashion editorial or a catwalk parade? What does fashion "do" within structures of narration and characterization? How does it relate to aesthetic, emotional, and cultural narratives? What makes dress and fashion such a fascinating subject for writers? Our contributors argue that fashion and fiction have long existed in close proximity; writers have been driven by their experience of fashion; fashion has been developed through and by literary tropes. The volume includes lively papers assembled from Australian, British, Swedish, German, and North American scholars. These papers capture the power of fashionable fictions, that apart from characterization, fashion in the novel frequently propels the plot and therefore reinscribes fashion's association with change.

Fictions and Clothing Forms

In his semiological exploration of fashion, *The Fashion System* (1985 [1967]), Roland Barthes famously asked: "Why does Fashion utter clothing so abundantly? Why does it interpose, between the object and its user, such a luxury of words (not to mention images), such a network of meaning?" (Barthes 1985 [1967]: xi). *The Fashion System* aimed, as Carter (2003) notes in his *Fashion Classics. From Carlyle to Barthes,* to "impart to the object, fashion, a coherent conceptual order" (Carter: 144). It was an assertion of semiology and structuralism over nineteenth-century sociology. Barthes believed that fashion was built on its use of confusing adjectives forming their own kind of taxonomy, one that lent itself easily to pseudo-scientific classifications—"type a: sporty; type b: avant-garde; type c: classic" (Van Leeuwen 1983: 34).

   The "real garment," the "represented garment," the "used garment," "communicating through clothes": these now familiar categories proposed by Barthes and his circles transformed the possible ramifications of the study of clothing. As Stafford notes in his translation of Barthes' fashion writings, the romantic notion of "inspiration," in everything from literature to fashion, was anathema to Barthes. The fashion system, then, demands that a "structured collective being precedes, and provides the foundation for, individual being" (Carter 2003: 145). Barthes forged a relationship between semiology, structural linguistics, and historical sociology, and the effect of his approach was to question the dynamic diffusion model proposed by sociologist Gabriel Tarde, the event-based history of clothing proposed by numerous nineteenth- and twentieth-century writers, trickle-down and aspirational notions propagated by Thorstein Veblen, and the seduction and eroticism model characterized by the writings of James Laver. Barthes resisted the allure of the notion of *zeitgeist,* of the corollary between an aviatrix and 1920s fashion, for example, and once in a round-table rather tersely commented, "I always resist linking historical content to clothing forms" ("Fashion, A Strategy of Desire," in Stafford and Carter: 88). To Barthes, history no longer documents the real but produces the "intelligible," and in this way he owed a debt to the *Annales* School of French history, of *lived* history (*histoire vecu*).

   Numerous essays in the volume presented here deal with the question of mass fashion and the democratization of style and taste in contemporary culture. Barthes gave much attention to texture and weightiness, a very important part of *The Fashion*

System. "So it is precisely its smallness, its finished look, its very substance as the opposite of the fluidity of fabrics, that makes the piece of jewelry part of fashion and it has become almost like the soul in the general economy of clothing, that is *the detail*" (Barthes 1961: 63). The authors gathered in this volume argue from precise detail, generally not for stylistic analysis alone, and for syntactic rather than lexical observation.

The anthology also brings together different strands of scholarship connecting the history and theory of fashion with that of the study of literature. These individually rich traditions have tended to be conducted in the academy adjacent to each other.[3] The first of these academic approaches is the tradition of interrogating literature for what might be learned there about the social and cultural changes signaled by fashion and the way in which such change was generated. This approach was present within the feminist scholarship that drove a part of the nineteenth-century or "Victorian studies" of the 1970s and 1980s, analyzing women's subjectivity and characterization through attention to choices of dress and demeanor. Such analysis, which often looked at the relationship between fiction, journalism, and social life and played particular attention to class—the figure of the prostitute or fallen woman, the seamstress, the lady of fashion—was also central to debates concerning the relationship of fashion to second-wave feminism. Such approaches structured a part of the first publication that attempted to comprehensively interrogate modern fashion as imaginative practice and social force, Elizabeth Wilson's *Adorned in Dreams: Fashion and Modernity* (1985). Wilson studied English literature at Oxford University and her text made extensive use of literary sources in order to demonstrate that fashion was an expressive cultural form and a significant part of the cultural life of any society. Indeed, her text commenced with an epigraph from George Orwell's *The Road to Wigan Pier;* a quotation from Lewis Carroll's *Through the Looking Glass: And What Alice Found There* opens chapter one. In concluding this chapter with the comment "Fashion is modernist irony," fashion sounds very much like literature in Wilson's influential model (15).

The second strand of scholarship addressed in this volume is the New-Historicist deployment of literary theory to reread historical practices texts as always contextual, neither timeless nor universal. Literary theory carries within itself a different agenda from an historical overview of literature. This scholarship, exemplified in the work of scholars such as Stephen Orgel, Anne Rosalind Jones, and Richard Stallybrass on the Renaissance, foregrounds fashion metaphors as central to literary tropes, the realm of poetics, and the shaping of societies through mechanisms such as race and gender difference (Jones and Stallybrass). These writers have recognized in the material culture of fashion, with its necessary focus on time and transience, something different from the study of an expensive majolica jar or a carved wedding chest. This significant methodological and ideological issue has been highlighted by Ulrich Lehmann (2000). At an important point in his text *Tigersprung: Fashion in Modernity,* Lehmann refutes the causal relationship of fashion and society: "Yet we cannot expect to ascertain historical facts merely from looking at clothes. This is not to say that no factual interpretation is possible; yet fashion will always remain too transient and ephemeral to simply explain historic causality—though its changes are very often anticipated ... it can never be seen as simply mirroring that society; instead, it projects forward" (299). In a critique of conventional models of dress and costume history, Lehmann argues in a significant note that the dress/costume history approach "makes clothing nothing but costumes within a linear historical progression—and thus goes against the fundamental characteristics of fashion" (473). The texts assembled in this volume support the principle that Lehmann espouses. They proceed from a range of methods and techniques; we note the dominance of cultural studies, art and design history, and design research among our authors. Through these approaches, we present a volume that is less about making fashion significant through its connection to overt political, social, and material concerns than linking fashion to its form, narrative and aesthetics.

Fashion in Novels: The "Reality Effect"

The men and women of Edith Wharton or Thomas Hardy, George Gissing, Leo Tolstoy, George Moore, Henry James, or Marcel Proust carry their stories on their backs, each outfit mapping their social and sexual conquests and their declines. How better to map Emma Bovary's doom than in her spending on fashion and frippery, each new garment or hat a harbinger of her inevitable fall, each fashion purchase accounted against her soul? This is what makes fiction so captivating: readers read on numerous levels and learn about the multifaceted world of the author through multiplying layers of meaning. As dress historian Aileen Ribeiro notes in her important study of the Stuart culture of dress, *Fashion and Fiction: Dress in Art and Literature in Stuart England,* "Literature conveys emotions and feelings about clothes that can highlight character and further the plot of a play or a novel ... Fashion itself can be said to produce fiction" (Ribiero 2005: 1).

These devices are not specific to the great social and psychological fictions of the late nineteenth century. From Jay Gatsby's gold and white aura in F. Scott Fitzgerald's *The Great Gatsby* to the street garb of Anthony Burgess's *A Clockwork Orange,* or modern Japanese fiction, clothes define, sustain, and give voice to social momentum and the stages of life. As Gabrielle Finnane's essay in this volume on Capote's *Breakfast at Tiffany's* and Sarah Gilligan's exploration of the *Matrix* films demonstrate, film audiences read these costumes avidly, their indicators and signs offering a visual subtext to the main plot. This reader participation foreshadows the participatory nature of contemporary fashion identity and realities of the marketplace.

In an essay in *Modern Fiction Studies,* Vincent Leitch argues for fashion as a form of contemporary cultural capital (Leitch: 112). Serving political designs, Leitch notes, fashion continues to consort "with hegemonic norms and domination;

its regulating force incites mainly conformity but sometimes resistance. To adopt a style (or uniform) is to choose a socio-economic milieu and a future." Many of the anthology's essays argue that this complex interrelationship between clothes and character forms one of the key narrative devices in fiction, offering what Peter Brooks (1993: 54) described as "a semiotics of bodily adornment and personal accessory" as a means of getting to "know" people. Writers want their readers to know their characters, forming a significant contractual expectation between reader and writer. What a character wears and how he or she carries his or her clothes speak to the reader in ways that a character's spoken words rarely could. Fashion is codified or endowed with meaning and a reader soon catches the writer's intent: a woman's downfall from silk to cottons, a young man's social rise through the cut of his coat, the slow stripping of clothing denoting a pecuniary decline or the startling makeover that carries a character from fledgling identity to full self-expression. This use of clothing-fashions Clair Hughes calls the "reality effect": they lend tangibility and visibility to character and context, generally simplified and "naturalized" within the construction of an imagined world. Such passages, Clair Hughes notes in her monograph *Dressed in Fiction* (2005: 2–3), "offer us one of the different pleasures of reading a text—different, that is, from simply following the plot." Dress, always in perpetual motion in a novel, underscores "dress in movement, in metamorphosis, unpredictable and treacherous" (11). Dress, with its power of "occult "alterity" ... and "subterranean power," prompts us to ask the difficult question, "How far are the surfaces we live with, contrived as they are to produce certain effects, also false?" (183).

Clair Hughes's essay commissioned for this volume, *Dressing for Success,* examines how fashion raises issues of identity, disguise, hypocrisy, sincerity, and seduction. How is dressing for success connected to the novelistic double lives of the nineteenth century? Hughes carefully avoids reductivism and asks instead how "'impressions'—visual, tactile or psychological ... are governed by material facts." In reviewing Hughes's extended study *Dressed in Fiction,* Lucy Carlyle noted, "Though literary style is frequently analyzed, the presentation of material style within literature is seldom investigated" (Carlyle 2006: 361). Professor Hughes's research on literary affect finds echoes in the grouping of essays that analyze genres of fiction as diverse as film (*Breakfast at Tiffany's* and *The Matrix*), the Japanese novel (Jun'ichirō Tanizaki's *Naomi*), the brand storytelling of "magalogs" (narrative catalogs), and the family photograph album.

Margaret Maynard's invited paper places an emphasis on representation. Maynard argues in *The Mystery of the Fashion Photograph* that within fashion, the word-image relationship is a space "of intrigue and mystery." Fashion photographers, Maynard writes, both responded to and shaped narrative strategies that developed alongside new lifestyle and marketing patterns in the twentieth century. "Fashion photographs are a form of modern writing," Maynard writes, "hovering in an uneasy space between linguistic information and the pictorial. Situated somewhere between representation and perception, often loosely contained within generic formulations, they constitute a system neither alphabetic nor fully aesthetic."

The chapters in the section "Fashion Texts and the Visual Imagination" form a type of "fashion-studies response" to the important exhibition *Fashioning Fiction in Photography since 1990* (New York, Museum of Modern Art, 2004). This exhibit explored how genres such as the snapshot and the cinema have provided dominant modes in recent fashion photography, with "story lines and interrupted narratives, which imbue the images with dramatic complexity as well as contribute to the aura of personal intimacy and authenticity" (Kismaric and Respini 2004: 12).

Through such diverse explorations, the essays in this section contribute to an understanding of the important shift toward a fragmented fashion intelligence in the years since rave culture and "grunge," the deemphasis upon "head-to-toe" unity in dressing. Contemporary consumers' personal expression has become more important than unified looks dictated by designers, and the new forms of fashion editorials that emerged in the 1980s are created precisely through new narrative combinations. Publications such as *Dutch, Purple, Tank, Self Service, Big, Surface,* and *Sleek* create editorials through combinations of text and image that build upon the legacy of *i-D, The Face,* and *Interview.* Our focus on fiction permits new connections to be made between the fashion industry and its reliance on cultural memory and ideas.

As all of the essays in the anthology demonstrate, "fiction" can be considered an expanded category—filmic and television narratives, adaptations, and self-fashioning through memoir, or writing the body through brand identity, cult identification, body patterning, and tattoo. Clothing appropriations create and enable cultural exchanges to emerge. Japan's contemporary "Lolita-goths," for example, bring a new reading to Nabokov's seminal novel and the ways in which his "nymphette" redefined adolescent identity in the 1950s and continue to play out on contemporary Japanese city streets. The exchange is a kind of palimpsest of fashion, the Japanese narrative fashioned above Nabokov's words. The fashion revolution of the 1960s provided new ways of reworking the dandy fashions of eighteenth-century England, evident in the social realist fiction of the sixties, from the stylish socioeconomic juxtapositions of Ken Barstow, Alan Sillitoe, and Lynne Reid Banks. But as our authors' papers also suggest, fashion and fiction are far from simply synonymous. As Margaret Maynard concludes in her paper, in fashion, "Unlike the thriller, a fully realized denouement is impossible. For desire to remain active, it is inevitable that the mystique of the purchased garment be dissipated."

Notes

1. *The Fashion System*'s difficulty as a piece of prose stands in contrast to Barthes's delightful short essays; the former has been called the *Moby-Dick* of structuralism. See Carter 2003: 144.

2. On the relationship of Barthes and Mallarmé see Andy Stafford, "Afterword," in Stafford and Carter 2006: 122.

3. Clair Hughes's bibliography (2005) provides a useful working list. For other analytical studies see Kuhn and Carlson 2007, Relihan and Stanivukovic 2003, Razek 1999, and Fortassier 1988.

Part 1
Fashion Tales and
the Visual Imagination

–1–

Dressing for Success

Clair Hughes

There is an eighteenth-century account of the French queen Marie Antoinette opening a court ball in "a blue dress strewn with sapphires and diamonds. She was young, beautiful, and adored by all—yet she was already close to the abyss." This passage was quoted in a review by Daniel Mendelsohn of Sofia Coppola's film *Marie Antoinette* to highlight what he felt to be the film's weakness: Coppola, he says, "gives you, as it were, the dress but not the abyss" (Mendelsohn 2006: 22). The verbal description of the queen's appearance was, in short, more telling, more dramatic than the film's gorgeous images. Mendelsohn's contrast with a written account raises the question of why so very visual a thing as dress should be considered within the context of literature. What do words do for dress? For the reviewer it was the suggestiveness of the words—the implication of depths below surfaces—that lent drama. Dress, said Roland Barthes (1983), is the ideal poetic subject: touching the body, it reveals the self, but also intersects with the social—conforming, rejecting, deceiving, or seducing.

But dress is also the most obvious signal of order and hierarchy in the new middle-class world that became the key subject of the novel. It is rank and status writ large. It is the expression of individual taste within social limits. It is the marker of ambition, self-respect, and respect for others. The gradations of dress distinctions as Europe shifts from a traditional aristocratic order to a new bourgeoisie are of endless concern to those who lived through these changes. And in the novel they find some of their most subtly ambiguous, questioning descriptions. In this essay, which concerns the ambitions of four fictional heroes, the abyss that awaits failure dogs their footsteps— successful appearances must be maintained. As Lucien de Rubempré reflects in Balzac's *Lost Illusions,* anguished by the sight of a Paris errand boy wearing a cravat like his own, "Have not such apparent trifles tormented men in brilliant walks of life? The question of costume ... is one of enormous importance for those who wish to appear to have what they do not have, because that is often the best way of getting it later on" (Balzac 1971 [1837]: 165). Lucien's ambitions must not appear to be those of an errand boy. What do these young men want, and how do they dress to get it?

Lucien is a central figure in my story. But I want to glance first at Goethe's heroes of 1774 and 1786, Werther and Wilhelm Meister, who, according to Franco Moretti's study of the nineteenth-century novel, *The Way of the World,* are early heroes of the European bildungsroman. As the title *The Sorrows of Young Werther* suggests, Werther's quest fails. But it provides a key garment in the history of dress, as well as in the history of the novel, in the shape of a blue coat. Indeed, "The Irrepressible Blue Coat" might be a subtitle for this essay, as we shall be seeing surprisingly many of them (Plates 1–2).

After an impassioned courtship of Charlotte, Werther learns of her marriage to another and puts a bullet through his head: "He was found lying on his back ... fully clothed, wearing boots and his blue coat and buff waistcoat." A letter to Charlotte states his wish "to be buried in these clothes ... you touched them and they are sacred" (Goethe 1989 [1774]: 134, 135). Werther's plain outfit in simple stuff, mark of the noble, natural man, is the English antifashion, diffused throughout Europe and based on country clothing: Werther's unshowy, substantial garments are a contrast and a challenge to the privileged luxury of the German aristocrats who had rejected him. Werther fails, but he is also a success. The best-selling novel caused young men of Europe to dress à la Werther, though happily they didn't often pull the trigger on themselves. The fashion inspired by this literary image, and reinforced by the neoclassical aesthetic, is *the* great change in dress on which the modern male appearance is based (Plates 3–4).

The bildungsroman is, according to Franco Moretti, "the beginning of modernity" (2000 [1987]: vii), and to be of their time is the central endeavor of its protagonists. "I can pick the right uniform for my century" (Stendhal 1991 [1830]: 336), says Stendhal's Julien Sorel—unfortunately, not always the one he wants at heart. With the late eighteenth century's new sense of historical time, there emerges also a concern with individual self-determination and its accommodation within society. The bildungsroman, Moretti says, is situated not only on the border between two epochs, "but on the border ... between the bourgeoisie and the aristocracy. It is the story of the young merchant, Wilhelm Meister, adopted by a small group of enlightened landowners, and Elizabeth Bennet's journey from Cheapside to Pemberley; of Stendhal's Julien and Balzac's Lucien, of Jane Eyre" (Moretti 2000 [1987]: viii). Ambitious girls will have to wait for another day, but I shall be looking at Wilhelm, Julien, and Lucien as well as William Thackeray's Pendennis—and at how they dress for success.

Heroic success is found not through labor, for the bourgeoisie endlessly worries over what it is to be a "gentleman.: Wilhelm Meister hopes to be a poet, but, dissatisfied with his efforts, he joins a group of actors as playwright. Among actors the question of costume presents itself. Wilhelm, until now in a featureless grey suit,

> ... began to think about his clothes. A vest which would have a short cloak thrown over it was a most appropriate garb ... Long knitted trousers and laced up boots seemed just right ... He acquired a splendid silk sash ... [and] had some pieces of muslin fastened to his shirt which ... gave the effect of an old-fashioned collar. A silk scarf ... was loosely

attached to the inside of his muslin ruff. A round hat with a brightly coloured ribbon and a big feather completed the disguise. (Goethe 1994 [1786]: 123, 124)

Wilhelm's avowed model is Shakespeare's Prince Hal—literature providing the preferred ambience of these heroes and Shakespeare's plays being then all the rage. The description's perspective, we note, is not distanced; it internalizes the act of trying on clothes. The sequence of garments, ending with a dramatic hat, reflects the business of dressing and checking effects. The long trousers and boots are very 1780, but the cloak, hat, sash, and ruff are filched from the theatre wardrobe; calling his costume a disguise suggests Wilhelm's uncertainty about the final effect.

After being wounded in a fight with robbers, Wilhelm is rescued by a beautiful lady, who wraps her "man's loose overcoat" around him: "electric warmth seemed to be penetrating his body from the fine wool" (Goethe, 1989 [1774]: 134, 135). She vanishes, but Wilhelm, declaring she is his Amazon queen, vows to find her again. Disillusioned with the actors, he is received into a society of philanthropic nobles. Werner, an old friend and member of this community, looks at him approvingly: Wilhelm's earlier appearance, he says, had perhaps been charming, "chest half-bared, big ruff ... round hat, short vest and baggy trousers—but I thought that outfit pretty close to a clown's. But now you look like a man" (Goethe, 1989 [1774]: 307). "Being dressed," Mick Carter has said, "never quite achieves the status of 'natural'" (Mick Carter, personal correspondence), a crucial concept for the Romantics. Wilhelm's new look is therefore unspecified; this manly look is somehow intuited and understood as "natural" by writer and reader.

Wilhelm is finally declared a "man." An oddity of the novel, however, is that its women wear male dress. Wilhelm's first love, Mariane, dresses as a soldier; the devoted Mignon wears a replica of Wilhelm's first grey outfit; Therese, to whom Wilhelm proposes marriage, supervises her estate in a man's suit—and there is the Amazon, in her electrifying overcoat. Is Goethe suggesting that courage, fidelity, efficiency, and philanthropy are moral virtues, embodied by women, that Wilhelm must love and acquire to achieve manhood? I am not at all sure what Goethe is trying to say here. The dénouement reveals that Natalie, one of the society of nobles, *is* Wilhelm's beautiful Amazon. His earlier liaisons are summarily dispatched to allow their union and the fulfillment of Wilhelm's "noble seeking and striving after betterment"(Goethe, 1989 [1774]: 325). We are hopeful that Natalie's electrifying qualities are not confined to her overcoat.

Wilhelm's theatrical guise is an aspect of self; not false, but incompatible with his socialization. Unlike Julien Sorel, whose desires fire the narrative of Stendhal's *The Red and the Black,* Wilhelm's ambitions are vague, passively expressed. Stendhal's heroes, according to the French critic Jean-Pierre Richard, do not wait for things to happen: "life [is] an untamed wilderness of sensations across which a pleasurable path must be carved ... sensation is a risk as well as a reward, the prize for courage" (Richard 1954: 20, my translation). Julien does not seek harmony with the Bourbon

Restoration society of 1830: under a performance of conformity he nurses rebellion and Napoleonic dreams of glory. Dress is the fabric of Julien's state of mind, a compliant mask, beneath which seethe intense emotions.

The novel's title highlights an apparently dress-related contrast: military red and clerical black—but nothing is that simple. The French Revolutionary Guard wore red, but so did the princes of the Church. Black clothed the lower clergy and had been the garb of tradesmen, but by 1830 respectable black was settling over the entire middle-class male population of Europe—a shift in meaning that reveals and conceals the trajectory of Julien's career. Sponsored by a priest, Julien leaves his peasant home to become tutor to the de Rênal family, where he is given a black suit: "the feel of clothes so unlike the ones he was accustomed to, put him in ... an abnormal state of excitement" (Stendhal 1991 [1830]: 34). Black dress, as we know, is overdetermined: "sexy, serious, and a little sinister," according to Anne Hollander (2002: 128); "conspicuous," John Harvey notes, "even if it says 'Don't see me! I efface myself'" (1995: 13). This mixture of drama and decorum serves Julien well: his "face as pale and gentle as a girl's" (26) is set off by black, but black's clerical associations also guarantee him harmless. It is not his suit, however, that seduces Mme. de Rênal, but his instinct for clean linen, a dandyesque concern very much of its time (Plate 5). When she sees "how extremely clean the young abbé's simple attire was," she thinks, "Poor boy, how does he manage?" (39).

Mme. de Rênal arranges a day of dizzying glory for Julien. She gets him a "beautiful sky-blue coat with colonel's epaulettes in silver" (Stendhal 1991 [1830]: 105) to accompany a royal progress through the town. Red and black may be the contrast of the novel, but blue seems to have special significance in a young man's color chart. Julien "felt on top of the world ... he was one of Napoleon's aides-de camp ... leading the charge" (107)—a costume of pure joyous fantasy. The day ends, however, in an encounter with a young bishop in purple robes and lace so costly that Julien stops in his tracks: "'So young,' he thought, 'and Bishop of Agde ... how much is the income?'" The sight of the bishop then surrounded by pretty girls "caused our hero to lose the last vestiges of his reason. At that moment he would have fought for the Inquisition" (109–10).

Exposure threatens his affair with Mme. de Rênal, and Julien leaves for a seminary. Success there leads to his appointment as secretary to the Marquis de la Mole in Paris. "You will wear a black suit," his superior says, "but like someone in mourning, not like a man in holy orders" (Stendhal 1991 [1830]: 224). Black, then, is the new black and Julien is sent off to shop. But despite a new wardrobe, humiliation lies ahead. On his first evening, the Marquis looks "in obvious pain at Julien's boots: 'I didn't tell you that every day at 5.30 you must go and dress.'" Julien looks confused. "I mean put on stockings!" This *is* confusing; but if we turn to Delacroix's portrait of 1827 of Baron Schwiter in semiformal evening wear, shoes, and stockings, we see the required look (Plate 6). The day's dress-injuries are not over, for when Count Norbert, the Marquis's son, enters in boots and spurs, Julien fumes;

"and I'm supposed to wear shoes, apparently like an inferior" (253–55)—at which point the reader may wonder who Julien thinks he is. On the other hand, we may find his nerve, or his naiveté, enlivening.

Julien quickly adapts to the codes of Paris society. "He has style without realising it" (Stendhal 1991 [1830]: 259), reflects Mathilde, the Marquis's daughter. A Parisian beau notes approvingly that Julien's coat is from Staub, the best tailor in town. If he wears a uniform at the behest of others, Julien now controls his effects, translating clerical garb into something else, something chic, something sexy. "The double life," Moretti says, is "the key to the modern personality ... If the narrator of *The Red and the Black* did not remind us from time to time of the colour of his attire, who would remember that Julien is practically a priest?" (Moretti 2000 [1987]: 87, 93). Being almost a priest is not quite the same as being almost a virgin or almost pregnant, but in Julien's case there is something of that on/off dichotomy that dress helps to clarify—or confuse.

Julien's performance seduces not only Mathilde de la Mole, but her father as well. His affection for Julien troubles his pride; that eternal black suit is a daily reminder of social difference. "Allow me, my dear Sorel," he says, "to make you a gift of a blue coat: when you see fit to don it ... I shall regard you as the younger brother of the Duc de Chaulnes." Julien's day becomes schizophrenic. Every morning, in a black coat, "he was received in the old manner. In the evening, with blue coat, the tone was quite different." But Julien is amusing all day, and so the Marquis, still uneasy, presses a Légion d'Honneur on him—"I don't wish to make you abandon your black suit ... when I see this cross, you will be the son of my friend, the Duc de Chaulnes" (Stendhal 1991 [1830]: 285, 286)—an award for services to tailoring, we might say.

When he then gets Mathilde pregnant, we await catastrophe. But not at all—these amorous detours, consequent on his increasing allure, actually seem to further his revolutionary aims. To protect family honor, Julien is accepted as Mathilde's suitor and made an officer in the Hussars (Plate 7). Triumphant, Julien becomes "one of the most elegantly-dressed young men in Paris" (Stendhal 1991 [1830]: 445). But nemesis beckons all the same: Mme. de Rênal sends a letter to the Marquis, denouncing Julien. He leaves Paris, finds Mme. de Rênal in church at prayer, and shoots her, twice. He is arrested and condemned to death.

In court, "dressed very simply but with perfect elegance," Julien attacks society for punishing in him "young men who, being born into an inferior class ... have the audacity to mingle in what the rich ... call society." Finally, in "a large blue coat on the floor" we see "what remained of Julien" (Stendhal 1991 [1830]: 528). Neither red nor black but shrouded in the coat of an officer and gentleman, Julien's dreams rest intact. Death is success, for in Julien's world of symbolic values there is no accommodation with the realities of mid-nineteenth-century France.

Is this the end of the Romantic hero, the death of Werther's blue coat? To judge from the opening of Balzac's *Lost Illusions* of 1837, it might seem so. Lucien

Chardon (later de Rubempré), provincial chemist's son with a small poetic gift, is invited to Mme. de Bargeton's salon, the center of Angoulême's cultural life. Lucien's sister uses her savings to buy him "a new coat from the most fashionable tailor. She embellished his best shirt with a frill" (Balzac, 1971 [1837]: 49). David, her fiancé, assures Lucien of his success: "You look like a gentleman in your blue coat with yellow buttons and your plain nankeen trousers." But at Mme. de Bargeton's, Lucien is uneasy, "for he was wearing boots ... Sixte de Châtelet [his rival] was wearing a dazzling white pair of trousers with straps under the feet, ... elegant shoes and stockings of Scotch thread ... a white waistcoat ... his black coat was commendable for its Parisian style and cut" (Balzac, 1971 [1837]: 71, 77). De Châtelet snubs Lucien, who vows revenge.

Although only seven years separate *The Red and the Black* from *Lost Illusions,* we have moved into a different social and aesthetic world. Images of Julien clothed were vivid but vague on detail. Balzac, on the other hand, tells us about stocking thread, trouser cloth, and straps. It is not just impressions of order that occupy Balzac: he loves detail in all its amplitude and ambiguity. In his *Treatise on the Elegant Life,* Balzac explains that as hierarchies vanished with the Revolution, "we have only nuances left ... those effects of a good upbringing ... that separate the man of leisure from the labourer." You can, he says, spot "the bureaucrat from the fraying of his sleeves ... the flâneur by pockets misshapen by the frequency with which he puts his hands in them ... the gold-buttoned jacket of the old-fashioned [provincial], or the dirty spencer of the miser ... these are the infallible signs of professions, of customs and habits" (Balzac (1998 [1830]: 75, 76, my translation). Such signs that might be revealed, might need to be concealed, or can be imitated (Plate 8).

Balzac, Henry James said, gives us "the machinery of life, its furniture and fittings" (James 1984, vol. 2: 97); but these "are described only in so far as they have a bearing on the action" (James 1984, vol.1: 608). In *Lost Illusions* clothes very nearly *are* the action. Lucien and Julien, for example, both have bad-shoe days: Julien, in shoes, resents the boots of the aristocratic officer; Lucien's boots are *de trop* in a literary salon. Julien's choices are constrained by his status as employee, but bourgeois Lucien, free to exercise his taste, is bent on revenge, literary success, and a new wardrobe in Paris.

Once there, Lucien sees that Louise de Bargeton is behind the times. And while she finds Lucien "singularly handsome," the cheap provinciality of his appearance is "prodigiously ridiculous" (Balzac, 1971 [1837]: 161). Lucien himself undergoes "two hours of torment in the Tuileries [over] the out-of-date cut of his coat, its dubious blue, its outrageously ungainly collar ... the buttons were rusty ... his waistcoat was ... grotesquely provincial ... only commonplace people wore nankeen trousers" (164, 165). Lucien's outfit can be identified in Madeleine Delpierre's study of French costume: wide trousers and shawl collars are typical of the 1820s; after 1834 the silhouette lengthens, collars and trousers narrow, and trouser-straps are de rigueur

(Plate 9). The cutaway coat in blue, green, or black with gilt buttons, popular in the first decades of the century, by 1840 was being replaced by the skirted frock coat.

Lucien runs to his hotel for cash to "re-equip himself from head to foot" (Balzac, 1971 [1837]: 168). When Stendhal's Julien goes to his room it is to check with himself that his actions accord with his ideals. But Balzac's Lucien suffers no inner doubts; social mobility is an end in itself, and he monitors his progress by going *out* into the city's public spaces—park, boulevard, opera—consumer parades of status symbols. Lucien attends the opera in his purchases: "a green coat, white trousers and a fancy waistcoat ... and a pair of very elegant, well-fitting boots ... feeling, however, a little restricted in the close–fitting apparel." His attention is caught by some young men "whose elegance today was that of yesterday and would be the same tomorrow. Lucien sensed that his appearance was that of a man who had dressed up for the first time in his life." "The most essential element of elegance," Balzac warns in his *Treatise,* "is to hide the means by which it is achieved ... Everything that strives after effect is bad taste" (Balzac 1998 [1830]: 56, 84). Looking round, Lucien realizes "with bitterness in his heart [that] he would have to visit a first-class tailor" (Balzac, 1971 [1837]: 169, 177, 180).

In the *Champs Elysées* he is cut by Louise, in a carriage, and a vision of Parisian elegance. "Rage and a lust of vengeance took hold of Lucien—'Great God! Gold at all costs! ... No! Not gold, but glory ... Hard work! I will win through! I will drive along this avenue in a barouche with a flunkey behind me!'" Lucien, like Julien, finds the answer at Staub's, where he orders a frock coat, waistcoat, and trousers. Later, reinvented, he returns to the boulevards where "he was so well-dressed, so graceful, so handsome that several women looked at him" (Balzac, 1971 [1837]: 187). But the chapter ends as Lucien weeps, alone in Paris, friendless and unprotected, and—lest we get sentimental—writing a begging letter home, for he has run through his own and his sister's funds for the year. In pursuit of a style that ensures success, Lucien chases a chimera always just ahead of him.

Lucien's "hard work" is hack journalism, theatre and book reviews in which opinions are sold for sexual favors or a fistful of tickets. Coralie, an actress, becomes his mistress and a witty article brings him celebrity. But fame is as short-lived as the fashion in cravats, and Coralie "[ruins] herself to provide her beloved poet with the elegant outfit of a man about town": a torrent of ornament follows, culminating in some "fabulous waistcoats to match the colour of his coats" (Balzac, 1971 [1837]: 439). But Lucien's colleagues plot the destruction of the intruder: his work is rejected; Coralie falls ill and dies. "The wretched provincial prodigy," as Balzac calls him, returns to Angoulême.

Louise patronizes Lucien again, flattering him with invitations. He sends a request for clothes to Paris: "I simply must have some Sunday best; I've nothing but rags," he wails. Louise and her cronies are in fact after Lucien's brother-in-law, David, owner of a profitable industrial process. Lucien betrays David at a party where he is the ne plus ultra of fashion: "his black, close-fitting trousers ... his grey silk open-work stockings, his elegant shoes, his black satin waistcoat, his cravat, everything in fact scrupulously ... moulded to his person" (Balzac, 1971 [1837]: 615, 619)—a last gamble on his belief that if you appear to have what you haven't, you will finally get it. Dress as a socioeconomic sign here collapses: impeccably clad but fooling only himself, Lucien heads for ruin. It is ironic that our image of Balzac, based on Rodin's statue, is that of an ungainly, untidy man. But the imagination, the écriture, of Balzac is another sphere occupied by the human comedy in which everything might count, and clothes, status, money, and good looks all restlessly fight for position. But the clothes in this case do not finally determine what the person is.

Balzac, Moretti concludes, has isolated in Lucien "the feverish and anarchic features of early capitalism ... [its] enigmatic alternations of success and ruin" (Moretti 2000 [1987]: 145, 146). Neither nobility, rebellion, nor taste motivates his dress-decisions: they are panic responses to fashion's maelstrom of images—he has no idea what he is doing, or why. In each dress-triumph lies failure, for he cannot distinguish signs from what they represent. His blue coat, so early discarded, tied him to family and place; subsequent costumes replace one another in headlong waste. There is no logical end to his ambitions or his costumes, and so, plucked from disaster by a sinister priest in black silk stockings, the novel ends in the coach to Paris—and Lucien's story is to be continued elsewhere.[1]

Lucien becomes the "mere hollow shape," eviscerated in Thomas Carlyle's satire of 1832, *Sartor Resartus*. Carlyle's target was dandyism, as embodied by Count D'Orsay, Disraeli, and Bulwer-Lytton. Lucien's ensemble at the fatal party is in what John Harvey (1995: 28) calls "the black style of dandyism," inspired by the "dashingly gloomy" hero of Lytton's best-selling novel, *Pelham*; a style that, according to the novel, only the well-born can wear. The new bourgeois world of the nineteenth-century novel is a European phenomenon whose concerns resonate from one country to another. England invents the dandy's outfit—and the English novel has its own dandies with their dress and class anxieties. We see them, for example, in Arthur Pendennis, another chemist's son, hero of Thackeray's novel of 1850, *Pendennis*.

On the death of his father, Pendennis (or Pen) is left in the hands of his mother and uncle, Major Pendennis, a successful military man. The major opens the novel "in the best blacked boots in all London ... and linen so spotless that Mr. Brummell himself asked the name of his laundress" (Thackeray 1999 [1850]: 1). The English country style, adopted by the French, had recrossed the channel to be refined by the Prince Regent's friend, Beau Brummell, into a style not unlike military dress—dark cloth coat, pale waistcoat, light close-fitting pantaloons, fine footwear, and clean linen. Linen indeed became the touchstone of a correct appearance: "[I]f you are economical with your tailor," the *Handbook of Etiquette for Ladies and Gentlemen* (Anonymous 1853: 144) says, "you can be extravagant with your laundress." The prince's profligate way of life, however, had brought the Regency period into disrepute, although, as Ellen Moers has pointed out, Victorian attitudes to dandyism were ambivalent. Frivolity was clearly wrong, but there was something attractive, even nostalgic, about the way dandies "made a success ... of absolute selfishness" (Moers 1960: 14), and, as Thackeray admits at the novel's close, "Ours is a selfish story" (Thackeray, 1999 [1850]: 719).

At the sight of a schoolfellow "in crimson and gold, with an immense bearskin cap on his head" (Thackeray, 1999 [1850]: 28), Pen, like Julien Sorel, is attracted to the army. But where Julien had longed for heroic *action,* Pen longs only for the *costume* and is easily distracted when he meets another old friend, Foker, "in one of those costumes to which public consent has awarded the title of "swell"" (36). The swell, a figure of the 1840s, vulgarized the dandy style: Foker wears "a scarlet shawl neckcloth ... a bulldog [pin] in gold ... a fur waistcoat ... a green cutaway coat with basket-buttons and a white upper coat with cheese-plate buttons" (36–37). Thackeray's own illustration of Pen and Foker together shows Foker in two waistcoats, check trousers, and a fat cravat; Pen's outfit has a Regency simplicity, updated by a stovepipe hat and bow tie of the 1840s. "Simplicity is the only distinction," *The Handbook of Etiquette* rules, "which a man of taste should aspire to" (Anonymous 1853: 140).

The "swell" was socially inferior to the gentleman, and Pen's response to Foker as role model is confused, for he is "not much more refined than in his school days." He enjoys Foker's account of university life, however, and decides to go to that novelistic invention, Oxbridge. Once there, he finds that "one or two very vulgar young men, who did not even use straps to their trousers ... beat him completely in the lecture room." This mismatch between sartorial and academic success does not worry him long, however. When he returns home, his cousin Laura notes the "quantity of fine new clothes he brought with him," and Pen appears "in wonderful shooting-jackets ... gorgeous velvet waistcoats, with richly embroidered cravats." Snooping round his room, Laura finds a dressing case "with silver mountings and a quantity of lovely rings and jewellery" (Thackeray, 1999 [1850]: 172, 212, 213). We see a paradigm shift here from the Brummell/Major Pendennis model to a new concept of sartorial success, that of the Count D'Orsay, arbiter of London society in the 1830s.

D'Orsay brought feminine softness, color, and gleam to Brummell's austerity; as Ellen Moers says, "[H]is dandyism was made from weaker stuff" (Moers 1960: 148). Pen, in his cravats, waistcoats, and jewelry, is not made of very stern stuff either. The image of Pen is now modeled on D'Orsay—his charm, his auburn curls, and, most importantly, his role as fashion leader, for this is what Pen effortlessly becomes: "When the young men heard ... that Mr. Pendennis had just ordered a crimson satin cravat, you would see a couple of dozen crimson satin cravats in Main street ... the jeweller was known to sell no less than two gross of Pendennis pins" (Thackeray, 1999 [1850]: 219).

Pen's ambitions are entirely self-indulgent and Thackeray does not downplay the cost of his way of life. But we also hear of Pen's exuberance, his pleasures and popularity, that "impeccable naiveté" that characterizes Baudelaire's Hero of Modern

Life. Not seduction, not revolution or revenge drives him. Nemesis arrives, nonetheless, in the form of unpaid bills. Pen fails his degree and returns home, with two gold buttons to his name. In failing to gain the qualifications necessary for productive work, Pen has rejected Victorian middle-class values and opted instead for the glamour of an ancien régime grandee.

Bored at home, Pen leaves for London to study, financed by his womenfolk. He is declared "a man of *ton*" and settles to a round of London amusements. He shares lodgings, however, with a third, and surely worthy, role model, George Warrington. The Major is startled by Warrington "in a ragged old shooting jacket ... drinking beer" (Thackeray, 1999 [1850]: 372, 362), but decides he is a gentleman. Warrington is Thackeray's Man in a Jacket, a figure he had created in 1841 in one of his antidandy articles, "Men and Coats," in which he turned "the manly, simple, and majestic" jacket into a moral symbol: "a man IN A JACKET is a man. All great men wore jackets" (Thackeray n.d. [1860]: 611). By 1850 the workingman's jacket was indeed working its way up the social scale, to finally become a part of the now-familiar suit. Thackeray's evangelical side was attracted to its homespun austerity, but in his fiction, his nose for the absurd ensures that jacketed worthies like Warrington do not prevail. A vignette of Warrington rescuing Pen's manuscript novel from the fire shows him in a hairy jacket against Pen's thinner coat. Warrington tells Pen he is "a molly-coddle ... spoilt by women," but these bracing remarks have no effect. On the success of the rescued novel, Pen, "in his very best chains, shirt-studs, and cambric fronts" (Thackeray, 1999 [1850]: 393, 435), becomes a literary lion.

Thackeray's increasing focus on jewelry is that novelistic preoccupation with extraneous detail "to convey the notion of frivolity" that Hollander (1978: 424) notes in relation to female dress in fiction (Plate 10). When Pen, in rakish mode, takes up with cockney Fanny Bolton, this focus intensifies. Parading with him in Vauxhall, she thinks how his "white duck trousers and white hat ... gold chains and shirt studs, gave him the air of a prince of the blood." He then drops her, but she can't believe that Pen is wicked—"the good, the great, the magnificent youth, with the chains of gold and the scented auburn hair" (Thackeray, 1999 [1850]: 626, 650). Her last sight of Pen is at Epsom races, in mourning for the death of his mother, but a mourning in which sex appeal is the calculated effect: "There he stood ... dandified, supercilious, with black crepe to his white hat, and jet buttons in his shirt front: and a pink in his coat that someone else had probably given him; with the tightest lavender gloves sewn with black ... the trinkets at his watch-chain, the ring on his hand under the glove, the neat shining boot" (748). The fashion details are almost shocking, and in terms of perspective and description in the realist novel, unsettling. "It is worth following the movement of the focalizer in the text," George Hughes says in his book *Reading Novels* (2002: 58). Fanny, though watching Pen from a distance, itemizes his appearance minutely: the closeness of her focus, unreal on the one hand, has, on the other, a bitter sexual intensity that is psychologically wholly real.

Retribution must surely follow this triumphant peacock display, for during the course of the novel Pen has run through his own, his mother's, and Laura's money in the sole cause of personal adornment and a good time. Failure has been overlooked, penitence intermittent, and sensible role models ignored. But Thackeray rewards Pen with an income and marriage to Laura. We last see him alone on his wedding morning "attired in a new hat, a new blue frock-coat [blue again] ... in a new fancy waistcoat, new boots, and new shirt-studs" (Thackeray, 1999 [1850]: 972). Is this an image of successful modernity?—"new" is, after all, repeated five times. Thackeray loves detail but he evades analysis. We never "go behind" Pen, as we do with the passions of Julien and the panics of Lucien, so, in Henry James's phrase, we must "guess the unseen from the seen ... trace the implication of things" (James 1984, vol. 1: 53).

Pen's look is neither that of the swell nor of the Victorian worthy; he opts instead for the style of the Regency Buck—distinguished and erotic. Why? There is, as Ellen Moers says, a strong personal element to Thackeray's treatment of Pen: "He had wanted to be Pen: what his mature self chastises ... is the dream world of his younger self" (Moers 1960: 207). Mario Praz calls Thackeray's attitude to modern progress "elegiac and melancholy"—the most successful parts of his novels "are always descriptions of the protagonist's youth" (Praz 1969: 240, 243). Thackeray cannot punish Pen for fulfilling his own dreams. The richer the image of Pen's youth grows, the more inexorably that of adulthood is drained. Warrington in his hairy jacket is, of course, the man Thackeray felt he ought to be; but, as he said of himself, "I am walking about in 1828 in a blue dress coat and brass buttons, a sweet figured waistcoat, looking at beautiful beings in gigot sleeves" (Thackeray n.d. [1860]: 440). And although Pen's wedding coat is now the unsexy frock coat, we might note that it *is* blue, the blue coat of Thackeray's lost Arcadia. Pen, like Stendhal's Julien, is caught between somehow accepting the world or remaining faithful to defeated ideals. Pen's solitary figure, in a blue coat, allows Thackeray's ideal to make a last stand, before the walls of Victorian domesticity close about him.

What makes these heroes most alive, then, obsessively concerned as they are with dress and success in a borderland between the ancien régime and a bourgeois society that leads eventually to industrialized modernity, is their inability to make sense of their worlds. They construct hierarchies; they imagine social orders, priesthoods, élites, military rank: necessary badges for entry into the heart of a new world, for success with money and affairs of the heart. The novel constructs and enriches our images of this process in all its bourgeois amplification and complexity: men become peacocks in blue coats, or dashing figures in the dance of black and red, or sex objects in lavender gloves and gold rings. Dress makes them and unmakes them; it writes them into their world and suggests them still for us. In our world, in which Bill Gates has made mandatory work wear of T-shirts and jeans, we can imagine through novels what brought us to where we are now. And the confusions around novelistic dress can remind us—forcefully—that we still don't know (dresswise) where we are now.

Note

1. After further adventures and many purchases, Lucien finally dies in *Splendeurs et Misères des Courtisanes* (1844).

–2–

Grisettes, Cocottes, and *Bohèmes:* Fashion and Fiction in the 1820s

Denise Amy Baxter

The categorical fictionalization of the bohemian as a recognizable social type first happened during the French Restoration (1814–1830), becoming codified later in Henri Mürger's text *Scènes de la vie de Bohème,* but also in the prints of Henry Monnier, Paul Gavarni, and, most notably, Octave Tassaert (1800–1874) in his lithographic series *Boudoirs et mansardes* or *Dressing rooms and Garrets* from 1828 and *Les amans et les époux* or *Lovers and* Spouses from 1829. Two examples, *MÉCHANT!. . . /WICKED FELLOW* (Plate 11) from the former series and *AH! POUR LE COUP, LA BELLE ENFANT!!/HA NOW J'VE CAUGHT YOU, MY BEAUTY!!* (Plate 12) from the latter may stand as paradigmatic examples for the whole. The titular taglines should be understood as carrying more than passing interest. For example, they are bilingual but not particularly well translated throughout. While the presence of both French and English reflects the dual publication of the lithographs, in Paris by chez Ostervald ainé quai des Augustins and chez Neuhaus rue Saint-Honoré, and in London by Carter, Roland Street, Oxford Square, the awkwardness of the English texts may have been intentional—certainly someone in Oxford Square would have been capable of catching the mistaken J'VE for I've—indicating the demonstrably French origin of both the print and the *bohème* and his feminine counterpart, the grisette, and their commodity status. Indeed, Jules Janin would later claim in his entry on "La Grisette" from *Les français peints par eux-mêmes: Encyclopédie morale du dix-neuvième siècle* that "de tous les produits parisiens, le produit le plus parisien sans contredit, c'est la grisette" (Janin 1862 [1840]: 9). Typified within Tassaert's prints and throughout her pictorial history by her simultaneous fashionability, purity, and venal sexuality, the grisette was recognizable by her dress and accoutrements more than by the narrative scenarios in which she was depicted. Indeed, the prints seem intended to document the grisette's modish attire and commodities in scenes of eroticized leisure, seemingly as object lessons demonstrating the linkages between commodity culture and the represented eroticism of the everyday, in which we may recognize the origins of our own conflation of goods, sexuality, and sources of the self.

Yet while fashion is the keystone of the recognition and therefore categoriza-
tion of these figures, it is at least in part a fiction of fashion. Indeed, insofar as
the attire depicted in these prints may easily be made to correspond with contemporary Restoration-era fashion plates, such as those from *Almanach des Modes,
L'Observateur des Modes, Le Journal des Dames et des Modes* or *Petit Courrier des
Dames, ou Nouveau Journal des Modes, des Théâtres, de la Littérature et des Arts*, we
must consider them to be recognizable as fashionable. Simultaneously, artistic production of the Restoration period—the time during which the former Bourbon mon-
archs were reinstalled in France following the Revolution and reign of Napoleon—is
most commonly associated with the aesthetic movement of Romanticism and its
tenets of extreme and emotional connotations of beauty. Yet recognizable within
Romanticism is the continuation of prior forms of representation, most notably from
the eighteenth-century, or rococo period, seen throughout nineteenth-century artistic
production, in both high art and popular culture. These include, most notably, scenes
of a genre identified as the *tableau de mode*, originated by Jean-François de Troy
in the 1720s–1730s.[1] Throughout these paintings, such as *La jarretière détachée*
(1724, private collection) or *La declaration d'amour* (1731, Stiftung Preußische
Schlösser und Gärten Berlin-Brandenburg, Schloß Charlottenburg), de Troy depicts
heroines playfully refusing the advances of equally fashionably attired ardent suitors, scenes in whose exactitude of color, cut, and decorative detail in which are
echoed late seventeenth- and early eighteenth-century fashion plates, are again revis-
ited within the Romantic era, making these representations both fashion and fiction
alike.

Due to Octave Tassaert's status as an immensely popular artist of the era who produced both paintings for the official *Salon de peinture*—most notably overwrought
melancholic scenes such as *L'Abandonné* (1851, Musée Fabre, Montpellier), in
which a woman, abandoned and pregnant, swoons at the sight of her former lover's
nuptials—as well as popular lithographs such as those in the *Boudoirs et mansardes*
and *Les amans et les époux* series, his depictions of the grisette offer key opportunities to investigate the relationships both between high art and popular culture and
between the Romantic era and the rococo, whose iconography is echoed in these
nineteenth-century popular physiologies.[2] More importantly, however, the images
and texts both beg the question: if these are intended to be representations of the
particularities of fashion and commodity culture, why resort to fiction, why return to
eighteenth-century tropes? How does the reception of commodified female sexuality change depending on both the era (rococo versus Restoration) and the medium?
The rococo source material, such as de Troy's *tableaux de mode*, was paintings,
quintessentially high art, and hung in the official Salon, while Tassaert's lithographs
were popularly collected. More significantly, however, an examination of shifting
representations of the grisette allows for a case-study investigation into the connection between depictions of venal sexuality, notably embodied in the fashionable and
the feminine, and the development of an aestheticized, commodity-based conception
of self.

The feminine type, the grisette, was known as early as the seventeenth century. In his 1690 *Dictionnaire,* Antoine Furetière defined her according to her attire and station as "femme ou fille jeune vêtue de gris. On le dit par mépris de toutes celles que sont de basse condition, de quelque étoffe qu'elle soit vêtue."[3] The 1694 first edition of the *Dictionnaire de l'Académie française* did not focus on the term's etymological roots[4] in the color grey but rather concurred with Furetière in its explanation of *grisette* as "Terme qui se dit par mépris d'une jeune fille, ou d'une jeune femme de basse condition. *Il n'y avoit que des grisettes à ce bal. il ne voit que des grisettes*" (*Dictionnaire de l'Académie française* 1694: 542). By the time she is again defined in 1782 by Louis Sébastien Mercier in his *Tableau de Paris* she was a beloved figure, emblematic of the city of Paris, her attire no longer "gris" and her situation no longer "basse."[5] By the Restoration Henry Monnier would, to no avail, search London for grisettes, asking: "Where are those naughty figures, those charming little faces, that would arouse the dead: I hunt everywhere for *grisettes.*"[6] Monnier could, of course, not find her in London because the figure of the grisette is embodied in the imbricated elements of the erotic, the economic, and the city of Paris.

In brief, the grisette earns her living manufacturing and selling goods for the Parisian fashion industry of which she is both consumer and product. She is herself able to partake in the fruits of capitalism, purchasing bonnets and sweets and attending the spectacles, while simultaneously being open to purchase in both image and body. The grisette was available to the consumer in physiologies and guides, which let their readers know that they too might be able to possess her in the flesh. Yet while the reader understands that the grisette might gain a portion of her living wage from the generosity of her lover(s), she is never condemned for it. Instead the reader is made to understand that, for a variety of reasons, the grisette is a good and honest girl, to the extent of becoming the ideal of the city of Paris. The grisette may, in fact, be read as an index of chronological change in the nature and conception of the commodification of venal sexuality. To that end we might explore three different historical definitions of the grisette from the physiologies, which denote her as an integral element in the knowledge of the city of Paris: Louis Sébastien Mercier's in his *Tableau de Paris* (1782) from the end of the ancien régime; Monnier's from his *Les Grisettes* (1827–1828), dating from the last days of the Restoration; and Gavarni's illustrations of the type in Louis Huart's *Physiologie de la grisette* and Jules Janin's entry from *Les Français peints par eux-même,* both dating from the July Monarchy.[7] While Mercier's text is set against the backdrop of the very inception of the market economy and its attendant fears, Monnier's depictions savor the glory of the grisette while giving her a slightly different form. Most noteworthy, however, is the aspect of nostalgia that consistently marks any discussion, or even visual depiction, of the grisette, as if by that stage of commercial development—whichever stage that might be—the grisette's innocence was no longer tenable. Throughout, however, the fashionable feminine type, and the grisette in particular, pervades the guidebooks, the fashion press, and, increasingly, high art as well, transforming what had been a simple seamstress into a marker of modernity and the construction of the modern self.[8]

In Mercier's textual account he claims that despite their meager existence, grisettes are more privileged than their bourgeois counterparts and that "la grisette est plus heureuse dans sa pauvreté que la fille de bourgeois" (Mercier (1994 [1782]: 338). This is because the grisette has what the *fille de bourgeois* can never attain, her freedom. Mercier, moreover, doubly blesses the grisette. Granting her the freedom to do as she will, free from the watchful eyes of aunts and grandmothers, Mercier forgives her for what he sees as inevitable moral peccadilloes: "La vanité, non moins mauvaise conseillère que la misère, lui répète tout bas d'ajouter la ressource de sa jeunesse et de sa figure à celle de son aiguille. Quelle vertu résisterait à cette double tentation?" (338). While Mercier recognizes the prostitutional aspects of the grisette's existence, he places the blame for these on what we might now term a patriarchally based market economy. The grisette escapes the label of sexual predator and, in Mercier's description, is no more than a simple, carefree girl. In the prerevolutionary era, the market is to blame; the grisette is innocent.

In the mythology of the Restoration, the grisette remains innocent, honest, and hardworking.[9] While she saves her money in order to marry the fiancé of her own class (a character who, ironically, never figures in the illustrations), she is considered loyal to both the bourgeois men whose attention she attracts on her promenade and her student lover. Henry Monnier, the grisette's chief illustrator of the Restoration period, who published his lithographic series *Les Grisettes* in 1828, clearly adored the type.[10] While Mercier absolved the grisette for her sins and laid blame on the unfair treatment of women in a newly expanding market economy, Monnier reveled in the woman, the market, and their glorious intersection in the form of the grisette.

Monnier's grisettes are shown in the trappings of the market. He represents them with leg-of-mutton sleeves, tiny waists, elaborate bonnets, and the finest bows. The grisettes, however, are shown as more than producers and consumers of fashion; Monnier makes it clear that they are themselves available for consumption, in both the content and the mere existence of his lithographic portrayals. Yet Monnier denies their active participation in this economic exchange. The grisette may gain financially from the bourgeois gentlemen whose stares she attracts, but Monnier makes it clear that the simple joys of love, rather than mercenary intents, are her goals. This is evident, first of all, in the physical type that Monnier depicts. She is not plain in her dress, but its nature, combined with her round head and unrefined features, make it clear that the grisette is no sophisticate. This is made especially clear in *Il veut m'épouser ... le scélérat!!* (Plate 13), Monnier's scene of two grisettes gossiping from the 1828 series. The girls' round faces and simple expressions let the viewer know that he has nothing to fear; these are not conniving vixens. In fact, the caption, which might be translated as "He wishes to marry me, the scoundrel!", lets the viewer know that the grisette is no gold digger. She is not trying to trap any man into providing her with home and hearth; rather, she is content with her free existence.

One of Monnier's grisettes graced the published edition of a popular song about grisettes, whose lyrics give credence to the contemporary prevalence of Monnier's interpretation of the type:

J'aurais bien pu rendre
Mon sort fortuné,
J'en ai tant vu vendre
Ce que j'ai donné ...

Mais simple et modeste,
Je ne veux pas d'or,
Et ce qui me reste
Je le donne encor ... [11]

The grisette may take money from her lover, but she is interested only in love. The goods of the market only increase her beauty. Her participation in it does not tarnish her reputation. She and the market, for Monnier, are both beloved, both quintessentially Parisian.

What had been for Monnier a simple and joyful type becomes, in the hands of Gavarni, almost beatific.[12] In his frontispiece to Louis Huart's *Physiologie de la grisette* (Plate 14), she is shown at work, sewing. Rather than concentrating on the task at hand, however, she is shown wistfully daydreaming. But instead of seeming lazy or distracted by trivial pursuits, the grisette resembles nothing more than a modern saint at reflective prayer, and indeed Janin describes her variously as "la noble heroine" and, ironically, "vierge sainte" (Janin 1862 [1840]: 14, 15). Or, as Louis Huart more succinctly explains and Gavarni's works illustrate, "La grisette est [une] bonne fille" (Huart 1979 [1841]: 7). This is not to say that the grisette represented has no faults. The nature of these faults, though, her illustrations represent as such relatively minor infractions that they serve only to increase her charm. As Huart explains, "Elle a donc aussi ses passions—mais passions assez innocents du reste, et la plupart du temps faciles à satisfaire" (33). She, for example, prefers flowers and marrons to more sophisticated goods.

Gavarni, in his frontispiece to "Des passions de la grisette," chapter V of Huart's *Physiologie de la grisette: Grisette eating cake in the paradis* (Plate 15), shows her leaning over the balcony at a spectacle, completely enraptured. While looking intently at the scene below, she presses a sweet cake into her wide-open mouth. Gavarni attempts to convince his viewer that the grisette is as she appears and that her virtue is unquestionable.

The idea of a grisette of unquestionable virtue does, of course, present its own problems because her lifestyle is, by definition, not conventionally moral. As Mercier and Monnier before him had, Gavarni's paired texts absolve her as follows: "A défaut de mari, elle accepte donc un amant; et les grandes dames, qui ont de tout en abondance, leur reprochent encore ce strict nécessaire" (Huart 1979 [1841]: 45). The crime then belongs to the practitioners of conventional morality, "les grandes dames," rather than the freedom-loving grisette, in a comparison similar to that between the grisette and the *fille bourgeois* in Mercier's account. The texts go to the seemingly ridiculous extreme of Huart's question: "La grisette est-elle plus fidèle que les autres femmes?" He further justifies the question with the claim that: "La grisette est naturellement fidèle;—seulement elle est fidèle à son amant ou à ses amants. Je m'explique encore:—elle est fidèle à *son* amant de seize à vingt ans,—et à *ses* amants de vingt à vingt-quatre ans" (104). But even this is said in a tone of explanation rather than condemnation. Whether it is to "son" or "ses amants," she is loyal and that is enough. Or, as the refrain to Pierre-Jean de Béranger's *Les infidélités de Lisette* points out, the grisette's infidelity is understood as part and parcel of her station, predicated upon a desire for simple luxury goods, ribbons chief among them. Yet despite these infidelities, Béranger's protagonist urges Lisette to remain a grisette.

> Lisette, ma Lisette,
> Tu m'as trompé toujours;
> Mais vive la grisette!
> Je veux, Lisette,
> Boire à nos amours. (*Chansons de Béranger* 1875: 119–22)

Yet while he would take pleasure in having her to himself, he would prefer her to remain faithful to type, and subsequently unfaithful to him. Further, even while the linkage between the bodily possession of Lisette and the exchange of material goods is made explicit in the song, she is consistently presented as joyous and carefree rather than basely prostitutional. Indeed, everything about the grisette in her July Monarchy incarnations is as good and sweet as her preferred cakes, to a point of questionable excess. For example, in Janin's brief history of a prototypical grisette named Jenny, Jenny overcomes all of the possible obstacles of her station in order to live—happily ever after. Janin concludes his anecdote as follows: "Ce qu'est devenue Jenny? Elle est devenue ce que deviennent toujours les femmes très-jeunes et très-jolies, heureuse et riche; elle est à présent ce que sont toujours les femmes très-bonnes, elle est très-aimée, très-respectée, très-fêtée" (Janin 1862 [1841]: 15).

In her dissertation "Classification, Containment, Contamination, and the Courtesan." Courtney Ann Sullivan argues that "Janin idealizes the *grisette* because she provides the artist with financial and moral support as well as sexual gratification without ever demanding anything in return" (Sullivan 2003: 13). She differentiates between the coding of the modern courtesan and the perception of both the ancient courtesan and the grisette within nineteenth-century French culture. In Sullivan's investigations she notes that while the modern courtesan was reviled, her ancient predecessor and the grisette were lauded. For Sullivan these laudatory descriptions demonstrate an aspect of nostalgia, and indeed descriptions of the grisette as "vierge sainte" and her status as "très-respectée" indicate an excessive romanticism about the grisette typical of nostalgia. Sullivan claims that "writers [such as Janin] glorify the *grisettes* … because they represent the golden days when aristocrats held the sole privileges over their courtesan lovers and *grisettes*" (20). Later she explains that

> given the political, social, and economic turmoil of the period, these writers extolled the grisette because she emblematized the static status quo. In sum, writers represented her as simple-minded, child-like, easily seduced, reliable and therefore predictable, set in her ways, self-sacrificing, phlegmatically accepting of her working-class origin, and completely devoid of any urge to protest her miserable, poverty-ridden lot in life. (89)

Certainly the grisette is not seen as the intellectual equal to the *bohème*. But in presenting her as a nostalgic type, authors such as Janin and artists such as Gavarni and Tassaert recognize the impossibility of an unfettered relationship between feminine sexuality and commodity culture within a market economy. The grisette, therefore, is always already of the past. Whether in the ancient régime, Restoration, or July Monarchy, the perception seems to be that while once there were grisettes, one can find them no more.

Yet if she is perceived as an element of the past, she is nonetheless fashionable. The grisette serves a purpose in the identification of the city. It is as if she is somehow both venal and good so that capitalism and Paris might also be so happily paired. But, at the same time, she is by the July Monarchy a reminiscent type, an ode to an already past innocence. In an attempt to distinguish between the incredible variety of venal types in the period from 1815 to 1870 (including the cocotte, *lorette, lionne, amazonne,* and *biche* along with the grisette), Beatrice Farwell argues in her series *French Popular Lithographic Imagery* for a chronological progression. She explains that "the *grisette* is essentially of the Restoration, the *lorette* of the July Monarchy, and the *cocotte* of the Second Empire. Among these women, the most respectable and the most innocent is the *grisette*."[13] Indeed, the differences between the grisette and the *lorette* seem evident with only a quick examination of this pair of Gavarni's *lorettes,* who utterly lack the earnest nature that so defines his grisette.[14] The cocotte shares in the *lorette*'s mercenary characteristics. But is the difference merely one of chronology? It seems essential here to return to the obvious. The grisette is fictional; she is a pictorial and literary type rather than a sociological reality.

The grisette might be understood as an attempt on the part of the public, whose purchasing power allowed for the proliferation of the type, to deny the implications of capitalism. That the grisette might be, in effect, bought and sold yet somehow remain innocent might allow for the possibility that one could escape the commodifying aspects of capitalism unscathed. The feasibility of this must have been less imaginable by the end of the Restoration when new, more calculating types began to take the grisette's place. The very name of the *lorette,* for example, stems from the church of Notre-Dame de Lorette, most significantly a newly constructed and patently bourgeois neighborhood, the ninth arrondissement, which was considered her chief habitat. The *lorette* therefore functions as herself, the speculative property; she is commodified space, in that her name implies as much as her purportedly mercenary if not downright prostitutional behavior. As Lucette Czyba explains, the term *lorette* "connote simultanément l'évolution des mœurs de la bourgeoisie contemporaine, les progrès d'une société de consommation, la mutation profonde de la ville, du cadre urbain, par suite de l'essor de capitalisme industriel et de la spéculation immobilière" (Czyba 1984: 107).

Similarly, at the same time as he was illustrating Janin and Huart's texts on the grisette, Gavarni was producing prints such as *Une loge à l'Opéra,* which show a decidedly different type of woman (Plate 16). In this image the two women attract the attention of several men, one of whom actually inspects the women with his monocle. In this scene there are none of the innocent elements seen in the illustrations of the grisette; these women are implicated in the interaction taking place, intend the attention they receive, and relish it. Unlike Gavarni's grisette, whom he shows engrossed in the spectacle (Plate 16), these women pay no attention to the Opera that we are led to presume is going on before them. They instead are the spectacle, as they intend to be. These women, *lorettes,* know their place in the market economy and intend to use it to full advantage. While Jenny the grisette might find happiness at the end of Janin's tale, by the middle of the July Monarchy and Paris's contemporary status as a capitalist capital, she must have seemed curiously out of date.

This might provide an opportunity to rethink both the grisette's fashionability and her fictional nature. The grisette's most famous incarnation came with Henry Mürger's articulation of her, now best known as Mimi, in his *Scènes de la vie de bohème,* first published in *Le Corsaire-Satan* 1845–1849, and first popularized as musical theater in a November 1849 production at the Théatre des Variétés. That the mythology retained traction is apparent in the canonic status of Puccini's *La Bohème,* and the more recent phenomenon of *Rent,* both its theatrical and filmic productions, and Baz Luhrmann's *Moulin Rouge.*[15] The bohemian and the grisette are inevitably depicted as antibourgeois.[16] Indeed, Luhrmann's taglines for the film, repeated throughout, "Truth, beauty, freedom, love," are in direct opposition to market capitalism. Or are they?

In all of her incarnations, the grisette is a nostalgic type. She is always already out of date, a throwback, an ode to a past innocence that is understood as no longer tenable. In opposition to the *lorette,* the cocotte, or the *demi-mondaine,* while venal, she is uncorrupted by her venality. Her attraction is in her patent fictionality. As a representation she is doubly fictional insofar as she is understood as outside commerce, outside bourgeois morality, but exists exclusively for bourgeois consumption. Returning to the prints of Tassaert and Monnier, it is evident that she is a product of the desires of market economy. Insofar as it appears as if the grisette is a fashionable girl, a contemporary type, an antiestablishment ideal, it is an appearance that caters to establishment consumer desires. While a part of the market economy as a producer of fashionable wares, she is herself a merely a fashionable construct, existing synergistically with the market.

This itself is not new. The precedent of a commodity-based self within representation came into existence along with the market economy. Following the collapse of the Mississippi Bubble in France, for example, newly liquid capital paired with rapidly proliferating luxury goods, allowing nontraditional elites to forge novel identities in the realm of representation—the primary site for this enactment being the female body. This may be understood as a restatement or reinterpretation of Flügel's famous argument regarding the great masculine renunciation, but recent scholarship seems to indicate that the theoretical displacement of representational splendor to the distaff side began earlier than Flügel believed and, I believe, had more to do with markets than politics.[17]

The nineteenth-century grisette may then be seen as fictional on another level. This Restoration-era figure takes both its content and its iconography from rococo precedents. But what of it? First, it seems evident that in the case of neither the rococo nor its Restoration reinterpretations do we have an attempt of lower classes to ape their betters. Instead, commodities are seen as constitutive in a positive rather than a compensatory sense. It is through these commodities that the self is crafted. By this I do not mean to suggest that the essential self is entirely a fiction and that we see merely a field of slipping signifiers in Baudrillard's simulacrum. Instead I believe that what we are seeing in Tassaert's lithographic representations, and their links with their rococo forebears, is the immediate conflation between sexuality and commodity culture, so that modernity itself is borne by the fashionable female, and that which constitutes her existence, as well as she herself, are for sale, and in these commodity choices, and feminine self-fashioning, the modern self comes into being and remains to this day.

Notes

1. Christophe Leribault's (2002) catalogue raisonné of the artist includes a brief consideration of the genre. *Jean-François De Troy, 1679–1752* (Paris: Arthena). See also my "Fashions of Sociability in Jean-François de Troy's *tableaux de mode, 1725–1738*," in Alden Cavanaugh, ed. (2007), *Performing the "Everyday": The Culture of Genre in the Eighteenth Century* (Newark: University of Delaware Press): 27–46.

2. See, among others, Dorothy M. Kosinski (1988), "Gustave Courbet's *the Sleepers:* The Lesbian Image in Nineteenth-Century French Art and Literature," *Artibus et Historiae* 18: 187–99; Murielle Le Guen (1997), "Une Acquisition du Musée de la Vie Romantique de Paris: *La Porte Fermée* (1855) Par Octave Tassaert," *Revue du Louvre* 1 (February): 59–63; "Octave Tassaert (1800–1874), Peintre des Larmes et de la Bonne Fortune," *Bulletin de la société de l'histoire de l'art français* (1998): 273–86; and "Un Nouveau Regard sur les Dessins

d'Octave Tassaert (1800–1874), Du Musée Léon Bonnat à Bayonne," *Revue du Louvre* 2 (April 2000): 77–84.

3. Quoted in Jennifer Jones (1996), "*Coquettes* and *Grisettes:* Women Buying and Selling in Ancien Régime Paris," in *The Sex of Things: Gender and Consumption in Historical Perspective* (Berkeley: University of California Press): 49.

4. For an interesting review of similarly constructed French words, see G. Gougenheim (1946), "Le Féminins Diminutifs en Français Moderne," *Modern Language Notes* 61, no. 6 (June): 416–19.

5. Louis Sébastien Mercier (1994 [1782]), *Tableau de Paris,* reprint edition (Paris: Mercure de France).

6. Henry Monnier cited in Novelene Ross (1982), *Manet's "Bar at the Folies-Bergère" and the Myths of Popular Illustration* (Ann Arbor: UMI Research Press): 43.

7. See Mercier, Janin, Louis Huart (1979 [1841]), *Physiologie de la grisette, vignettes de Gavarni,* reprint edition (Geneva: Slatkine Reprints). See also Ernest Desprez (1832), "Les Grisettes à Paris," in *Paris, Ou le livre des cent-et-un* (Paris: Librairie Ladvocat): 211–37.

8. Denise Z. Davidson (2005), framing her article with a description of the fresh-faced grisette, discusses the ways in which public legibility functioned in Paris in the post-Revolutionary era and notes the imbrication of class, sexuality, and representation in ways that have influenced my own arguments. See "Making Society 'Legible': People-Watching in Paris after the Revolution," *French Historical Studies* 28, no. 2 (Spring): 265–96.

9. For the most thorough investigation of types, including the grisette, in the print culture of nineteenth-century France, see the work of Beatrice Farwell. See, among others, *The Image of Desire: Femininity, Modernity, and the Birth of Mass Culture in 19th-Century France* (Santa Barbara: University Art Museum, University of California, Santa Barbara, 1994); and *French Popular Lithographic Imagery, 1815–1870* (Chicago: University of Chicago Press, 1981–1998).

10. For Henry Monnier see, among others, Edith Melcher (1950), *The Life and Times of Henry Monnier, 1799–1877* (Cambridge, MA: Harvard University Press); Jessie G. Marash (1981), *Henry Monnier: Chronicler of the Bourgeoisie* (London: Harrap, 1951); and Daniel Gerould (1981), "Henry Monnier and the Erotikon Theatron: The Pornography of Realism," *Drama Review* 25, no. 1 (March): 17–20.

11. *La Grisette, Chanson de Mr. F. de Courcy, mise en musique par Charles Plantade et dédiée par les auteurs à Mr. le Général Marquis de Talouët,* c. 1830, reproduced in Farwell, *French Popular Lithographic Imagery,* Vol. 2, Plate 4F7 and p. 16.

12. For Gavarni see, among others, Therese Dolan (1981), *Gavarni and the Critics* (Ann Arbor: UMI Research Press); Aaron Sheon (1984), "Parisian Social

Statistics: Gavarni, *Le Diable à Paris,* and Early Realism," *Art Journal* 44, no. 2 (Summer): 139–48; and Marie Joseph François Mahérault (2004), *Gavarni: Catalogue raisonné of the Graphic Work* (San Francisco: Alan Wolfsy Fine Arts).

13. Farwell, *French Popular Lithographic Imagery,* vol. 2, 16. For any earlier attempt at classification, but from the theatrical perspective, see Sidney D. Braun (1946), "The Courtesan in French Theater (1831–1880): An Attempt at Classification," *French Review* 20 (2, December): 161–66.

14. See Maurice Alhoy, *Physiologie de la lorette.*

15. The grisette as the paramour of the bohemian retains its fascination. For academic inquires see, for example, Valerie Steele (1988), "The Working Woman as Artist, Aristocrat, and Erotic Fantasy" in Steele, *Paris Fashion: A Cultural History* (New York and Oxford: Oxford University Press): 70–75.

16. For explorations of bohemianism, see both Jerrold Seigel's classic text, *Bohemian Paris: Culture, Politics, and the Boundaries of Bourgeois Life, 1830–1930* (New York: Penguin, 1986) and Mary Gluck's more recent *Popular Bohemia: Modernism and Urban Culture in Nineteenth-Century Paris* (Cambridge, MA: Harvard University Press, 2005).

17. See, in particular, Reed Benhamou (1997), "Fashion in the *Mercure:* From Human Foible to Female Failing," *Eighteenth-Century Studies* 31 (1): 27–43.

–3–

Clothing, Class Deception, and Identity in Late Nineteenth-Century Fiction

Rosy Aindow

The emergence of a modern fashion industry in the second half of the nineteenth century transformed the way in which the British population, particularly people from lower-income groups, conceptualized clothing. As the work of historians such as John Benson and Gareth Shaw (1992: 31) and W. H. Fraser (1981: 62) has shown, developments in garment production, marketing, and retailing allowed these groups to make and buy clothing that adhered closely to fashion trends during this period. Although fashionability had certainly existed for large parts of the population since at least the eighteenth century, at least in terms of accessories and trimmings, it is reasonable to claim that more general fashionable forms, silhouettes, and clothing items became more widespread during the nineteenth century. Among the bourgeoisie, the fear that such developments would lead to a democratization in dress pervades contemporary cultural discourse. Given that the bourgeoisie was a group that carved out its social position in relation to such commodities, fashionable dress was the perfect vehicle through which to express wealth and leisure. It followed that any process that widened the demographic of fashion was perceived—although not necessarily realized—to be a potential threat to the existing social hierarchy. In the words of the contemporary observer Ada Heather Bigg (1893: 238), "To follow fashion [was] to claim equality."

As an expression of predominantly bourgeois sensibilities, the novel was crucial in the articulation of these sartorial anxieties. Authors such as Thomas Hardy and George Gissing register these cultural concerns when dealing with the permeability and instability of class boundaries in their respective novels *The Hand of Ethelberta* and *In the Year of Jubilee*. As Arlene Young (1999: 2) suggests, the novel was the medium in which dominant nineteenth-century bourgeois social values and attitudes were formulated and expressed. In these novels, characters that occupy a precarious social position and dress in fashionable attire come in for particular criticism. Moreover, it is the relationship that these fictional women, rather than men, have with their garments that proves most problematic. While this is not to deny that men, in reality, were also fashionable consumers—the work of Christopher Breward (1999) has done much to address the misconception that men did not engage in fashionable consumption—it is the literary register that is of interest here.

In Hardy's *The Hand of Ethelberta,* Ethelberta is condemned by her family for marrying above her social station. Ethelberta has harbored dreams of improving her situation throughout her childhood. Much to the disapproval of her family, she insists on getting an education and pursuing a career as a governess. Here, Hardy clearly draws on familiar nineteenth-century representations of the governess that emphasize the figure's ambiguous position in the employer's household: she is employed primarily as a servant but must also possess the education and manners of a lady. The young and beautiful Ethelberta captures the attentions of her master's son, Petherwin, a union that results in marriage. Returning as a widow to the town in which she grew up, Ethelberta is now identified as a lady. Furthermore, this position is explicitly announced through her fashionable clothing.

These sartorial details are the subject of great interest in the small, provincial community. The milkman, in conversation with the local picter, identifies Ethelberta as a "figure of fashion" (Hardy 1876, vol. 1: 4). Similarly, when Ethelberta's childhood friend Christopher Julian—a local music teacher—is anonymously sent a book in the post, he inquires after the sender at the local post office. When pressing the clerk as to whether he knows the woman, Julian specifically asks, "What does she wear?" The response immediately suggests Ethelberta, or Lady Petherwin, as she is now known: "A white wool jacket with zigzags of black braid" (32). As Vanda Foster (1984: 97) notes, "Light colours trimmed with dark braid or piping, together with fringes and narrow pleated flounces, are characteristic of 1868–1875," pointing to Hardy's emphasis on Ethelberta's adherence to contemporary fashions.

Importantly, Ethelberta's garments signal the social distance that now stands between her and her family, particularly her brothers, Sol and Dan, and her sisters, Pictoee and Cornelia. Sol and Dan refuse to openly associate with Ethelberta when they are in their working clothes, thinking it will cause both parties embarrassment. Pictoee and Cornelia, however, are a little more accepting of the differences that exist between them and their sister. After all, the girls benefit from Ethelberta's situation and receive her castoffs. Indeed, Ethelberta uses her exposure to the latest society fashions to educate Pictoee. When Ethelberta leaves for London, she continues to send her clothing back to the provinces, telling Pictoee "how to make up anew, in unobtrusive shapes, the valuable wearing apparel" (Hardy 1876, vol. 1: 204).

As a wealthy woman living in the metropolis, Ethelberta is able to assume a position of superiority in terms of her sartorial knowledge. Throughout the nineteenth century, high fashion was associated with city life, which itself became synonymous with modernity and novelty. London's reputation for style was due in part to the presence of the major fashion houses and dressmaking establishments. It was also where many of the famous fashion publications were located: with the explosion in the number of titles in the late nineteenth century, it was only natural that they should gravitate toward the capital. By comparison, the provinces were regarded as something of a sartorial backwater where older fashions persisted. Ethelberta chides her sister Cornelia for wanting a "flare up around her head on a Sunday," explaining that "it is … rather too brilliant in colour—blue and red together, like that? Remember, as I often tell you, people in town never wear such bright contrasts as they do in the country" (Hardy 1876, vol. 1: 259). Cornelia's preference for red and blue is clearly related to her provincial background, but it also points to the problematic relationship between clothing and sexual conduct. In contemporary literature, a penchant for bright colors—particularly among lower-class women—was often employed as a euphemism for prostitution, the ultimate means of attracting attention to the body. As Alison Victoria Matthews (1999: 177) suggests, this is precisely Lizerunt's fate in Arthur Morrison's novel of 1894, *Tales of Mean Streets*. Lizerunt expresses similar color aspirations to those of Cornelia. Her husband buys her a hat with "the reddest of all the plushes and the bluest of all the feathers" (Morrison 1894: 41).

In muted tones, Hardy's heroine is very much distanced from these debates. The "dove-coloured material" of Ethelberta's dress "with a bonnet to match [and] a little tufted white feather" (Hardy 1876, vol. 2: 264) clearly signal her elevated social (and sexual) position. Significantly, however, in much the same way as the prostitute, Ethelberta is still viewed as a commodity by her future second husband, Lord Mountclere. Indeed, her fashionable appearance is subtly understood to be the reason for his obsessive attraction. Mountclere has a taste for fashionably dressed women, evident in his vicarious reading of fashion publications such as *Le Follet*. As one might expect, *Le Follet* was relatively expensive; according to Margaret Beetham and Kay Boardman (2001: 221), it was a monthly publication with a cover price of 1s 6d. The fact that a single man would receive this title at all also sets up suspicion as to precisely why the household is subscribing in the first place, in that it alludes to an absent wife.

Ethelberta's sartorial appearance is, however, essentially deceptive and ambiguous. While she is the widow of a wealthy man, she is also the daughter of a butler. As the painter Ladywell (who dines in London society) suggests in the opening stages of the novel, "fashion is false" (Hardy 1876, vol. 1: 82). Despite protestations to the contrary, it is obvious that Ethelberta takes great pains to hide her origins. As she explains to Christopher when Sol and Dan do not acknowledge her in public: "They are painfully off-hand with me, absolutely refusing to be intimate, from a mistaken notion that I am ashamed of their dress and manners; which, of course, is absurd" (193). While confirming Ethelberta's words Christopher's reply, "Absurd, of course" (193), suggests a degree of skepticism. This skepticism about Ethelberta's motivation is echoed elsewhere in Hardy's "comedy in chapters." With a carriage no longer at her disposal, Ethelberta is ashamed at making a long journey on an ass when Lord Mountclere proposes a trip to a local castle in the initial stages of their relationship. Groaning "at her inconsistency of being ashamed" (54), she leaves the creature to graze before she meets Mountclere and his friends. As such, she makes no claim to the creature when the group encounters it: "The pride and emulation which had made her what she was would not permit her … to take upon her shoulders the ridicule that had already been cast on the ass" (54).

The narrator's reference to emulation here is significant. Ethelberta's desire to better her position—facilitated primarily through her respective marriages—is condemned by her father, Chickerel (and of course, this condemnation is eventually given credence with Ethelberta's discovery that she has married a man who already has a wife). Chickerel conceives his daughter's enterprise as one motivated by material possessions. Interestingly, he draws specifically on the trope of dress to demonstrate Ethelberta's betrayal of her class:

> Young men will rather wear a black coat and starve than wear fustian and do well … What she should have done was glorify herself by glorifying her own line of life, not by forsaking that line for another. Better to have been admired as a governess than shunned as a peeress … but it is everywhere the same in these days. (Hardy 1876, vol. 2: 263)

While Chickerel's warning refers to young men's pursuit of fine clothes, his message specifically implicates Ethelberta. In the closing stages of the novel, Sol similarly laments,

> Berta, you have worked to false lines. A creeping up among the useless lumber of our nation that'll be the first to burn if there comes a flare. I never see such a deserter of your own lot as you be! But you were always like it, Berta, and I'm ashamed of 'ee. (Hardy 1876, vol. 2: 271)

Referring to his sister as Berta Chickerel rather than Ethelberta Petherwin, Sol highlights Ethelberta's dual identity, a division that is evoked by dress throughout the narrative. When Ethelberta wishes to visit her father's workplace anonymously, for example, she is identified as "a woman dressed in plain black" (9) rather than a lady in fashionable dress, as if black somehow grants her immunity from the world of fashion. Dressed in this way, Ethelberta knows that she will not incite attention from unwanted observers. As "Sylvia" (1876: 13), the author of *How to Dress Well on a Shilling a Day,* observes, "A blue dress is often recognised as an old acquaintance, when a black, or even a grey [dress], may pass unrecognised." Just as Ethelberta's fashionable appearance allows her to move in respectable society, Ethelberta utilizes the garb of the working woman to facilitate another form of disguise.

Ultimately, Ethelberta pays a high price for social mobility. The discovery that her second husband, Lord Mountclere, is already married leaves the reader in little doubt as to the treacherous nature of her enterprise. The role dress plays in expressing these concerns in Hardy's novel is significant, however, in that it prefigures wider sartorial anxieties in late nineteenth-century fiction: those that transcend geographical location and are used instead to illustrate the social ambiguity inherent in a particular group rather than an individual. In George Gissing's *In the Year of Jubilee*

(1894), a scathing critique of the emerging suburban class, the French sisters believe that their fashionable dress is indicative of their new social position and, concomitantly, their rise up the social ladder. While Hardy's allusions to fashion suggest a method of deception, Gissing presents the notion that these women deceive themselves through the acquisition of fashionable clothing.

One of the first things the reader learns about the French sisters—the daughters of a deceased Camberwell builder—is that they are "fashionable" (Gissing 1894: 2). Indeed, even the name French points to an association with style. Beatrice French enters the narrative under this very supposition: "Then a bedroom door opened, and a lady in a morning gown of the fashionable heliotrope came downstairs" (2). When Beatrice's sisters are introduced, the reader is exposed to a more overt rejection of their clothing. Fanny's clothes are "showy and in a taste that set the teeth on edge" (3). The fact that Fanny also plays music hall tunes on the piano confirms the social ambiguity expressed in her garments[1]. Because Beatrice shares the same household with Fanny, the two sisters are understood to occupy a similar social level. In this sense, Beatrice's fashionable heliotrope is intended as a critique of her appearance rather than evidence of high style. As the narrator remarks:

> The ineptitude of uneducated English women in all that relates to their attire is a fact that is not to enlarge upon. Beatrice French could not be regarded as an exception, for though she recognised monstrosities, she very reasonably distrusted her own taste in the choice of a garment. (240)

The narrative emphasizes the lack of education in the French household: "They spoke with a peculiar tongue, the product of a sham education and mock refinement grafted upon a stock of robust vulgarity" (Gissing 1894: 7). There is a sense that their mannerisms are contrived in much the same way as their clothes. "That they used a finer accent than their servants, signified only that they had grown up amid falsities, and were enabled by the help of money, to dwell above stairs, instead of with their spiritual kindred below" (7). Indeed, the relationship between Beatrice's sister, Ada Peachey, and her servants reveals the distinct similarities between the two parties. Ada finds it increasingly difficult to deal with her servants, with the reference to "rows" (5) illustrating the lack of mutual respect and social boundaries. By virtue of her position in society, Ada is simply not equipped to deal with such problems. She is unaware of the complexities household management presents, a skill that women from the middle and upper classes were presumed to take on with ease. As an anonymous writer in the *Lady's World* (1887: 242) observes, impertinence on the part of servants can be excused only if a mistress "forgets her position, and speaks harshly or unwarrantably to her servants in the first instance." The writer is "sure," however, that the reader of this particular journal would never do this, and so her "remark does not apply to present circumstances" (242). Ada's behavior challenges such an assumption.

These problems are reflected in Ada's dress. She sees no necessity in dressing appropriately for breakfast, entering the room in

> a costume which, at any season but high summer, would have been inconveniently cool. Beneath a loose thin dressing-gown her feet in felt slippers, showed stockingless, her neck was bare almost to the bosom, and the tresses of pale yellow, upon which she especially prided herself, lay raggedly pinned together on the top of her flat head. (Gissing 1894: 3)

As the advice offered by "Sylvia" (1876: 16) suggests, dressing for meals was an essential practice in respectable households, illustrating a desire to appear well dressed at all times of the day and not only—as Ada does—when going out in public. This façade of respectability extends to the interior décor of the Peacheys' home: the drawing-room has a few "show-volumes" and "half-a-dozen novels" belonging to Mr. and Mrs. Peachey, respectively. Thus, the Peacheys' claim to respectability lies entirely within the burgeoning commodity market. Even their furniture is "less than a year old" and the drawing room is full of "pretentious ornaments" (Gissing 1894: 5).

As Ellen Bayuk Rosenmann (2002: 47) suggests, clothing and furniture performed a similar function in Victorian narratives, as they both fell under the category of commodity. These two commodities are often linked in contemporary discussions of the emerging demand for such goods. As Arthur Baumann (1888: 293) notes in the *National Review*:

> an enormous class of persons are interested in cheapness and quickness of production; cheap clothes and cheap furniture ... give pleasure to a large number of excellent people. In Gissing's novel, Beatrice French intends to capitalise on this demand for cheap goods, setting up a Dress Supply Association, which sells low cost fashionable garments. As she explains to her sister Fanny; "the thing is to persuade [the customers] that they're getting an article cheap" (Gissing 1894: 12).

This demand comes from members of their own community—people who they claim acquaintance with despite their apparent vulgarity—Mrs. Middlemist "until a year ago ... adorned the private bar of a public-house" and Mrs. Murch has "something to do with the manufacture of infant's milk" (Gissing 1894: 90–91). Both women have recently come into money, finding themselves transported from the upper working class into the lower echelons of the middle. With their lack of sartorial awareness, these women constitute an ideal target audience for Beatrice. While Beatrice herself, of course, does not profess to be particularly knowledgeable (and promotes her business by wearing the clothes she capitalizes on), she simultaneously has the foresight to recognize the faults of the women who surround her, the predominant fault in this instance being the attempt to appropriate the sartorial signs of the middle and upper classes.

In this sense, Beatrice displays the skepticism of Ethelberta's father, Chickerel, in Hardy's *The Hand of Ethelberta.* Indeed, throughout Gissing's novel, Beatrice displays rather masculine attributes, particularly in her pursuit of enterprise. Luckworth Crewe, the manager of an advertising business, refers to Beatrice as a "good fellow" (Gissing 1894: 93) on one occasion, and the pair often talk "business" (94). As a result, there is, perhaps, a wider point here to be made about the way in which fashion is considered and approached by male characters in *The Hand of Ethelberta* and *In the Year of Jubilee,* novels that were both written by men. In Gissing's novel, the character of Stephen Lord raises increasingly vocal concern for his son Horace, who spends too much time in the company of Fanny. Despairing at Horace, he exclaims: "After all your education, haven't you learnt to distinguish a lady from a dressed-up kitchen wench? ... What were you doing all those years at school, if it wasn't learning the difference between real and sham" (40). Lord's notion of the real and the sham feeds into a larger discourse that fashion is primarily a deceptive surface. Moreover, this surface is employed primarily by women as a means to deceive men.

This theme is encountered elsewhere. For example, in Hardy's later novel, *Jude the Obscure,* the principle applies not simply to garments, but to any method of female adornment that falls under the guise of fashion. Hardy's narrator draws explicit attention to the use of false hair by Jude's wife, Arabella: "A long tail of hair, which Arabella wore twisted up in an enormous knob at the back of her head, was deliberately unfastened, stroked out, and hung upon the looking-glass which he had bought her" (Hardy 1896: 68). Arabella justifies this purchase to Jude, claiming that false hair is often worn by those among the "better class ... I bought it just for a fancy ... Every lady of position wears false hair—the barber's assistant told me so" (68). Jude finds this extremely difficult to believe. Just as Ethelberta draws attention to the discrepancies between provincial and city fashions, Arabella offers this distinction as an explanation for Jude's naiveté. She acknowledges that she has enough hair "as country notions go. But in towns the men expect more" (68). The comment also, of course, inadvertently reveals her objectives in dressing in this way. In the course of their discussion, Arabella discloses that she has worked as a barmaid in town. It is while she occupied this position that she was encouraged to buy the hair piece: "some people put me up to getting this" (68). Like Mrs. Middlemist in Gissing's *In the Year of Jubilee,* the allusion to the pub registers Arabella's lack of respectability. As the barmaid was considered to be a particularly flirtatious character in the popular imagination, the occupation also alludes to Arabella's moral character. The fact that she has adopted false hair in order to fulfill male expectations confirms these suspicions in Jude.

Yet Jude clearly finds Arabella attractive during their courtship, indicative of how fashion can easily mislead men. "Arabella looked so handsome amid her untidy surroundings" (Hardy 1896: 50). Her clothes represent a certain degree of sensuality that Jude is keen to explore. As Arabella exclaims when she takes off her jacket and hat, " 'Don't touch me, please,' she said softly. 'I am part egg-shell.' ... She began unfastening the collar of her gown" (63). Jude is amazed to discover that she carries a "cochin's egg" wrapped in wool in her bosom, and she draws it out for him to see. A tussle ensues for the egg and "they looked at each other, panting; till he rose and said: 'One kiss, now I can do it without damage to property'" (63). Arabella's appeal instantly disappears when Jude discovers that she wears false hair, however. "A little chill overspread him at her first unrobing" (68). Jude feels let down by Arabella; she has seduced him using false means: "'What—it wasn't your own?' he said, with a sudden distaste for her" (68). As the narrator remarks, some women have "an instinct towards artificiality in their very blood, and became adept in counterfeiting at the first glimpse of it" (68). These words are mirrored elsewhere in the contemporary periodical press. According to an anonymous writer in the *Cornhill Magazine* (1894: 408) on the subject of "powder," "its sole result is to draw attention to [women], and to provoke the secret comment that the woman who uses it is trying to make herself agreeable by deception."

While there is a certain degree of naiveté in Jude, the male voice elsewhere in late nineteenth-century fiction believes himself more adept at recognizing the artificial nature of female fashion. In Gissing's novel, Lionel Tarrant adopts this position when faced with the prospect of marriage to Nancy Lord. When courting, Lionel and Nancy have very different perspectives on their relationship, differences that are articulated through dress. Nancy believes, for example, that she has a certain degree of grace, exemplified in her choice of garments:

> Without attempting to rival the masterpieces of fashion which incited envy or wonder from all observers, [Nancy] thought herself nicely dressed ... Her taste in garments had a certain timidity that served her well; by avoiding the extremes of mode and in virtue of her admirable figure, she took the eye of those who looked for refinement rather than for extravagance. The unconsidered grace of her bearing might be recognised by all whom such things concerned; it by no means suggested that she came from a small house in Camberwell. (Gissing 1894: 109–10)

Nancy's father has encouraged both his son and daughter in these pretensions, exposed, perhaps, in the family's surname. A more accurate indication of Nancy's real social position is her friend, Jessica Morgan, a customer of Beatrice French's Dress Supply Association: "[Jessica's] dress, formerly neglected to the point of untidiness, betrayed a new-born taste for fashionable equipment; she suddenly drew attention to it in the midst of serious talk, asking with a bashful smirk whether Nancy thought it suited her" (Gissing 1894: 264). Nancy instantly condemns Jessica's appearance, despite Jessica's claims that "it is the very best cut [and] by dressmakers from Paris" (264). Jessica is clearly overjoyed by these new purchases, but Nancy feels "her diminishing regard for Miss Morgan had suffered a fresh blow" (264). While Nancy cannot contemplate why Jessica would want to dress in such a way, there is an implication that this response implicates Jessica as a potential threat. Earlier in the novel,

Nancy observes that while Jessica's position is "unfortunate ... at least [she] did her the office of relief by contrast" (110). Now the situation has altered.

Unlike the French sisters and Jessica, who patronize the association, Nancy believes she is positioned outside this pursuit of cheap fashionable dress. As a result, she can legitimately attract the attention of Tarrant—a "gentleman." Yet Nancy's stance is ultimately an act of self-deception. Tarrant in fact considers Nancy to be "in every respect his inferior" (Gissing 1894: 146). Tarrant likens Nancy's character to that of a barmaid, highlighting the reality of her position and her proximity to the ignorant Mrs. Middlemist (and, perhaps, to Arabella in Hardy's *Jude the Obscure*): "He would as soon have contemplated taking to wife a barmaid. Between Miss Lord and the young lady who dispenses refreshment there were distinctions, doubtless, but none of the first importance" (146). While these comments expose the difficulties inherent in Tarrant's own social position—his father's "squandered estate" does not provide him with sufficient income and the money came originally from trade— they also reveal his ability to read her "taste in garments" accurately. Just as Nancy believes that Jessica's clothing associates her with the vulgarity of the Dress Supply Association, to Tarrant Nancy herself evidently belongs

> to the social rank only just above that of wage-earners; her father had a small business in Camberwell; she dressed and talked rather above her station, but so, now-a-days, did every daughter of petty tradesfolk ... She would marry some hapless clerk, and bring him to bankruptcy by the exigencies of her "refinement" (145)

Thus the ensuing relationship between Tarrant and Nancy reveals the complexities of the late nineteenth-century marriage market. Nancy clearly intends to utilize her dress as a means of obtaining the best match. Just as Ethelberta is able to maintain her position in society by virtue of appearance, Nancy believes she is sending out a positive financial and social message to potential suitors through her garments. As Joel Kaplan and Shelia Stowell (1994: 108) suggest with reference to Cicely Hamilton's play *Marriage as a Trade,* "personal adornment ... is less a matter of vanity or 'romance' than business calculation. Women, under patriarchy, simply acquire the skills needed to pursue the careers to which they have been apprenticed." In other words, while these fictional women are condemned—at least initially—by characters such as Tarrant, there is a sense that men themselves are responsible for the stronghold of fashion.

Within the works discussed, fashionable clothes are troped as a means of moving—or attempting to move—up the social ladder. For characters such as Ethelberta Petherwin, the desire to dress well is explicitly identified by her father as her motivation for marrying above her station. While Ethelberta's respective marriages go some way to legitimize her fashionable consumption, they simultaneously alienate her family. The sartorial differences that exist between Ethelberta and her brothers, for example, emphasize the problematic nature of her appearance. By assuming different clothes, Ethelberta is able to make the transition between lady and working woman swiftly and effectively. Hardy's narrative, therefore, points to the deceptive qualities of dress, and more explicitly how lower-class women are able to utilize these attributes in order to achieve—and in Ethelberta's case maintain—their social ambitions. Women such as Nancy Lord, Jessica Morgan, and the French sisters in Gissing's *In the Year of Jubilee,* however, play a slightly different game in the late nineteenth-century suburbs, exposed as engaging in a form of self-deception that makes, of course, their fashionable consumption so vulgar. The fact that male rather than female characters articulate these concerns most directly—Nancy Lord's comments about Jessica's dress clearly indicate her own lack of self-awareness— suggests that this is as much a debate about gender as it is about class. By emphasizing the ability of men in these works to recognize the social tensions inherent in fashionable dress, the threat fashion poses to the structure of late nineteenth-century society is, to some extent, contained.

Note

1. The middle class considered the music hall a vulgar institution because of its roots in working-class culture and, by extension, its association with drinking and prostitution.

—4—

Novelist as Stylist, Designer as Storyteller

Sophia Errey

What fascinated the truly modern artist was fashion's mystique, its understanding of historical, even archaic expression and—what Benjamin came to emphasize—its sense of the mythic, which offered a counterpoint to the threat of modern reification and rationalization as well as providing a vehicle for aesthetic experience.

Lehmann 2000: 213

Marcel Proust's *À la recherche du temps perdu* is an eight-part novel of thousands of pages, published sequentially over fourteen years but in gestation for even longer. Current fashion shows last for less than twenty minutes, showing garments developed over six to eight weeks. Their lifespan in images and publications is barely nine months before they are submerged in the relentless schedule of the fashion calendar. Yet despite the apparent contrast between the grandiose achievement of the novel and the ephemerality and triviality of the shows, it is possible to trace affinities that are reciprocally revealing. What the novel and the shows share is the capacity to engage us with a creative vision.

Proust creates an illusion of reality, immersing us so profoundly, yet so delicately, in a constructed world that his characters come to assume an independent existence veiled from our sight, as they are veiled from the understanding of the Narrator of the novel. The briefly glimpsed details of the form of fashion show, sometimes described as a spectacle show (Duggan 2001), may appear as bizarre, fantastic, and inaccessible to the viewer as the puzzling manifestations of others' behavior appear to the Narrator. Yet novel or show are both compelling in stamping a creative vision on us, revealing a consistent inner core beneath apparently arbitrary and willful variations.

Just as Proust argued that his details were not important in themselves but were "a full theory on memory and knowledge" (Festa-McCormick 1984: 177), so the elements apparently casually deployed in the presentation of clothes collections may offer a key to a coherent universe.

Clothes have long been recognized as a highly significant leitmotif in Proust's writing—indeed, Valerie Steele (2006) has suggested that if assembled into a single text, clothes-related passages would form a book of their own—and book-length studies have been devoted to exploring such passages and their relationship to the oeuvre as a whole. While Steele is a notable exception, the majority of such studies have been by writers well versed in literature and history but with little expertise in fashion.

It is well documented that Proust questioned friends about the details of outfits and ensembles worn or observed by them, and he also consulted photographs and artworks of an earlier period than the time at which he was writing. At the most banal level, in a work in which time is crucial to meaning, evocations of previous styles serve as exemplary chronological markers. Well-to-do Parisians who constituted the primary social milieu of the novel's setting were undoubtedly keenly attuned to the observation of changes in fashion, and to subtle details of stylistic variation. While references to such changes may have been comprehensible to Proust's earliest readers, the writer's allusions, which are couched in passionately Ruskinian detail rather than presented as descriptions of complete outfits, may prove puzzling to later readers. Only through a thorough historical knowledge of ensembles from the 1870s to the early twentieth century can we reclothe the characters from head to toe, rather than in elusive shreds and patches—here an impression of color, there an evocatively named hat or trim. Perhaps this is why albums of photographs or paintings of the period have also played a large part in Proustiana.

Proust assumes—and compels us to assume also—that clothes both reveal and mask individuals both unwittingly and as a matter of deliberate choice. As extensions of the body they function as indices of desire—that of the Narrator and that of the characters—and desire is a notorious distorter of vision. Attempts to read ensembles as signifying systems have proven abortive and a reading of Proust readily demonstrates why; the signs read by the Narrator are revealed as at odds with both others' readings and the intentions of the wearers.

From the rich range of material in the text I will focus on two characters and associated sets of references in which evocation and cultural coding are deeply implicated, since these mechanisms are foregrounded in late twentieth-century fashion shows.

The painter Elstir, the quintessential visual artist of *À la recherche du temps perdu*, appears first as the vulgar buffoon Monsieur Biche but is later shown as a brilliant painter and intelligent man with excellent taste in dress, a taste that the young Narrator lacks. The Albertine of the first period at Balbec, whose taste in music the Narrator considers execrable, is already able to appreciate the refined simplicity, achieved at great cost, of the clothes that Elstir has had made for his wife. She avidly absorbs the artist's comments on Venetian brocades and on the actress Mlle. Léa's "little white sunshade" (Proust 1999: 704), which stimulated the artist's "exquisite taste" and creative powers.

From the mid-nineteenth century couturiers had adopted the "legitimating codes of art to distance themselves from the vulgarities of commerce" (Watson 1999); what is sometimes considered to be a recent rapprochement of art and fashion has deep roots. Indeed, the modernist myth of the artist underpins, and simultaneously is refracted through, the tropes of creativity that are fundamental to the architecture of *À la recherche*. The Narrator, then, while aware of the limitations of Albertine's education, and secretly amused by her betrayal of such limitations, defers to her taste in clothes. The involuntary revelation of her contempt for him in her response to his ignorance of the difference between an haute couture dress and that from "an ordinary shop"—"An enormous difference, my good little man!" (Proust 1999: 705)—prefigures her later restless chafing under his control as he struggles to placate her and buy reciprocal emotion by gifts of expensive clothes, notably the designs of Fortuny. The themes of money, clothes, and the desired other are inextricably joined, then as now, each enflaming the other in the delirium of consumption.

The clothes designed by Mariano Fortuny function as an emotional crux for the Narrator, since they are linked with his desire to travel to Venice, where the Fortuny atelier was situated. He conveniently blames his neurotic resistance to undertaking the journey on Albertine, imagining that maintaining his control of her is the reason he is forced to remain in Paris ordering her Fortuny gowns. Their patterns and scent both soothe and exacerbate his longing for the dream city that he imagines through the lens of his knowledge of artworks.

Fortuny drew on a wide variety of historical styles of dress and ornament, including Greek, Renaissance, and oriental sources. These references helped to confer a timeless status on the designer's work, placing it in the realm of art rather than fashion and undergirding its ongoing collection by museums and art galleries as well as private collectors and wearers.

For the Narrator, Fortuny is linked with a brooding shadow of loss and separation as well as creativity and renewal, a metaphor for both the novel as a whole and for fashion with its perpetual annihilation and rebirth. He soothes himself with the notion that Albertine cannot leave him because "It was in a week's time that she was to try on the new Fortuny gowns" (Proust 1999: 1903), but as he embraces her the stiff fabric of her dress figured with coupled birds, symbols of death and resurrection, "ces oiseaux fatidiques," offer him a presentiment of her imminent flight from his grasp (Proust 1999: 1904).

The model of the archetypal "feminine" woman, the very embodiment of alluring contradictions, is established by the Narrator in the figure of Odette de Crécy. In the account of her life and liaison with Swann while the Narrator is still a child, she is presented as the seductive counterfoil to the nurturing care of the boy's mother and grandmother. Significantly, this woman of the demi-monde is characterized strongly in terms of her clothes and her immediate environment, which appear in an ambiguous synthesis as extensions of her role and personality. At her very first appearance in the novel she is "la dame en rose" (Proust 1999: 68–71), her soft pink dress implicitly associated with luxurious shimmering flesh, and wears pearls, gems often regarded as specifically feminine but also associated with the indoor life of the kept woman (471). In keeping with the fashion of the period, but also consonant with her class and position, Odette is consistently linked with orientalist allusions (182, 472) including a décor featuring chrysanthemums and Japanese and Chinese objects and, later, indoor gowns of oriental stuffs. Even now, when the orientalist associations of submissive femininity as well as exotic escapism seem to have been laid bare, they continue to exert a powerful fascination for designers.

Later, as the wife rather than the mistress of Swann, Odette is presented as an admired, elegant figure with a distinctive personal style: "She need only 'hold out' a little longer in this fashion and young men attempting to grasp her outfits would say: 'Mme Swann is a whole period in herself, isn't she?'" (Proust 1999: 490). In a following passage, deliberately positioned as ambiguous in time, the writer reflects on the details of outfits. He evokes an avalanche, a "profusion" of "delicate reminders." These apparently useless trims, lace, braid, trinkets, edgings, "that row of little satin buttons which buttoned nothing and could not be unbuttoned," are not only the "individualité vestimentaire" of an individual, but suggest the "delicate and spiritualized mechanism of a civilization" and encourage the writer's thoughts to linger over them. His detection of "an imperceptible air of being a costume, and insinuating itself within present-day life like an undecipherable reminiscence of the past" confers on Odette a fictitious nobility and "the allure of some historic or romantic heroines"—a distinct echo of the Narrator's first impression of "la dame en rose" as an actress (490–91).

The historical traces embedded in the eclecticism of nineteenth-century fashion have continued to haunt clothing to the present day (Clark 2004), with, in addition, an enormously enhanced exposure to source material via publications and museum collections. Fashion is renewed by recourse to any and every source that can stimulate and nourish the efforts of designers and makers and the desires of the consumer. Our imagination refracts the words of the novelist through vaguely remembered images of nineteenth- century costume, layered with glimpses of fashion plates and paintings—but also with film and theater costumes and later reworkings. The hint of panniers in Odette's dress, recalling an ancien régime luxury but also alluding to revivals of that period in the nineteenth and early twentieth centuries, inhabits a world of remembrance in which past and present are inextricably confused.

Odette excuses the romantic "costume" elements of her attire with the comment that, as she doesn't play golf, she doesn't wear "sweaters"—the word appears in English in the novel (Proust 1999: 491). One of the most profound evolutions in clothing forms in the last century has been the rise to dominance of so-called sports clothing. While this now totally dominates the market, it has not completely extirpated the production of more formal and elaborate dress, notably in French haute couture, where designs are most frequently damned as "costume," theatrical exercises unsuited to what is usually labeled modern life.

In spite of the bitter denunciations launched by Yves Saint Laurent and Pierre Bergé against contemporary designers, and vehement protestations that with Saint Laurent's retirement in 2002, haute couture was effectively dead, the process of making and showing prototypes of made-to-measure garments biannually in Paris persists and indeed currently seems to be undergoing something of a renaissance.

It is not difficult to understand how the aspect of Proust's oeuvre characterized by Edmund Wilson (1928, cited in Horyn 2007) as "the last fires of a setting sun" appealed to Saint Laurent, particularly in his later career, but clearly many other aspects of the novel and the novelist possessed a particular attraction for the couturier. While allusions to Proustian characters and atmospheres are undoubtedly present in the designer's collections, they are subtle and indirect. It is interesting to speculate on the relationship between the theme of cross-dressing in Proust and in particular women in men's clothing, and Saint Laurent's innovation of *Le Smoking* with its radical exposure of the gendered codes of modern dress.

While the designer's claim to having read *À la recherche* annually is hardly unusual, the use of astutely managed wealth derived from his design activities to create a Proust-themed retreat in the Villa Gabriel in Normandy from 1979 is much more extraordinary. What is remarkable about these interiors, at least in reproductions, is their deathliness, a sensation of embalmed time. Alicia Drake speculated, "Perhaps it was the emptiness of the house, or the contrived references that gave it such a sorrowful atmosphere" (Drake 2006: 280). This mournfulness and fixity in the object-crammed rooms is at a great remove from both the freshness of Proust's writing and the vigorous life of the catwalk in the shows of Saint Laurent at the height of his powers in the 1970s and those of his successors in the field.

The commencement of ready-to-wear presentations in 1966, with Saint Laurent's Rive Gauche label as one of the earliest participants, implied a decisive break with the traditions of haute couture. Although this innovation has been linked with the beginning of the staged "performance" show, as opposed to the restrained *défilé* form with a demure file of expressionless models pacing before the audience, a style many designers still use, the origins of the former lie much earlier. Recent writers have traced the roots of the extravaganzas staged from the 1980s onward to beginnings in the early twentieth century (Evans 2000, 2001; Troy 2003). Worth used live models in Paris in the 1840s and the presentation in which they walked before a seated audience began to be supplemented from around 1909 by thematic scenarios. The English designer Lucile (the trade name of Lady Duff Gordon) was probably the first to use this format, and also the first to name garments or ensembles. In Paris, Poiret began to use similar techniques around the same time. From the 1890s close relationships between designers and actresses were established. Leading ladies would often commission a personal wardrobe independently of the stage designer to wear as costume, and "fashion plays" in which the action revolved around fashion houses and shows—a genre later exploited in film—were popular. Actresses and stage scenes also figured prominently in magazine illustrations, both sketched and photographed. Ginger Gregg Duggan (2001: 23) has commented that elements used in contemporary shows—models, location, theme, and finale—that "translate well into fashion periodicals, feeding into the fantasies and aspirations of the readers," also apply to their earlier counterparts. Proust's well-known passage on the Princesse and Duchesse de Guermantes at the Opéra (1999: 776–79) implies that their dazzling appearance is as arresting as, or even trumps, the action on the stage, and the young Narrator's intense fascination with actresses is entirely consistent with the period.

From 1936 to 1939 Schiaparelli, a designer much studied by Saint Laurent and some recent designers, produced ten themed shows in which accessories and details of the outfits closely reflected the chosen motif—for example, the circus—and music, lighting, and choreographed movement were all designed to reinforce the effect. In the 1950s Mary Quant also used music and exuberant movement but additionally had the models carry objects related to the clothing references—posies for mock rustic shepherdess dresses or a shotgun for a Norfolk jacket. This may well have been inspired by the use of conventionalized props in photography, which already had a long history. The practice of "styling" photography sessions, involving both the creation or modification of a setting and the accessorizing and combining of garments—developed rapidly with the establishment of new and innovative publications such as *The Face* and *i-D* in the 1980s. As this activity became increasingly professionalized, to the point where it can be formally studied (Dingemans 1999), designers often supplemented their in-house team with freelance stylists, particularly for the all-important collection presentation staged for the press rather than for private buyers.

From the later 1990s it has become common for an individual to work as a freelancer for a designer or indeed several designers as well as on photographic series for magazines and on advertising shoots. While on the lower rungs of the ladder the work typically involves gofer jobs, sought-after individuals deemed to have creative talent have increasingly been given name credit. Not only do individuals work for a variety of clients, but also the lines between set design, artistic direction for film, live shows, and publications are increasingly blurred. In an interesting example, Annie Liebowitz photographed actors for the annual Hollywood portfolio of *Vanity Fair* published in March 2007. It was decided to stage a series of film noir-type scenes, with Michael Roberts as stylist and Vilmos Zsigmond as cinematographer—both widely known and admired figures in their fields. Liebowitz commented, "The styling was impeccable. I almost cried when I saw Abigail Breslin in that little French coat at the cemetery. The coat and that little beret were transforming" (2007: 168).

This shoot conformed to the "dramatic" fashion show as well as to a genre of photography explored in the exhibition "Fashioning Fiction in Photography Since 1990" (Museum of Modern Art, New York, 2002), not only in its capacity to evoke emotion, but also in its implied, but plotless, narrative. To some disapproving—but not unmoved—observers, these shows appear to be decadent, pretentious spectacles, empty of anything but a vitiated version of unashamed consumerism and lacking even the pretext of exhibiting wearable garments. However, the claim made by Alexander McQueen, "I design a collection with the staging, music, casting, hair, and makeup in mind—one complete vision if you like" (Bridget Foley's interview of

McQueen quoted in Karimzadeh and Socha 2006: 108), offers a clue to the powerful dramatic impact such shows can achieve. Just as the details of clothes Proust offers us are in no way dispensable or meaningless, so the staged presentation ideally succeeds in initiating us into a unique vision of the world, with all elements working together to create the experience. The effect is to offer the viewer, either present at the show or in a reduced version through the abundant images, both still and moving, available within hours of the show taking place, a concatenation of multilayered, multireferential images that, like Proust's characters and places, linger and grow in the mind over time. Proust's metaphor of an unfolding memory as a Japanese paper flower expanding in water is an apt one for this experience, for the time of the twenty-minute show, in that not only does it compress the immediately preceding work of the atelier, but in notable cases many elements of the particular universe of a designer and team expand in retrospect.

While Mugler, Kenzo, and others produced spectacular shows in the 1980s, the current designers particularly identified with this mode are McQueen and John Galliano; I will focus on examples drawn from the career of the latter.

The expression "fashion moment" has been degraded in the last few years, but a show consistently accorded this status by experienced fashion writers and professionals is the autumn/winter 1994/95 collection presented by Galliano in Paris, urged on by supporters, including Anna Wintour of USA *Vogue*. It was a last-ditch attempt by Galliano to try to regain his precarious footing in the fashion system after a rocky decade in and out of solvency. The venue was an elegant, historic, but dilapidated mansion loaned for the occasion by São Schlumberger. The show, pulled together in just fifteen days, consisted of only seventeen garments made primarily of black satin-backed crêpe, the most suitable yet affordable fabric that the designer could source (McDowell 1997: 166, 169–70). The style of the clothes evoked oriental and late nineteenth-century themes along with more recondite allusions—for example, a sleeve form based on a photograph of Palestinian bread makers. Beautiful though they were, they lacked the technical resources and sophistication of both reference and atelier skills available to Galliano in his later career at Givenchy and Christian Dior. What seems to have made the show so memorable was the integration of the elements. The hats, by Stephen Jones, and borrowed diamond jewelry complemented clothes displayed by some of the best models of the time. The house was dressed with fallen chandeliers, rustling dead leaves, and a deployment of seating throughout the space so that the models passed close to, and interacted with, the audience. A telling detail was the invitation, which was accompanied by a rusty key, a perfect symbol of the spatial, temporal, and erotic vistas the show sought—successfully, it would appear for many—to offer.

Galliano's graduation show from the Central Saint Martins School of Art in 1984 already demonstrated his absorption in a realm of occluded personal references, solidly grounded in detailed research but immersed in private fantasies stimulated by film and what ultimately became a formidable knowledge of fashion references.

These predilections were undoubtedly stimulated by his association with Amanda Greaves (later Amanda Lady Harlech), who had read literature at Oxford and who acted as muse and stylist until 1996. Her journals, and the later book compilations put together by the design team that detail inspirations and visual references, suggest the richness but also the consistency of the designer's vision. Galliano has always claimed that his much-commented on appearances at the end of each show are the result of his total immersion "living and breathing" the atmosphere of the collection. These appearances are now professionally styled, but their often undeniable strangeness tends to undergird claims of a compelling personal viewpoint as well as being calculated for the potential publicity they attract.

For many of the 1990s collections Galliano and his team concocted a heroine and an often highly improbable story line involving romantic trials and perils. The heroines were inspired by classic examples of extravagant personae, chiefly of the past—the Marchesa Casati, Kiki de Montparnasse, Diaghilev ballerinas—allowing both subtle and obvious references to historical costume, like Odette's hints, to appear through contemporary dress. The models were encouraged to throw themselves into acting a part, and the shows were presented in elaborately dressed sets designed by specialists, notably Jean-Luc Ardouin and Michael Howells, experienced stage and film designers.

They attracted increasingly strident criticism, particularly after Galliano was appointed to design women's wear for Dior in 1997. From 2001 to 2006 there was a progressive, although uneven, diminution of what commentators often derisively referred to as theatrical elements, particularly in the ready-to-wear, less so in the couture. Under the direction of Alexandre de Betak's production group, used for many Paris shows, the Dior presentations began to approximate much more closely the classic parade on an elevated runway. While the Dior ready-to-wear of October 2006 was by Galliano standards ultraminimalist, the March 2007 Dior show and the designer's eponymous line show abruptly rebounded, following a triumphal haute couture show in January 2007, to the drama, role-play, and opulent seduction of earlier shows, again under the direction of Michael Howells. Interestingly, the unusually integrated January 2007 collection was related, like the 1994 show, to Puccini's Madama Butterfly and refracted orientalism through a dizzying plethora of both overt and subtle references.

Galliano is unusual in having each model show only a single outfit, allowing for a prolonged and elaborate preparation of hair and makeup that often paradoxically obliterates the model's individual features. The effect is to present the models as manifestations of a single person, or, since the shows are frequently broken into groups or sets, of a small number of wearers, whose wardrobe-revealed personalities are amplified in each successive outfit in a manner parallel to the progressive revelations in Proust, a method that, to quote Diana Festa-McCormick (1984: 3), "foster(s) a feeling of expectancy, awaken(s) the imagination, and maintain(s) an incessantly renewed sense of novelty."

Fashion, like analysis, is interminable. While the collection show compresses a huge expenditure of time and energy—a single couture outfit typically requires hundreds of hours of work—into a brief flash, the next collection is already in genesis as it concludes. It is not necessary to subscribe to the theoretical justifications of Roland Barthes's statement that "Proust is a complete system for reading the world" (Barthes cited in Bowie 2001: 154) to understand his contention that we are confronted with a text that proffers us an experience of merging against a critical distance. Similarly, in the most successful examples of the staged show, we are offered the pleasures of clothing not simply as material garments but as a mode of dream.

The Mystery of the Fashion Photograph

Margaret Maynard

There can be something immensely powerful and visually arresting about a glossy fashion photograph. Its verve moves us, perhaps more than sexuality does. Great fashion images engage the viewer aesthetically (or by overt grittiness, voyeurism, sensationalism, or even excess ordinariness), but they also play with our minds. It is a truism to say advertising draws attention to its products by manipulating the viewer. But how does this happen? The focus here is on engaging upmarket, sometimes avant-garde, concept shots of women, mostly so-called editorial images, at the heart of glossy magazines, bearing in mind that fashion photographs are created, oriented to, and restricted by the status order of the magazine (Aspers 2006: 7, 70). The images of concern are those bookended by commercial or rag-trade photos in which the informational logic of mass advertising and the actual look of garments are the most important, as opposed to fascinations of a different order. My question is what makes certain high-end photos eye-stopping, what gives them their strange thrill, their compelling intrigue, and why is this important? What is it about some images that evoke in the viewer a desiring state of mind? Many examples here come from Australian fashion magazines and editorial photography, but this is a worldwide phenomenon.

Part of the response is that magazine editors and photographers formulate complex strategic and creative associations, or disassociations, between image and textual narrative that deliberately bring the imagination of the viewer into play, often in ways beyond sexuality. However, such photos, which independently have enigmatic stories, or more often derive from image/text relationships, lack resolution, unlike TV ads that frequently purport to solve consumer problems (Dyer 1982: 10). The spectator/reader is thus moved by hard-to-pin-down qualities. The highest order of fashion image has the inscrutable at its heart. Resulting emotions engender self-contained, even self-created experiences of a kind of unspecific fashionability. This may or may not be an immediate conversion to consumption.

Swedish photographer Mikael Jansson's stunning high-energy image of a model lying beside a pool for *French Vogue* (June 2004) stirs the imagination via a tale of anxiety and residual enigma. A male swimmer is in a dramatic act of grasping the woman—is it a predatory or a rescue shot? The subject ensures we "experience" its lack of clarification intensely. Watery connections and bathing are a repetitive subject for fashion imagery—also in art history with links back to classical times. An electric and brilliantly colored photograph by Paul Fullbrook for Australia's *Mode* magazine (Winter 1979: 84) shows two skiers racing down the slopes at a perilous angle, snow flying, causing us to gasp at the uncertainty of the story's possible ending. Such elements of narrative remind us to an extent of Barthes's familiar words from *Camera Lucida* (although not illustrative of it), in that they "prick," disturb, or punctuate the image, spurring our desire. They engender an affecting response (Barthes 1981a: 32).

Women model their fashioned selves on celebrities as well as photographic fashion models. It goes without saying that glamour, a genre of representation, a discursive effect, and a form of commodity, lies at the heart of most fashion images where its paradox of accessibility and exclusivity is most apparent. However, my claim is that intriguing storylines make high-end editorial images only tangentially a force for consumption. Rather, it is ambiguity that confirms their self-contained desirability. Feelings or emotions entrap the viewer (frequently ensured by reassuring subject clichés that I will pursue in this chapter). These emotions propel readers to participate vicariously in the fantasy, sometimes even to visualize themselves as a star in the show, but not necessarily to act on the emotion.

An image of model Gemma Ward photographed in Greece by Justin Smith for *Vogue Australia* (September 2004: 150–51) has this ambiguity. It is part of an editorial called "Vogue: The Odyssey" and implies a lengthy journey with no end in sight. The model, in knee-length ruched-up and loosely flounced skirt and thin-strapped top, leans back perilously from a naked classical statue while clasping the statue's muscular right arm. Could this image refer to the impossibility of a subject offering herself unsuccessfully to a statue lover immersed in his own self-involved act of heroic struggle? Or is it a good theme, which fit well with the staging of the Athens Olympic Games? The dress is stunning, but what might come of this unsatisfactory relationship?

Anne Marsh, in *The Dark Room,* argues that photography is a performative medium in which the camera produces a dynamic discourse of desire at the intersection between scientific (the known) and the magical (the unknown) (Marsh 2003: 17). The result is dramatic fiction, a *tableau vivant* involving viewer, subject, and operator. Marsh's definition is useful, derived from a trilogy we find in Barthes' *Camera Lucida* (1981a: 13), and might be readily transposed as a way of understanding fashion photography. This definition is brilliantly explicated by the image of Caroline Drury modeling on a Hollywood set circa 1960 (Plate 17) by highly regarded Sydney photographer Laurence Le Guay.[1] Relying on a longstanding, modern advertising trope, it juxtaposes the polish of high-end female fashion with sleek motoring technology. Le Guay's presence is indicated by proxy via his photographic lighting apparatus turned away from the subject, with double viewers (allegedly Roger Moore in the passenger seat[2] of the latest Ford Falcon Thunderbird and the photographer doubling as ourselves). There is a third mysterious person in the passenger seat of the other vehicle. Importantly as here, when a curious indeterminacy is strategically employed in a fashion image, the reader/spectator is offered the chance to play a subjective role and thus intervene in the scenario. So mystery (as opposed to fantasy) in fashion photography is not just glamour and aesthetics, it is also a reading experience to do with open-ended dramas, specifically set up to lack a bounded point of view. This scenario of us looking at someone who is looking at a model offers possibilities, not conclusions.

At stake are four major issues: first, the structure of fashion magazines; second, narrative and the shifting shape of editorials; third, genre; and finally the role of the spectator.

In terms of the first, ideas from Michael North's book *Camera Works* (2005) are useful to examine. In this book, North talks about popular photography in the early modern period. He suggests it offered hope of a new kind of democratic writing with light—a system neither purely linguistic (that is, descriptive or alphabetic), nor purely pictorial (the aesthetic), to an extent readable but often haunted by unresolved strangeness. As a visual language it hovers in what he calls a utopian space, an impossible, unfixed imaginary "somewhere" (North 2005: 4). This new form of communication, neither writing alone nor picturing, was felt to reach the mind directly (5). Photographs, he comments, were regarded as a kind of code. Like a hieroglyph they were felt to bypass spoken language and reach the mind directly through the eye.

North does not deal with fashion photos per se, as he is considering too early a period. But it is useful to think of his ideas in relation to high-impact fashion photography, in which image consumption is an instant thing, arising from a utopian (or today sometimes a dystopian) space, stemming from an association between narrative and image. We see this in disturbing images of a black model at night in various states of dress disorder by French photographer Rachel Bank for issue 67 of *Oyster* (2007: 120–27). The editorial is called "The Dark Hour," with all that entails. The space or "gap" I am alluding to is coded as mysterious or thrilling—one of anxiety as here, or of pleasure perhaps or even frustration, as with the Justin Smith image.

Another example is the arresting *Vogue Australia* image (Plate 18) (January 1985: 63), part of a twenty-page editorial called "Magnetic Centre" by Michel Comte (New York), the magazine cover inscribed *Primal*. Here a white cotton Linda Jackson V-back dress and white organza poncho are shown on a model whose face is mysteriously obscured and who is wearing bracelets decorated with pseudo-Aboriginal designs. Many of the sequence images are captioned with words like "Diaphanous dreamtime," "Fabric of the land," "Rock painting for the body," "Ayers Rock hunter and gatherer, wrapped from the heat," "white goes walkabout," and so on. Words and images together hint at the excitement of traveling to a remote environment but also back in time to an exotic and strange location, a mainstay for fashion photography.

North is not unusual in pointing to ways in which photography and language entwine. Many writers have done so. W.T.J. Mitchell regards the relation of photography and language as a paradox; it is, and it is not, a language (Mitchell 1994: 284). Quoting Burgin, he notes that photography is always mediated by words (stories); it is invaded by language the moment it is looked at. The intention here is not to enter into such general theorizing about photography and language. We have Barthes's landmark book *The Fashion System* (and its focus on how related elements or components make up fashion) to thank for much writing on word/image relationships. His central category is "represented clothing" separately ordered or coded into image-clothing and written-clothing. Images, he claims, provide fascination, slipperiness, and vagueness but need language to bring fixity and the immobilization of perception (Carter 2003: 150). "Image-clothing can most certainly be *fashionable* … but it cannot be *Fashion* directly," for it is only an attribute (as quoted in Carter: 150).

This separate ordering of different parts of fashion can seem disagreeable, but it needs noting, as do arguments claiming photography to be one kind of a mark-making technology rather than a medium of communication (Maynard 1997: 57). I would also like to mention critical rethinking of Barthes and Burgin, offered for instance by Hughes and Noble in *Phototextualities,* bringing the cultural context and photographer back into the picture (2003: 14). Suffice it to say that we need to acknowledge current multidimensional approaches to photography and current views of the complexity of verbal/visual tensions and intersections between photos and text that produce understanding. Barthes suggests that fashion images provoke fascination (1981a: 17) but also that the presence of language acts to stay perception, thus cementing meaning as fashionable (Carter 2003: 150). Language in fashion photography does not impose such fixity; rather, a dynamic space is created via visual associations with nonspecific, often troubling stories, and the combined enigma offers an immediate invitation to engage.

Clive Scott in his book *The Spoken Image* says that the problem of fashion images is that they are theatrical and artificial and do not present as reality; on the other hand consumers must negotiate with this falsity and be convinced of the real possibility of a purchase (1999: 144–45). Unlike in thrillers that climax to a conclusion, no such thing happens in the fashion photos under discussion. Here the inscrutability of the image and/or editorial sequence is clearly the driver of a desire that may have incidental connections with the purchasing chain. This is not product placement per se.

In these captivating fashion images, a kind of drift takes place in a gap of indeterminacy, an imaginative space open to viewers' interpretation. In this regard it is interesting to consider celebratory Rankin's[3] photographic "keyhole" advertising campaign for Elle McPherson's Intimates lingerie range in 2003, which drew a lot of criticism for being sexually offensive. The models were photographed as if seen via a peep show. Situated in different interior settings, they have bodies but no heads. Elle's rather arch take on this was that was she was aiming for ambiguity, not voyeurism. She wanted to stress the notion of the unfinished story—everyone has a personal story, she said, and it is up to the beholder to interpret what they see: "We invite the viewer to enjoy the intrigue and draw their own conclusions." On the Web site, the viewer leafs through a virtual book titled "Intimate Stories. An Anthology," which contains six short stories, three of which are anonymous.[4]

One particular story, "The Illusion" by Sandra Bernhard—a celebrity actress, comedienne, and writer—is as abstruse as it could be. It reads, "Dreams were filled with the past; she hesitated, waiting for the door to unlock. Where had he gone? 'Only to post a letter home.' Maybe she should have sensed it ... distracted by intimacy yet longing for space, she breathed deeply when he ..."

Fashion Magazines: Their Format and Structure

Fashion photography is about cultural status, and all fashion magazines have their own particular identity, their own complex niche formula. These elements are related to paper quality, target readers, and sales volume. Fashion magazines also sell fashion ideas to maintain the shape of this identity and rank themselves in a hierarchy of cultural capital. Today in Australia perhaps *Vogue Australia* and *Oyster* are at the top, with *Doingbird* and *Cream* as more avant-garde and *Marie Claire* lower ranked. This magazine niche status was the case fifty years ago, with *Vogue Australia* a conservative, high-class magazine compared to the more relaxed *Flair* commencing in 1956, *Pol* from 1968, and *Rag Times* and *Mode* from 1977, with *Pol* and *Rag Times* being the most adventurous. Fashion photographers creatively orient themselves to this hierarchical difference.

The cover of a fashion magazine until the 1970s, and sometimes continuing, was usually a close-up of a beautiful model's face. Such a cover carried its own expectations and very specific functions in attracting readership, combined with the use of devices such as heavier paper. The cover and opening pages are something that McCracken suggests serve as an interpretative lens that leads the reader into the magazine and helps increase its circulation (1993: 96). But at the heart of fashion magazines lie editorial photos, shoots that offer opportunities for a narrative of some kind and can have up to twenty pages, though more likely nine to ten. There can be several in one issue. The tone of these are devised by the fashion editor, responsible for ensuring they are compatible with the cultural "frame" of the magazine, probably assisted by ideas pitched by photographers. Editorial images are often supported by the slightest emotional trigger word; appealing and hyperbolic adjectives; repetitions, synonyms, and alliterative lines; incongruous themes; enabling and or subverting captions; loosely related story moments; or even free-floating images of nonspecificity. We may scarcely be aware of the words or stories, given the heightened power of images over text. Equally interesting is that photographers could slip between image making, writing, and editing. Wendy Adnam was fashion editor, article and interview contributor, as well as stylist and photographer for the progressive *Rag Times* from 1977 and became editor from issue number 7 (May 1978) to 1981. Rennie Ellis took fashionlike photos called "Street Life" for the same magazine in the 1970s and was also a feature writer.

In avant-garde magazines the editorial story may be nonexistent and may rest solely with the name of the celebrity photographer. In the highly adventurous Australian fashion magazine *Doingbird,* central narratives can be absent. In issue 10 of 2006 David Armstrong is credited with a portraitlike series of twenty-one images (no page numbers) that variously credit garment designers. In this issue there is such an eclectic mix of fashion, landscape, street styles, interviews, essays, news, and art photos that the category "fashion photograph" has morphed into something totally different from fifty years ago. Here the name of the well-known photographer, very prominently shown at the start of a series of images, actually replaces the role of the connecting editorial theme. The editorial has slipped away, and the name of the high-profile fashion photographer has taken its place, providing in fact the narrative glue.

On other occasions, editorial representations may be formally overwhelmed by text, as in Michele Aboud's editorial "Cinderella—Today's Ice Princess" for *Vogue Australia* in March 1996. One image (p. 145) of a modest young woman in a demure long white gown is overlaid with a block of heavy black text. Part of this reads, "Bridal styles are stale. To steal these looks from story books, white goes beyond the pale." Modern consumers are visually highly literate. Fashion stories are formed of course via visual references but also particularly by literary cross-referencing or homages, as we see here, to fairy stories, poems, films, and so on, adding further complications to our understanding of visual consumption.

Editorial images were customarily chosen by client or editor, from a series of contact prints. The small contact is a citation plucked from a number of sequential shots, editorialized into a narrative. A Sportscraft advertisement (*Vogue Australia* March 1966: 21–24), by David Franklin (who worked in Sydney until 1962), mimics a film-strip but could equally well reference these photographic contact prints. The predigital fashion photograph (before the 1980s) was, and is, notionally the equivalent of a block of type (North's hieroglyph).Today digital image making can take the place of the contact. Digital images are further types of fictionalized and derealized scripts; another novel category of writing. Without physical dimension, unhinged from the actual, they can perhaps more potently convey stirring and imagined states.

Fashion photography is a collective process, although since the 1960s photographers have enjoyed celebrity status to one degree or another, certainly evident today. "Naked Ambitions," a dramatic, film noir-like nine-page editorial of uncertain yet ominous storyline for *Oyster* (issue 67, 2007: 102–10), is by Mikael Vojinovic, sensational French/Yugoslavian celebrity image maker, and shows the photographer as chief protagonist in the image/story nexus (Plate 19). Vojinovic describes himself as one of fashion's newest criminals, and his Web site tells us that "Naked Ambitions" is his personal slogan. Many of the editorial fashion retailers have names like "Operations," "Agent Provocateur," and "Noir," adding to the thriller theme of the series. Yet despite the photographer's celebrity, a broad collaboration is still acknowledged. The editorial has what amounts to film credits: stylist, hair artist, makeup artists, production credit, casting person, and lastly the model.[5]

The understory of image making is of great interest, though not of primary concern in this essay. Suffice it to say that fashion imagery is only part of a dense web of meanings linked to the production and consumption marketing cycle in which they exist. This often unrecognized level is constituted by pragmatic issues linked to camera technology, economic factors, interpersonal interactions, marketing values, and the changing face of the publishing industry itself. Most importantly, the "backstage crew" makes the intrigue possible.

The most interesting fashion images seem to obscure, even hide, their raison d'être, their commercial links. Sometimes details of commercial or designer retailers are minute, relegated to the back of magazines or even absent. It is possible their absence energizes desire by strength of visual impulse. Clive Scott argues in *The Spoken Image* that photos interact with titles and captions (although still maintaining differences) but are more semantically rich the more speechless they are (Scott 1999: 11), for instance, "The Birds and the Bad Apple" series of fashion images by photographer Julia Kennedy with illustrations that accompany them by Laura Quick, which feature in the Gallery segment of *Cream* (2007 March/April/May: 40–49). No retailers are named and there is no text except to say it is a fairytale, recently animated by video director Neil Coxhill, plus soundtrack. Kennedy says, "We do these stories for the fun of it at the moment ... but we're hoping to get work off the back of them" (41). So an ambiguous concept, with a Web presence as well, generates a general sense of intrigue that circulates freely as fashionability but doesn't necessarily correlate with a designer or retailer.

Narrative and the Shifting Nature of the Editorial

Pictorial/textual and word relationships in fashion magazines have undergone manifold historical modifications dependent on period tastes, the class of magazine, and improved printing and production methods, giving magazines options to create new priorities. In editorial photography stories can be born less from the runway than from psychological or intriguing concepts that are conceived by the photographer, the stylist, the commissioning fashion editor, or any combination of these.

Narrative can deal with events as they occur, as a temporal unfolding of events or where there is a causal subject relationship between images (Richardson 2000: 110). In fashion photography the latter is more usual but seldom deterministic. Sometimes in the 1980s one finds highly evocative works, like Robert Butcher's editorial series in sepia on grainy paper called "Wild Weather" (*Mode* June/July1980: 113–29). It is reminiscent of the mystery of the moors and the gloomy weather of nineteenth-century novels, or perhaps melodramatic historical novels like *Jamaica Inn* (1936) by Daphne du Maurier. This strangeness has been seen more recently in the "Industrial Chic" editorial for *Marie Claire* (July 1996: 96–101) by Greg Delves, a Melbourne photographer who now lives in New York. The minimal listing of retailers in thin typewriter print almost looks like stray pieces of metal. The mesh belt (on p. 98) intrigues as it doubles as a snake on a rock, and the whole series maintains this opposition, even lack of clarity, between metal and natural landscape, a repetitive cliché for jewelry ads.

The idea of using editorial stories in fashion advertising is usually credited to Baron de Meyer in the 1920s, hired by Condé Nast for *American Vogue* in 1913. This concept of a fashion story is found in embryonic form in Australia about the same time. Fashion photography in this country was somewhat slow to develop, beginning seriously a little before the First World War and hampered by a poor-quality magazine publishing industry. Considered a mechanical medium, half-tone fashion photos were often slotted into unrelated slabs of text in newsprint magazines and newspapers. The images were one-offs, not editorials as such. Text, if it existed, was reserved for details of clothing retailers and hat shops. By the 1920s, and occasionally even prior to the First World War, proto-editorials emerge, chiefly as photos grouped around a common event, theme, activity, or type of clothing or centered on a season such as spring. They sometimes include a short story line. Accompanying images of "Mid Winter Modes" celebrating wool, advertised by Farmer's Sydney department store (*Home* June 1, 1921: 31), a tennis outfit is described as being a striped cape of brushed wool "to throw over your sweater as you come heated and triumphant from a successful 'set' of tennis."

As fashion photography became more "artistic" during the pictorialist twenties, textual copy sometimes matched photography's poetic, sometimes evocative style, adding a new dimension of beguiling salesmanship and occasionally but not always romance. An image from *Home* (December 1921: 41, Plate 20) is captioned: "She unfurls her picturesque Japanese sunshade of shower-proof oiled paper to keep the golden sungleams from the rival gold of her check-trimmed Jumper in loosely woven artificial silk. And never were checks and stripes more cleverly combined than in the box pleated skirt of cream gabardine …" Advertising language at this time is liberally laced with French terms such as *articles de Paris, toilette, charmante,* and *distingué*.

Anne Hollander sees the 1930s as a key moment for the capability of the camera to capture the passing moment and hence to capture unfinished dramas of acute tension (Hollander 1991: 46). In Australia various forms of editorial continued on and off into the 1950s; note that the country's first dedicated fashion magazine, *Fashion,* started only in 1947, and *Vogue Supplement for Australia* followed in 1955. After the war and into the 1960s, when fashion photography had developed a more defined professionalism, photographers Le Guay and Athol Shmith, who worked for *Vogue Australia* and *Flair,* situated models against slums or downmarket areas, raising the enigmatic stakes. But sometime in the 1960s relations between writers and photographers shifted, and editors began occasionally to exploit the possibilities of narrative in more complex ways.

Le Guay was responsible for a wonderful double-page example in 1960, "Untitled (Fashion Queue with Masked Child)." It is of a mix of travelers, both fashion models and others, in a bus queue. Held by the Art Gallery of New South Wales, it has the status of high art (the title was given to it by the gallery, which ironically adds to its mystery). It is a double spread that concludes a six-page editorial for *Flair* magazine called "How to Stand Out in the City" (August 1960: 34–39). It has retail bylines and descriptions of the actors' roles below the image on the page, but not their names. Le Guay doesn't casually interject models into a background of everyday street scenes, as did many American and British photographers. He deliberately stages a mix of fashion and everyday documentary: different ages, sexes, and economic conditions suspended in time, appearing both contrived and also snapshotlike. It is a combination of ironic humor laced with the macabre offered by the masked child. The significance of this work appears to lie in its hard-to-pin-down visual quality—its mix of street wear and high fashion, models and everyday commuters, all fostering an unsettling quality.

Radical magazines in the 1960s and 1970s often totally changed the nature of editorials by turning storytelling into something deliberately literal. Photographers such as Rennie Ellis ran so-called "Street Stories" in *Rag Times*. Yet even this move to the prosaic is intriguing. In some cases the prosaic commercial image/text deliberately cross-fertilizes fashion photography with actual mystery stories, but resolutions are vague. Peter Gough's sequence of photos (*Pol* April 1970: 17–21) tells the dramatic tale of feared counteragent Edwina Maloney and how to get a $1,000 painting past the Ratbags, a dreaded gang of Melbourne thieves. This task is finally handed over to two masters of female disguise, one of them being Robert Fritzlaff, the very designer whose clothes are featured. A story shot in the autumn/winter 1960 issue of *Australian Fashion and Beauty* magazine (45–47), "The Case of the Wanted Fur, a Fashion Who Done It," was devised by Don Joinson and scripted by Nicky Molyneux with images by Henry Talbot (a major Australian fashion photographer). It tells how Jones, a simple "fellow," had his heart stolen by five women who had succumbed to the glamour of furs and are in the dock charged with possession. Jones, the story tells, "just didn't have a chance." It is similarly didactic but still runs the line, "What's Your Verdict?"

Whereas movie celebrities endorsed fashion products in the 1920s and 1930s, by the 1960s fashion dramas could cross-fertilize with novels as well as cinema narratives. In a 1963 "Men in Vogue" supplement for October *Vogue Australia,* an editorial appeared entitled "A New James Bond," shot in Paris as if in a casino, by Helmut Newton (*Casino Royale* was filmed four years later, in 1967). Here we see Newton's wife taking a part as well as Ian Fleming starring as M, the self-consciously literal and filmic sense of a fashion thriller dramatically at work.

Aside from temporal stories, there is more often a loosely causal subject relationship in editorial images. A good example is Greg Barrett's "White Magic" editorial (*Mode* April/May 1980: 28–44), with a range of unrelated sites—tennis courts, Luna Park, and flower stands. There is no story, but the theme of magic and whiteness runs throughout, conjoined with a sense of the carnivalesque. Once practical possibilities for printing true and fast colors became common in the 1950s the focus on a single color (here white) became one of the most long-lasting clichés of fashion photography. More interesting as an editorial series are Karin Catt's brilliant images for *Marie Claire* (February 2000: 118–27), "Mothers Little Helpers," highlighting the perennial problems women have juggling work, fashionable dressing, and domesticity (Plate 21). No greater discrepancy could be imagined between a "litter" of babies, nappies, and leopard-skin accessories. Moving through various backyard sites are other images: a model tripping over a baby's drink bottle, a baby playing with a sequined handbag, and a purse spilling out a mix of pacifier, teething ring, and cosmetics. The story intrigues; we don't understand its implications, and the drama remains unresolved. Which will triumph: biology and motherhood, or style?

Genre

Some of the strangeness of fashion photography is paradoxically held in check by generic expectations, its clichés. Lipovetsky alludes to this in talking generally about the culture industries that conform to the fashion system when he notes the standard and formulaic attitudes to small novelties that he calls "an adventure without risk," as opposed to the inventiveness of the radical avant garde (1994: 177). We speak categorically of the "genre" of fashion photography as having coherent histories, practices, and expectations, allegedly predictable qualities, something in common, a norm that may organize viewers' responses (Palmer 1991: 113). But the status of genre is not as essentialist as might be imagined. Genres are not made up of sets of ingredients. They are rhetorical practices, informed by provisional, external engagements and framing procedures that play with relational contrasts. In other words, to consider fashion images as generic is to understand them as constituted by sets of regularities, sufficient to mark out particularities, but at the same time without entirely consistent rules (Freadman and Macdonald 1992: 25–26, 43). Various differences exist, being "ceremonial" frames or boundaries, which for fashion photography may be variability of captions, layout, and technical procedures; the overall size, type, and marketing style of the magazine itself; as well as the photographers' lens selection, camera angle, cropping layout, and choice of location (Alvarado 2001:154).

So fashion image making as a genre is located in a shifting and dynamic matrix between image and text defined by "impurities." But fashion stories (subsets of the genre of fashion photography) also spring from generic triggers that tend to be highly conservative in subject and settings, like the cover girl and fashion associated with cars (and other technology like airplanes). Other clichés include the exotic, the weather, colors, and especially water locations such as the beach or pool scenes, cityscapes, erotica, the downmarket, the melancholy model, and so on. But repetitive formalities and secure containments seem the precise mechanism that allows the enigmatic free rein. They assist the viewer's subjectivity to range more widely in constructing a story. Curiously this formulaic element is what Radnor has found to lie at the heart of romance novels—the fantasy of repetition is as important as the fantasy itself (1995: 71–72). So there is some irony in that the open-ended dramas of creative fashion editorials are made reassuring, sometimes predictable, by their generic, even clichéd regularities or subject coherences.

Even the blank lack of engagement of the most photogenic models, their self-absorbed disdain and sense of unattainable perfection, which allegedly fuel desires of consumers beset by feelings of inadequacy, have their place. While not all models necessarily offer this (with regard to male models Entwistle [2000] shows it is more often a certain quirkiness that takes the photographer's eye), their disengagement, sometimes their seeming anonymity, provides a blank canvas that further fuels imprecise and intense longings.

The Spectator/Reader

Fundamental to the popular psychology of selling from the early twentieth century was the belief that consumers, especially women, were susceptible to visual stimuli. Today this theory now applies across genders. Anne Hollander's famous view that shifts in the "look" of fashion are based on representational impulse, appealing directly to the imagination through the eye, is a tangential facet of this concept. Hollander claims the pressure of visual needs has nothing to do with social communication, culture, or ideology. Artists or photographers do not invent new fashions; they create compelling looks, and these necessitate the need for change (1978: 350). I agree to a great degree with Hollander, but in my view, the compelling "look" comes from an observing eye tempted by the enigmatic, held in check by genre, and tempered by text and narrative.

While accepting Hollander's thesis about the significance of the look, one needs to take further account of the beholder. We all know viewers variously decode fashion photographs. The consumer is actively engaged in taking control of the process by which she or he is represented (Radnor 1995: 178). Various types of magazine audiences are skeptical and critical, attaching different meanings to fashion imagery, as Diana Crane shows in *Fashion and Its Social Agendas* (2000: 208). But we need to realize that different responses can be due to opportunities offered by unresolved narratives. The enigmatic allows viewers an opportunity to slide into an authorial seat, not just indulge in passive looking (if this indeed ever occurs). In such a position, they momentarily exercise control via their own imagination, writing themselves into the story. They also self-create the mystery, which is their part in the construct of fashionability.

Readers come to fashion image-texts (editorials) with generic expectations, which reassure. Imprecise narratives with formal aesthetic qualities, the "wow" factor of the look, its setting and no-plot story, create a powerful effect, drawing the viewer into the scenario. This imprecision mirrors popular fiction, including TV sitcoms, for instance, for which there may be no single author, and audiences collaborate by inserting their own personal readings. This creates a system of orientations that circulate between audience, text, and industry (Palmer 1991:125). Desire and meaningfulness are triggered when the beholders are aesthetically convinced and vitalized by the enigmatic gaps between image and story, and they are encouraged to fabricate their own personal links between the casual montage of events. Comfortable subject clichés enhance this freedom to imagine. If consumption does occur, regret may sometimes follow, or even a sense of loss after buying, thus generating the need for further fashionable imaginings.

In commercial fashion photography, desire is triggered if the photographer, in sync with a narrative, creates an enigmatic yet thrilling space hovering between what we see and something unknown: one of intrigue. This urges the viewer to personalize her or his emotional involvement. It is my contention that the unspecific mix of unsettled and unsettling space created for, and by, a desiring subject is what makes fashion imagery so effective. This does not necessarily mean the viewer will be a fashion wearer. A fashion photograph remains an enigmatic thing. One may look, yearn for, but not necessarily buy.

Notes

1. Dating has been partly based on the style of the motor vehicle as well as the fashionable outfit.
2. Information given to the author by former fashion model Caroline Drury.
3. The photographer's full name is John Rankin Waddell.
4. <www.intimate-stories.com>, accessed April 2007.
5. Models started to be regularly credited by their full names only in the 1970s but still mainly as "cover girls."

–6–

The Fashioned World of Andrea Zittel

Tim Laurence

Since the middle of the last century artists have expanded the boundaries of art practice as they have been confronted by and ultimately engaged with increasingly pluralistic environments. Art practice is no longer bounded in traditional aesthetics but centered in the creation of significant ideas. It is within this context of idea-based art practice that design as art has developed. This phenomenon is now generally referred to as design art. An artist who exemplifies this practice is Andrea Zittel.

Under the pretext of offering solutions to the maladies of contemporary life, Zittel creates art that crosses the traditional boundaries of artistic practice. Her practice skips across areas of design: architecture, interiors, furniture, product design, and clothing. My focus here is on the last of these, her apparel works, a strand of her practice that she has explored continuously over her career.

Zittel is best known for her range of artworks that deal with issues of contemporary human living or habitation. These works are varied in substance and substantial in number; however, they all follow a common purpose, to pose solutions to problems found in contemporary life. Zittel first developed this interest in life's problems while completing an MFA at the Rhode Island School of Design; at that time her work focused on defining the role of the artist in contemporary society. She did not wish to add to "the artistic glitter of the world"; rather, she wanted to concentrate on "non-creative works" (Zelevansky 1994: 29). She has maintained this noncreative approach to her work ever since, always creating objects that bear the aesthetics of industrial production. Her most publicized works to date that clearly illustrate this idea are her *A–Z Living Units* (1992–1994), steel-framed plywood units that combine sleeping, cooking, and living in one self-contained object. These works went into a type of serialized production initially for friends of the artist and later for exhibition and purchase. Zittel exhibited her first *A–Z Living Unit* at Andrea Rosen Gallery in a two-person exhibition with Simon Leung in October 1992. In text reminiscent of advertising propaganda, originally written as catalogue text, Zittel, on her Web site, describes the background to her *A–Z Living Units*:

> This structure was the first attempt to satisfy the often conflicting needs of security, stability, freedom, and autonomy. Owning a Living Unit created the security and permanence

of a home that could then be set up inside homes that other people owned. It provided freedom because whenever the owner wanted to move s/he could collapse it and move the unit to a new location. (Zittel 2006)

Zittel's claim that her *A–Z Living Units* could change the lives of their users, giving them order and thus "security, stability, freedom, and autonomy," parodies the ideals of modernist architects and designers who fervently believed that design could change the world. Most art commentators took these solutions for living as a serious engagement with design, due to the extensive nature of the works she produced in the early 1990s and the fact that she never strayed from her stated aims of delivering "security, stability, freedom, and autonomy." Zittel became known as the artist who solved life's problems, but with compulsive vigor and determination. This problem-solving meta-narrative is reinforced by the artist's use of a fictionalized corporation, *A–Z Administrative Services (an Institute for Investigative Living),* through which she developed and exhibited her works. *A–Z Administrative Services* offers life-changing experiences to the purchasers of its products, her works. *A–Z* products are diverse in nature but share a goal in liberating their owners from the restrictions and drudgery of their everyday lives.

Andrea Zittel's art practice can be divided into three distinct themes: the theme of habitation, the theme of apparel, and the dual themes of leisure and escape. Within the theme of apparel she has created two to three ranges of garments every year since the early 1990s, each range comprising one dress worn exclusively by the artist (or purchaser) for the duration of the season. Her garments, like all of her works, focus on the utilitarian and draw references from the design avant-garde of the early twentieth century. I am focusing here on Zittel's apparel works as a way of exploring the contradictory messages in her practice: on the one hand paying homage to avant-garde design principles while simultaneously reflecting their failures through her extensive use of irony and humor.

I will elaborate upon on her constructed corporate identity, *A–Z Administrative Services,* from which her works are made and distributed. Zittel uses this as a conceptual device to distinguish her works as art. *A–Z Administrative Services* first appeared in 1992 when she took on a project "to institute some self-imposed conditioning" (Zittel quoted in Connelly 2000: 88) for a fellow artist and friend, Jon Tower, whose level of personal disorganization was affecting his ability to function in the world. Zittel formalized what may have been her first commissioned work by sending her friend a letter of confirmation.

Dear Mr. Tower,

We would like to offer you a systematized apparel program to eliminate disorder and confusion in your daily attire dilemma. Our company has chosen a prototype based on your social position, reputation, and occupation which we feel will be suitable for your needs ... However, first we ask that you review the A to Z commitment plan.

In exchange for a new life of order and efficiency we only ask that you be prepared to adhere to our guidelines. No slacker will be tolerated.

A–Z Administrative Apparel (Morsiani and Smith 2005: 69)

The commission letter offers an example of both Zittel's artistic subtext of control and order as well as her use of humor. The letter blatantly parodies consultancy agreements used by designers and is formalized by her use of the corporate persona *A–Z Administrative Apparel.* This letter was the first use of her corporate persona. At that time Zittel was in regular need of industrial materials, plywood, steel, and hardware, to construct her furniture-based works and was finding that her youthful California accent did little to convince New York trade suppliers of her serious intent. Ostensibly to be taken more seriously by these suppliers, Zittel created her own pseudo-corporation, *A–Z Administrative Apparel.* The name she finally settled upon, *A–Z Administrative Services,* uses her initials, A and Z, to represent a dictionary of possibilities, with a truly generic suffix, Administrative Services, that she considered to be less specific to her earlier choice, Apparel (Zittel 2006). All of Zittel's works since that time have been branded with her A–Z corporate prefix and at exhibition are usually accompanied catalogues disguised as A–Z promotional catalogues, flyers, or videos. The language used in these works is akin to advertising propaganda in that it extols the virtues of the works as life-changing to the purchaser. *A to Z Administrative Services* thus becomes a fictional supplier of Zittel's art and at the same time a source of commentary on her practice.

The concept of *A–Z Administrative Services* borrows from the American commercial landscape of the mid-twentieth century when trusted manufacturers of household essentials produced detailed catalogues of their extensive product ranges that were distributed door to door or by mail order. Trevor Smith sees in *A–Z Administrative Services* a reference to the ACME company immortalized in Chuck Jones's Roadrunner cartoon series (2005: 40). Whatever the exact reference, the association to labor-saving gadgetry of the 1950s is clearly Zittel's objective.

In 1991, in response to a need to wear something respectable for her job at the Pat Hearn Gallery and faced with very limited funds, Zittel created a very stylish uniform that could be worn every day of the week. The resultant garment was later integrated into her artistic résumé as *A–Z 1991 Spring Summer Uniform,* the first work of a collection titled *A–Z Six-Month Personal Uniforms* (Figure 6.1).

Initially Zittel created a new uniform every half-year, one for summer and one for winter. Some of the garments were quite complicated in design and used a number of different fabrics and styles. By 1995 Zittel realized that all her uniforms to date had been stylistic variations of one idea (Schumacher 2003: 71). She then decided to set herself some guidelines for her garment designs. Zittel described her search:

I had looked around at the numerous rules that had already been made by other designers, particularly the Russian Constructivists. Their idiom that "geometric patterns maintained the integrity of/ the fabric (which was woven in rectangles)" was arbitrary in one way, lucid, and sensible in another. As a way to push this rule to its absurd yet logical conclusion I decided to take the position that all dresses should only be made from a rectangle … almost as if the fabric had been sliced from the bolt. The most interesting thing about the rectangular format is that the creative variations became almost limitless—it was possible to achieve the effect of either a prom dress or a blacksmith's apron with just a few suggestive details. (Zittel 2002: 78)

There is a clear link between the uniforms and Zittel's *A–Z Living Units*. Her reference to rules connects her apparel works to her other lifestyle works, all of

Figure 6.1 *A–Z Uniforms* 1991–1994. Installation view, Andrea Rosen Gallery, New York, Gallery 2, January 23–February 21, 2004.

which have been informed by rules such as time efficiency, as espoused in Fredrick W. Taylor's *Principles of Scientific Management.* The rules that Zittel set herself on this occasion intertwine rational avant-garde design methods with absurdity. In the first instance it is absurd to preserve the rectangle of cloth as a truth to the machine that created it yet rational in that the simplicity of the design makes for a garment that is ideally suited to Zittel's clothing needs. In adhering to this strict rectangular rule, she overlays a major limitation to her creative freedom. This limitation, and the consequent difficulties in working with it, is the kind of perverse challenge central to Zittel's practice.

In 1995 Zittel extended her program of personal uniforms into limited produc-tion as *A–Z Personal Panel Uniforms* (Figure 6.2). This series was continued until 1998. *A–Z Personal Panel Uniforms* follow the basic principles and rules developed by Zittel and are constructed from a rectangle of cloth, suspended from the body by shoulder straps, and tied at the back with another pair of straps. The finished product resembles a pinafore worn over a wraparound underskirt. The panels come in a variety of colors and fabrics. Some are multicolored and composed of overlaid rectangles sewn together to form a large rectangular panel. This seems to contradict Zittel's pure adherence to the single rectangle.

In an A–Z exhibition brochure Zittel developed for the *A–Z Personal Panels,* anyone purchasing a customized garment is instructed to wear only this item and either discard or store away all other garments in their possession for the duration of the experiment, the time being determined by the purchaser, who may with-draw from the agreement at any time (Schumacher: 72–73). Zittel assumes that in

Figure 6.2 *A–Z Personal Panel Uniform* 1995–1998. Seven uniforms of various fabrics. Emanuel Hoffmann Foundation, permanent loan to the Öffentliche Kunstsammlung, Basel, Switzerland. Instal-lation view, *A–Z Uniforms* 1991–2002, Andrea Rosen Gallery, New York, 2004.

restricting their garment choices to a single item, owners of an *A–Z Personal Panel* will feel liberated from the nuisance of having to decide what to wear and the dictates of fashionable dress codes. Wearing an *A–Z Personal Panel* will prove a genuine enrichment to the owner's life. Zittel is presumably being ironic in suggesting that liberation comes from such extreme restrictions and in using words such as "experiment" and "genuine enrichment" (Schumacher: 73). There is an underlying absurdity in the idea that a collector buying one of these works would participate in the experiment.

Zittel continues to produce one garment a season—however, she now divides the year into three seasons and produces special garments for particular activities; recently she produced a hiking uniform. Since 1998, she has incorporated a number of variations to her restrictions on the cloth and the making of the garments. In the first of these, *A–Z Raugh Uniform* (pronounced raw), she was informed by her Raugh philosophy, that the easiest way to keep things ordered and clean is to create them with disorder in mind. Thus, Zittel reduced the garment's construction to fabric lengths torn from a bolt of cloth, wrapped around the body, and secured using diaper pins. In *A–Z Single Strand Uniforms* (Figure 6.3), Zittel replaces a single piece of cloth with a single continuous length of yarn and uses needlepoint and crochet techniques to create shapes that still maintain, according to the artist, the same purity as the rectangle.

Figure 6.3 *A–Z Single Strand Uniform* 1998–2001. Twenty uniforms of various fibers. Emanuel Hoffmann Foundation, permanent loan to the Öffentliche Kunstsammlung, Basel, Switzerland. Installation view, *A–Z Uniforms* 1991–2002, Andrea Rosen Gallery, New York, 2004.

Most recently, the *A–Z Advanced Technologies: Fiber Forms* (Figures 6.4 and 6.5) were constructed from handmade woolen felt. These garments are tubelike objects without seams formed to the shape of the body and secured with safety pins. Zittel refers to this traditional craft practice of felting as a progressive technology in that the basic nature of the material is used in a unique way. It seems that with each edition of her garments the rules become even more idiosyncratic, yet all her garments are both wearable and stylish.

These apparel works are where Zittel most skillfully creates and uses rules, making them and then breaking them. The concept behind the uniforms is the single element, but the rule is amended slightly with each iteration. In one way this is design innovation, assuming that the original restriction was placed on the designer; you must not cut the cloth or you risk losing the integrity of the piece. It is almost like a game in which the rules develop each time it is played.

A particular challenge for Zittel with her Uniform Series was finding new ways of constructing her garments and interpreting technologies while adhering to the principle of her rule. Each technique seems to require more labor than the previous one and explores an even more fundamental or traditional form of making: from commercially available dyed cloth cut from a bolt, to piece-dyed and printed cloth, to hand-crocheted garments, and finally to body-shaped felting. Unlike the pioneers of the avant-garde, who exploited the machine's potential for economical and efficient production, Zittel avoids the machine like an Amish pioneer. In her apparel works, Zittel repeats the visual qualities found in her early habitation works. These works share an aesthetic that is premodern, and in contrast to the machine made aesthetics expected of modernity.

Interestingly, in a recent interview Zittel said that she always thought about clothing as being a form of public art; when you wear clothing it becomes one of the most practical ways to display something (Zittel quoted in Colomina, Wigley, and Zittel 2005: 55). Zittel's garments have become part of her artistic persona, and indeed, each time Zittel is seen, it is in one of her garments. In this way she brings her work out of the gallery and into the public arena.

The culture of consumerism and consumption is a backdrop for much of Zittel's work. Zittel's apparel works challenge consumerism and the cultural dictates of the fashion industry. By adapting constructivist design methodologies for her own rules to materials and making, she uses modernism to reinforce her antifashion message. As with her more recent habitations works, Zittel uses her garments as a statement on personal freedom from control and restrictions to individuality. That is, in this instance, by breaking with the societal requirement for multiple and regularly changing fashions, she liberates her users while simultaneously restricting them to one uniform look—a paradox. There is much irony at work here, in particular the idea that by embracing restriction, the individual finds freedom and liberty.

In this instance, conformity to a personally constructed style liberates the individual from conformity to the culture and dictates of fashion etiquette. The *A–Z*

Figure 6.4 *A–Z Fiber Form Uniform* (olive shirt). Courtesy artist and Andrea Rosen Gallery, New York.

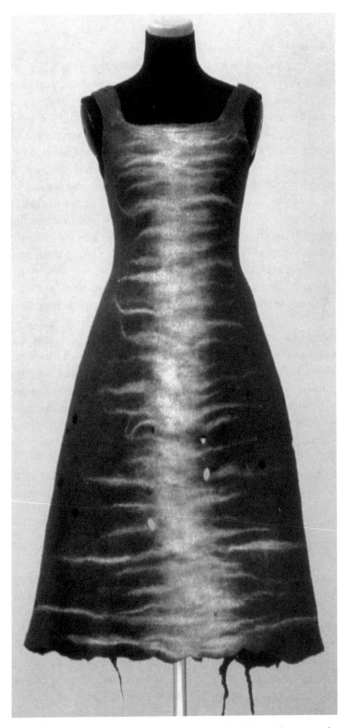

Figure 6.5 *A–Z Fiber Form Uniform* (green and white dress). Courtesy artist and Andrea Rosen Gallery, New York.

Personal Panels and *A–Z Advanced Technologies*, like much of her earlier work, accentuate contemporary issues of waste and excess that are endemic in contemporary societies. Ironically, while Zittel's garments offer to the purchaser freedom from the fashion industry, they attract similar prices to those of haute couture. This is another contradiction in Zittel's work in that, while ostensibly the works offer simple solutions to everyday problems, in reality they parody simple economical solutions. Those privileged enough to purchase a Zittel garment would have an income level that would shield them from many mundane everyday problems. It is more likely that her purchasers have little desire to be liberated from the dictates of the fashion industry. However, Zittel's most recent incursion into the world of fashion is *a–z smockshop* (http://www.zittel.org). This is a not-for-profit venture for the artist; rather, it generates income for other artists whose work is either noncommercial or not yet self-sustaining. The smocks are designed by Andrea Zittel and produced by a group of smockers who reinterpret the design based on their own individual skill sets, tastes, and interests. The smocks retail for $250–$400, so Zittel is making her works available to the average consumer, again throwing her social agenda into question.

We can understand Zittel's practice in terms of its engagement with, and reference to, a number of art and design movements. The movement with which Zittel is most often associated is architectural modernism. I will explore the claims various critics have made and examine the different ways Zittel connects with the ideas and practices of architectural modernism. I will then examine Zittel's connection to more recent art movements: performance art, conceptual art, and pop art.

Zittel's connection to modernism drew extensive comment from critics, particularly during the first ten years of her practice, when her most notable works were her habitation works. For example, Joel Sanders discusses Zittel's work and what he saw as its aesthetic connections with the work of some early twentieth-century modernists.

> While Zittel's proposals for contemporary Spartan living would seem to situate her within the masculinist tradition of the heroic modern architect, confident in her/his abilities to forge a rational world through the creation of standardized artifacts that obey universal human needs, her status as a contemporary female artist makes it ambiguous as to whether Zittel intends her interpretation of modernist austerity to be read as prescription, parody, or critique. (Sanders 1996: 16)

Sanders is not alone in reading the contradictory messages about modernism in her work: paying homage to avant-garde principles while simultaneously reflecting their failures. Jan Avgikos, in her review of Zittel's *Purity* exhibition—the same works Sanders referred to—could not determine whether Zittel was offering a critique of "arch modernism" or whether she believed in and promoted its "obvious defects" (1994: 88).

Modernist design is a broad descriptor for a series of art and design programs, manifestos, and movements that developed in the first half of the twentieth century in Europe. A number of critics, and Zittel herself, have made references to one or several design movements that fall under the rubric of modernism: the Bauhaus, the Russian Constructivists, De Stijl, and as well as the work of Le Corbusier. Architectural historian Charles Jencks has noted that these art and architectural movements shared a number of idealist principles. First was the idea that design should be an instrument of social change, that the living, working, and social environment of the average person should be enhanced through design and that this could be achieved through utilizing the technological advancements of the age. Jencks refers to this as the idealist tradition of the heroic period of architectural history (1973: 29).

Unfortunately, the social and environmental effects from the "heroic period" of architectural history have not been as universally beneficial as had been postulated. The legacy of this period of architecture includes, alongside the icons of modernity, a number of buildings and public spaces that, rather than enhancing people's lives, have been blamed for creating cultural and social problems rather than curing them. This is most visible in public housing and urban consolidation projects from 1950 to 1970, when across the world, working-class areas were razed and replaced with ubiquitous high-rise apartments. While most of these projects were successful in raising quantifiable standards of living, they were less successful in developing autonomous communities or enhancing local cultures.

In contradiction to the aspirations of modernist architectural theorists, modernist architecture in many instances has been used by governments and planners as an instrument of social engineering. Critics have seen this controlling side of modernism as a defining feature of Zittel's work. Avgikos argues that in her *Purity* works Zittel's "touch is robotic—intolerant of vulnerability, weakness, and indecision" and questioned whether this was a deliberate critique of modernism (1994: 88). Robbins takes a different position, reading Zittel's messages of control in her *A–Z Living Units* as a deviation from modernism:

> The units she designs are less about their modernist lineage or materials than about maintaining control. Modernism projected its goal of universal betterment, but Zittel individualizes it, bringing life management to a personal scale. (2000: 41)

That Robbins ignores the controlling aspect of modernist design demonstrates an uncritical reading of the movement. Zittel's works assist and direct the purchaser in a number of living functions but are so prescriptive that they limit the user's freedom. Avgikos is correct in reading the accentuated control in Zittel's work as a critique of modernism; however, the criticism is presented via a parody of the control meted out by modernist designers. All of her garment works were developed to answer personal needs, but the utility of the works is overlaid with humor.

As I indicated earlier, Sanders questioned whether Zittel intended her work to be read as a prescription, parody, or critique of modernism. I believe she engages with modernism through all three of these modes. On the face of it, particularly with her *A–Z Living Units* and *A–Z Uniforms* Zittel subscribes to modernist intentions and processes, yet because of the humor in her work such prescriptions must be read as a parody of modernism and as a subtle form of critique. Zittel skillfully avoids directing her viewer to a single reading; rather, the ambiguous nature of her engagement enjoins the viewer on a cycle of reflective enquiry.

For example, Zittel has refuted the assertion that her works, in particular her *Purity* works, were controlling, countering that her aim at the time was not to impose rules on anyone unless they wanted rules. Zittel has also expressed disappointment that the rules she has developed and upon which she based her works were neither tested nor subverted by her purchasers (Zittel quoted in Colomina et al. 2005: 55). This disappointment is valid only within the meta-narrative of *A–Z Administrative Services* as a service-provider to consumers. Outside this narrative, this would be an ingenuous claim by an artist. The viewer of a Zittel work in a gallery has no opportunity to either physically test it or comment on the rules on which the work was based. The viewer is an observer rather than a user of the work. In a gallery context, the viewer is presented with both the merchandising narrative from *A–Z Administrative Services* and a Zittel object; the work combines both of these elements. The viewer can either take the work at face value as a product that offers life-assisting properties or reflect on the claims made for the works by *A–Z Administrative Services,* but the viewer cannot actually test the works. Even if the gallery allowed the viewer to touch the work, testing can truly occur only in the context for which the work was created, that is, in the home of the collector, but even the collector is unlikely to test the work. As Trevor Smith has noted, a collector would be unlikely to either physically test or amend their A–Z work, as the value of the work is derived from its authorship, not its usability; if the work were amended it would lose its status as an original work. As I noted previously, it would not be likely for owners of Zittel's garment works to actually wear the garments as prescribed by Zittel (Smith 2005: 46). So for these reasons Zittel's works will not be tested, but neither will they be used. It follows, therefore, that Zittel's works will never be controlling, as the works are not acquired for their usability.

Zittel's connection with modernism goes beyond her constructed narrative to include her art process, her use of technologies, and the overall aesthetic of her works. Zittel's process simulates the design process developed by modernist designers, that is, identifying a universal need and then developing an aesthetic and functional product to satisfy the need. Zittel continually creates new functional pieces to solve her life problems, and these form the basis for new artworks. These problems all share a common theme in that they all place constraints on personal freedom. Once she identifies a problem she creates a rule to define yet resist this constraint, and finally she develops an object to ritualize the rule. Her one-garment-per-season rule, together

Plate 1. Philipp Otto Runge, *Self Portrait,* 1805 (oil on panel). Hamburger Kunsthalle.

Plate 2. George Cruickshank, *Tom and Jerry and Dr. Please'em's Prescription,* 1820. Private Collection.

Plate 3. Louis Léopold Boilly, *Portrait of a Man, possibly Monsieur d'Aucourt de Saint-Just,* c.1800 (oil on canvas). Musée des Beaux-Arts, Lille.

Plate 4. Henri (Karl Ernest Rudolf Heinrich Salem) Lehmann, *Portrait of Franz Liszt,* 1839 (oil on canvas). Musée de la Ville de Paris, Musée Carnavalet, Paris.

Plate 5. Jean Auguste Dominique Ingres, *Amédée-David, Comte de Pastoret,* 1823–26 (oil on canvas), 40½ × 32¾ in. (103 × 83.5 cm). Estate of Dorothy Eckhart Williams; Robert Allerton, Bertha E. Brown, and Major Acquisitions endowments, 1971.452, The Art Institute of Chicago. Photography © The Art Institute of Chicago.

Plate 6. Eugène Delacroix, *Louis-Auguste Schwiter.* © The National Gallery, London.

Plate 7. Théodore Géricault, *Officer of the Hussars,* 1814 (oil on canvas), Louvre, Paris.

Plate 8. George Cruickshank, *Tom and Jerry at a Coffee-Shop near the Olympic,* 1820. Private Collection.

Plate 9. Men's Morning Dress, 1840. *Le Petit Courier des Dames,* Paris. Private Collection.

Plate 10. *Young Man of the Harcourt-Hillersden Family,* c. 1835–40 (pastel and gouache). Private Collection.

Plate 11. Octave Tassaert, *Boudoirs et Mansardes (Dressing-rooms and Garrets): MÉCHANT! … /WICKED FELLOW,* 1828 (lithograph). Bibliothèque nationale de France, Paris.

Plate 12. Octave Tassaert, *Les Amans et Les Epoux/Lovers and Spouses: AH! POUR LE COUP, LA BELLE ENFANT!!/HA NOW I'VE CAUGHT YOU, MY BEAUTY!!,* 1829 (lithograph). Cabinet des estampes, Bibliothèque nationale de France, Paris.

Il veut m'épouser..... le scélérat!!

Bible par H.e Gaugain et C.ie rue vivienne N.9 et chez B. André, r de la Monnaie N.11

Plate 13. Henry Monnier, *Les Grisettes dessinees d'apres nature: Il veut m'épouser ... le scélérat!!,* plate 6, 1828 (lithograph). Bibliothèque national de France, Paris.

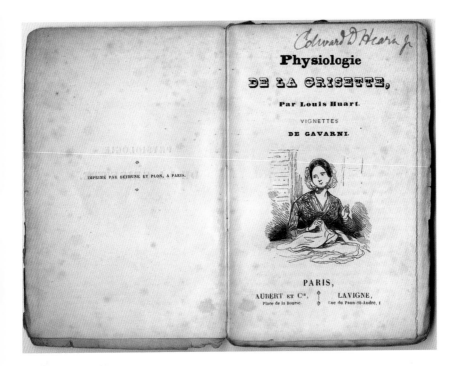

Plate 14. Paul Gavarni, frontispiece to Louis Huart, *Physiologie de la grisette* (Paris: Aubert, 1841).

Plate 15. Paul Gavarni, in Louis Huart, "Des passions de la grisette," chapter V of *Physiologie de la grisette: Grisette eating cake in the paradis* (Paris: Aubert, 1841), 32.

Plate 16. Paul Gavarni, *Une loge à l'Opéra* from *La Mode,* Revue des modes, January 22, 1831, plate 115. Bibliothèque National de France, Paris.

Plate 17. Laurence Le Guay, *Fashion illustration* (Hollywood), circa 1960. Gelatin silver photograph, vintage, 49.0 × 39.2 cm. Gift of the artist. 1980. Collection: Art Gallery of New South Wales. © Estate of the Artist. Photograph: Ray Woodbury.

Plate 18. Michel Comte, courtesy I-Management Ltd.

Plate 19. Copyright © Mikael Vojinovic; with permission Mikael Vojinovic.

Plate 20. Advertisement for Farmers Department Store, *The Home,* December 1921. Private Collection.

Plate 21. Photo: Karin Catt.

Plate 22. Vampire Attack from A&F's "The Vampyre's Kiss." © Bruce Weber, All Rights Reserved.

Plate 23. Gladiator from A&F's "Summer 2003 Magalog." © Bruce Weber, All Rights Reserved.

Plate 24. Nude from "Summer 2003 Magalog." © Bruce Weber, All Rights Reserved.

Plate 25. Amanda Stonham and Catherine Harper, civil partnership day, September 2, 2006, Brighton. Private Collection.

Plate 26. Amanda's mother, Eileen Stonham, in the bronze lamé cocktail dress, circa 1950s. Private Collection.

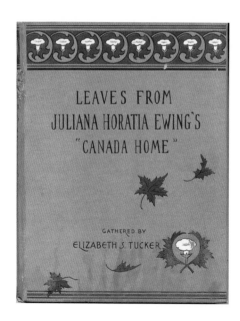

Plate 27. Book cover, 1896. Private Collection.

Plate 28. Dress with Aesthetic Movement influence (*Delineator*, September 1900: 297). Private Collection.

Plate 29. Mainstream fashion (*Delineator,* December 1899: 628). Private Collection.

Plate 30. Audrey Hepburn, circa 1950. Photograph: Antony Beauchamp.

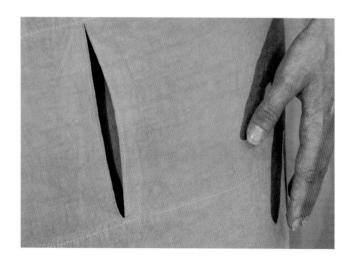

Plate 31. *Front.* Photograph: Dagmar Venohr.

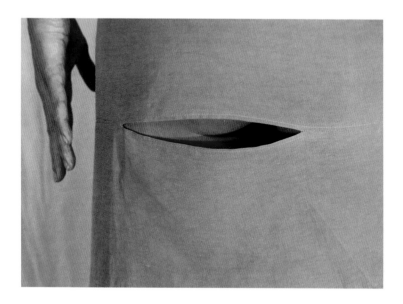

Plate 32. *Back.* Photograph: Dagmar Venohr.

with the rules she places on making her garments, exemplifies this process. When Zittel took the lease on her Union Street studio, she faced the problem of living in an industrial space devoid of any cooking or bathing facilities. On analyzing her situation, Zittel decided that the convention of dedicating a room solely for bathing and elimination, a bathroom, was an unnecessary constraint; as she put it, "Bathrooms were tyrannical." This became a rule. She then invented objects that "would liberate your body" from the necessity of using the bathroom, such as the *A–Z Bed Pan* (Smith 2005: 47). Zittel's process deviates from modernist design in that the needs that she identifies are idiosyncratic rather than universal, coming from Zittel's personally developed set of problems and rules and the products that she develops. Her objects, while aesthetically pleasing and functional, actually create new problems that the artist ignores. How and where does one dispose of the wastes contained within the *A–Z Bed Pan* and the waste buckets of the *A–Z Cleansing Chamber?* In this regard, she parodies a modernist design process by making her process; she builds her idea on an absurd premise and creates an equally absurd set of problems from her solutions.

In understanding the significance of parody in Zittel's work it is useful to consider the broader aspects of humor in her work. She has referred to the "dark humor" in her *Purity* works, specifically the "scatological references" she made in her *A–Z Comfort Unit*" (Zittel quoted in Colomina et al. 2005: 52). The *A–Z Pocket Property,* she has said, was a darkly humorous commentary on "the way our culture constructs and then capitalizes on human longing for freedom, autonomy, and isolation" (Zittel 2002: 20). Critics have ignored this aspect of her work. Her works from 1995 are more obviously comic, maybe light humor rather than dark, to use her qualification. Humor ensures that these works are not read in a literal way; rather they are signals to the viewer that there are more complex messages in the works that require thought and reflection. Examples of humor in her work include presenting an aluminum casket that resembles a space-age freezer that one enters to escape the world, the *A–Z Escape Unit;* a fiber-glass float that will ensure the user is stranded at sea without a paddle, the *A–Z Deserted Island;* a supersized rodent that one enters to scream abuse at the world, the *A–Z Prairie Dogs.*

As I noted previously, Zittel's engagement with modernism can also be understood through her use of modern technology and modernist aesthetics. Fundamental to modernist practice is the idea that the machine must be exploited to its fullest potential and that it is most efficient when employed to create multiples; serialized production is privileged over artisanal production. Modernist aesthetics are consequently mechanistic and devoid of decorative embellishments that might conceal the structure and fabric of the object. While Zittel's works are aesthetically modernist and appear to be produced using serialized processes, in reality the works make limited use of such production techniques; rather, each work is made unique, either by traditional techniques of making, or through customization for the purchaser. Where works are produced in series, for example, *A–Z Living Units, A–Z Travel Trailers, and A–Z Escape Vehicles,* only certain elements of these works are common; all pieces are differentiated in some way. Thus Zittel implies a modernist design program of serialized production but actually employs traditional artisanal techniques. In Zittel's process, she returns to first principles to find nontechnological solutions to solve her problem. In fact, she deliberately avoids the use of postindustrial devices. Jerry Saltz has commented on this technological contradiction in Zittel's works:

> The problem is that while it looks early modern, her works suggest a pre-modern condition without plumbing, toilets, zippers, or buttons. Zittel questions everything, so you start to, too, which is good; she can really make you think about the way you live your life. She leaves you puzzling over whether her objects are as functional as she claims they are. (1994: 100)

Saltz's comments highlight the artist's use of contradictory messages, her use of a modernist aesthetic that implies mechanized production, and her use of "premodern" or nonmechanized components. He also notes the critical aspect of Zittel's work in stimulating the viewer to question the work's functional claims. A fundamental issue in Zittel's works is that they leave the viewer "puzzling over" the utility of the object and their own need for objects and technologies. In fact, Zittel's works encourage reflection on necessities, because they all question basic human needs, whether they are for habitation, apparel, or leisure time. Zittel's work thus deliberately accentuates basic needs and, through implication, excessive desires.

Rainald Schumacher interprets the concern with needs and desires as related to ecological sustainability. The minimal amenity offered by the *A–Z Living Units,* Schumacher believes, could be read "as a correction of a lifestyle which, as we all know, is leading the earth's resources to the brink of exhaustion" (2003: 68). He draws a connection between this aspect of the artist's agenda and the social ideals of modernists. In his reading, he ignores the critical side of Zittel's ecological stance, that the lifestyle of rampant consumption is the result of modernist design's compulsive invention of both human needs and products to satisfy the needs.

Bourriaud, in discussing artists from the 1990s, believes that social utopias and "revolutionary hopes have given way to everyday micro-utopias and imitative strategies" (2002: 31). This seems true for Zittel, who has bypassed the social utopian vision, preferring to concentrate her work on simple ways to "improve" the everyday world. Her micro-utopia is the here and now stripped of excessive needs, consumption, and waste, although the problems she creates might counterbalance the utopian vision. Zittel's works draw attention to the wasteful excesses of the West's contemporary capitalist culture and recall the innocence and simple values and systems of an earlier time. In all her works there are statements about waste. Her subliminal messages are consistent: don't waste space, don't waste material and energy, don't waste time, don't waste clothes, don't waste your leisure, and don't waste your fantasies. Her works provoke a desire to never waste a minute. Zittel has said of her work that working as a designer from the position of an artist is not a new strategy and was the position of groups like Bauhaus, the Russian Constructivist and De Stijl ... My departure from these movements occurs when I work with the dilemmas and the contradictions that their work unearthed. (quoted in Weil 1994: 22)

Zittel is critical of the flaws and failures of modernist movements; however, as she indicates here, she is also indebted to modernism—that is, she works with the problems modernism unearthed.

The exclusive focus on Zittel's relation to modernism is a narrow reading of her work. Zittel comments on the dilemmas of American consumer culture, a culture that has developed alongside modernism, with the idea that utopia exists in the form of the American dream. At the same time Zittel's work recalls traditional cultural tropes of the American home, the trusted small business, the family vacation, and the pioneer's frontier.

Smith believes that central to Zittel's practice is her exploration of forms of sociability, "the 'self' in relationship to the greater whole" (2005: 38). I believe that sociability underpins her whole practice and is manifest in a number of ways that distinguish her artistic process from those of other artists of her generation. Her studio practice commingles with her public engagement. As Smith noted, her working process is sociable and has more in common with workshop critique, design iterations, and prototyping than the stereotypical artistic process of prolonged isolation in a studio followed by a brief public exhibition. Sociability is also apparent in the "customized" aspect of many of her works; her collaborations with her purchasers is a process of creative negotiation that results in a unique work.

I referred earlier to the performative aspect of Zittel's work. Lynn Zelevansky believes that Zittel, like performance-oriented artists, uses her body to "test the authenticity of her art in the world" (1994: 33). Clearly, Zittel uses her life and her body as testing sites for her works, but whether she does this to test her works' authenticity, as Zelevansky claims, or simply to promote her works to the world, her works are nonetheless performance oriented.

This is best demonstrated through three works, the *A–Z Personal Panels,* the uniform series that she wears exclusively for several months of each year; the *A–Z Time Trials,* created when Zittel lived for a week in a basement space without any references to time, and recorded the patterns and rhythms of her life on time-lapse video; and *A–Z Pocket Property,* her floating concrete island that she lived on for a week.

However, this is not the only way in which Zittel's work engages with performance art. Zittel is the embodiment of a controlling designer, a performance in its own way and seen most clearly through her pseudo-corporation *A–Z Administrative Services.* It is within the meta-narrative of *A–Z* that the heroic modernist designer operates, offering perfect solutions to the day-to-day problems of the world. In this narrative, Zittel acts out the role of the caring yet omnipotent designer; the gallery or museum becomes a product showroom and the collector a consumer of useful products. Zittel maintains this narrative outside the traditional institutional engagement of formal exhibitions through regular updates on her *A–Z* website as well as through interviews with journalists and critics.

A–Z Administrative Services also has precedents in conceptual art, where artists have created pseudo-organizations as part of their works, for example. the faux art museum Marcel Broodthaer created for his work, *Museum of Modern Art, Eagles Department* 1968–1972. Another connection to conceptual art can be found in the artist's use of publications from *A–Z Administrative Services,* such as *Personal Profiles Newsletter,* the posters for *Raugh,* and the A–Z brochures that accompany Zittel's exhibitions. These works recall the use of advertisements, billboards, and one-off magazines that some conceptual artists use as the venues for their work.

Associations can also be made between Zittel's practice and that of Pop artist Andy Warhol. Zittel's focus on American consumer culture follows on from Warhol's pop-art fascination with iconic American consumer graphics. Like Warhol before her, Zittel has developed an affected artistic persona and in operating out of her *A–Z East* and *A–Z West*—Zittel's combined art studio, home, and public "laboratories for living"—she offers a "good housekeeping" version of Warhol's *Factory,* in which artist, patrons, critics, and the public interact around her art. The *Thursday Evening Personal Presentations* in the *A–Z Personal Presentation Room* could be seen as a 1990s version of Warhol's Factory happenings. Finally, Zittel's recently published *Things I Know for Sure* can be likened to Warhol's publication of *The Philosophy of Andy Warhol (A–B and Back Again).*

In drawing these connections to performance art, conceptualism, and pop art, I am not suggesting that Zittel's work should be read as either conceptual art or pop art. Unlike the conceptual artists of the 1960s and 1970s, and even some of her contemporary design artists, Zittel's aim is not for her art to disappear into everyday life. Zittel, in conversation with Allan McCollum, outlined her own criteria for what makes something art:

> Art, to me, is all about perception. Historically it was usually a form of visual perception, but now this has expanded to a more cognitive kind of perception. An artwork allows you to understand something in a new way. (McCollum and Zittel 2002: 10)

Zittel follows her definition rigorously, having spent the last fifteen years creating art that allows us to understand the things we think we know in new ways. Zittel's design art reeducates us on how to inhabit the world. Partially hidden behind *A–Z Administrative Services,* she offers us an ongoing narrative of the pressures and restrictions that contemporary consumer society places on us. Through her works she shows us how to survive in the world, or more specifically, she shows us how to take control, escape from pressures and restrictions, and enjoy freedom. While other design artists raise issues about day-to-day living in their works, she is the only artist who attends to such issues exclusively, holistically, and humorously.

Part 2
Crossing Cultures, Queering Cultures

–7–

Tanizaki Jun'ichirō's *Naomi*

Toby Slade

In Japan fashion functioned as the most easily accessible grammar and vocabulary of modernity. As in many other countries, the desire to act "modern" and to be part of modernity could most simply and immediately be fulfilled by means of clothing. Such a situation was possible because fashion involves the acceptance of change as a value in itself. The idea of reflexivity—the continual reexamination and reevaluation of knowledge in every sphere—is essential to modernity, whose central precept of progress brought the end of certainty (Giddens 1991). Scientific and technological advances and social and economic reforms created anxiety rather than the reassurance of traditional sources of knowledge. Without adherence to absolutist, and often arbitrary, Confucian epistemology, the Japanese population sought new means of knowledge production and new sources of information and facts. Far from resulting in certainty, this led to continually changing social and cultural practices and fads—fashions.

Fashions in ideas and those things that become repositories for ideas, especially clothing, are also the repository for conceptions of individual and collective identity. Within modernity progress was constantly sought, yet constantly questioned, undermined, and remodeled (Wilson 2005b). This feature of modernity, the reflexivity of continual reappraisal, arose before most of the trappings of industrial modernization reached Japan. The physical experience of urban mass culture that reordered the aesthetics and fashion-life of this society came later. This historical process began in 1868 with the beginning of the Meiji period and continued during the Taisho period (1912–1926).

It was in this Taisho period that Jun'ichirō Tanizaki, perhaps Japan's second most loved author, after Natsume Sōseki, wrote *Naomi*. This mordant and witty, *Lolita*-like story of love and obsession was scandalous because Naomi was a *moga* (a modern girl) who defied Japanese tradition in dress, etiquette, and morality. It is a story on the Pygmalion theme of a husband who tries to make his young wife into a "Western-style" beauty but cannot control the outcome. She bobs her hair, wears the latest Western clothing and cosmetics, and emulates the Hollywood starlet Mary Pickford. It is a tale of the rapidly changing popular culture of Japan between the First World War and the Great Earthquake, of the revues and movie theaters of

Asakusa, sea bathing at Kamakura, and the cafés and dance halls of Ginza. But most of all it documents the change in what was most important for Tanizaki and Japanese men: the way Japanese women could "be" women. It is also a story of seduction, not just of a foolish man by the beguiling foreign clothes of his faithless young wife, but of the seduction of one culture by another. Again and again in this story, as in Japanese arts more broadly, fashion exemplified the vocabulary of modernity, to embody the fear and excitement of all those new things that came with the modern world.

There are particular events that make the history of Japanese sartorial modernity unique in global culture and are relevant for understanding the significance of *Naomi* as a document of the formation and character of early modern Japanese fashion. First, there was the matter of the unique nature of Japan's seclusion and subsequent reopening, in which the ideas and influences of modernity arrived simultaneously. This was quite different from the gradual transition during the Renaissance and the Enlightenment, when Europe and later North America adjusted from a feudal order to a modern one. In Japan this transition had to happen very quickly, and there was a certain amount of cultural chaos as a result. The varied and subtle intertwinings of traditional aesthetic concerns and the myriad influences flowing into Japan from the West were still the central cultural issue when Tanizaki wrote *Naomi* in 1924, some sixty years after the Meiji restoration first lifted the restrictions on general cultural interaction.

A second major historical event that shaped the history and fashions in the novel and in Japan, although never mentioned in the text, is the Great Kanto Earthquake of September 1, 1923, which killed somewhere on the order of 142,000 people and destroyed 540,000 homes, but which was also a major catalyst for the modern rebuilding of Tokyo and, significantly, the replacement of much destroyed clothing with more modern styles (Seidensticker 1991). A famous anecdote about Tanizaki, outside the city at the time of the earthquake, states that his first thought was elation that the city, and by extension Japanese society, could at last be remade in a truly modern way. This was a thought for which he later felt guilty, because it occurred to him before the safety of his wife and child, who were still within the burning city Tanizaki 1934).

At the beginning of the restoration period it was the stated policy of the Emperor Meiji to take the good and not the bad of the promising new cultures of Europe and America. The *Bummei kaika* (Civilization and Enlightenment) policy saw former samurai elites performing Western dances in tails and bustle-dresses at specially built pavilions to demonstrate their capacity and eagerness for foreign-defined "civilization." Later, through the advent of advertising and technologies such as cinema, the enthusiasm for all things foreign was able to spread to lower classes as well, spawning the age of Taishō low-*bunka* (culture; Jansen 2002). An expression of modernity, which previously required learning one of the European languages and prohibitive amounts of study, travel, and resources, could be made in the far simpler and more accessible form of local consumption. This was the age of "Modern Boys" (*Mobo*) and "Modern Girls" (*Moga*), in which Tanizaki, noticing the enormous consequence these things held for Japanese identity and society, wrote *Naomi*.

There was an ever-present association in Japan between modernity and the West, which was perhaps a product of the period of seclusion and the history of an island nation. Tanizaki battled with this association, and thus his dreams require the progress and development of Tokyo to be in a "truly" Western style. However, Tanizaki later became disillusioned with his vision of a splendid flapper-age rebuilding, writing of the "stick girls," female gigolos—who, like walking sticks, attached themselves to men, in this case young men strolling in the shopping district:

> But what effect has all this surface change had on the customs, the manners, the words, the acts of the city and its people? ... Westernization has not been as I foresaw. To be sure, there have recently appeared such persons as the stick girls of Ginza, and the prosperity of bars and cafés quite overshadows that of the Geisha quarters ... How many women and girls wear Western dress that really passes as Western dress? In summer the number increases somewhat but in winter you see not one in ten among shoppers and pedestrians. Even among office girls, one in two would be a generous estimate. (quoted in Seidensticker 1991)

While the earthquake did not have the totally reforming effect Tanizaki desired, a contemporary, Nagai Kafū, viewed more generously the changes in the cafés of Ginza, depicting them as modern in *During the Rains* (*Tsuyo no Atosaki;* Kafū 1994). He saw the cafés of Tokyo as being outposts of the *demimonde* and viewed their sensitivity to new fashions and tastes as thoroughly modern. Tanizaki did not see changes in customs and manners as Kafū did, distinguishing between surface appearances and deeper change. For Tanizaki it was not enough that women wore modern styles; they had to fully assimilate them. The female character had also to satisfy him, as in his novel *Naomi,* in which the *moga* title character even appears to change her face and body to look more European, an attraction for which the narrator despises himself.

Writing also in the 1930s, Kawabata Yasunari (2005) was more interested in physical change, and is perhaps a subtler chronicler of it, than Kafū or Tanizaki. Kawabata noticed minor details such as the underwear of young girls playing in a Tokyo park to be modern in style. These types of debates—by men—over Japanese and Western female beauty seem to miss the point of assimilation. Too busy with abstract notions of the feminine, the contemporary Japanese city female changed, and yet they do not know how and when to ascribe the shift. Are there suddenly too many, or too few, *moga*? Modern girls seem to be very limited in number but enough to challenge the entire system and to capture the popular imagination in celebration, condemnation, or just plain confusion. Like their flapper sisters in Europe and America, their challenge is so radical that in the reaction against them the pendulum swings far back the other way. In Japan there was a return to traditional dress, notably in the nationalism of the Second World War and the period immediately preceding it. In the larger scheme of things the emancipation of Japanese women, both conceptually and sartorially, was something irreversible; the *mogas* and their clothes were the pioneers of that revolution.

Tanizaki had great enthusiasm for popular culture: "This is an age of democracy ... arts reflecting aristocratic tastes will increasingly be confined to narrow interests," he claimed. But Tanizaki also loved the traditions of Kyoto and wrote the famous essay "In Praise of Shadows" about Japanese aesthetics as an art of seduction, as opposed to the Western aesthetic system of bringing into the light (Tanizaki 1977). He wrote a great deal about women, including an essay entitled "Kyoto: Her Nature, Food ... and Women" (Tanizaki 1934). The Kyoto-type woman, according to Tanizaki, was softer, more elegant, and warmer than Tokyo's, with a beauty that was the product of art, tradition, elegance, and sophistication. But his fiction is not constricted by fashions or by clichés. He sought to understand the paradoxical nature of human behavior.

One of his early works on the theme of women, for which he became famous in 1910, was the short story "Shisei" (*The Tattooer*), in which a drugged girl lies asleep while the artisan creates his masterpiece upon her (Tanizaki 1996 [1910]).[1] Tanizaki renders both the scene and the passage of time with a traditional Japanese poetic sensibility. Sunlight reflected from the river beyond the windows bathes the sliding screens and the body of the girl in golden ripples. As the tattooer, Seikichi, paints upon the canvas of the girl's back, the spring sky darkens, the moon rises, and he has to work by the light of a candle. With the spring morn dawning, Seikichi looks down on the completed spider that sprawls on the girl's back, embracing her, and as the girl returns to consciousness the tattooed spider seems to writhe with her body movements. The mundane is never far from the poetic. In his essay "In Praise of Shadows" he wrote, "Beauty must grow from the realities of life ... We Japanese find it hard to be really at home with things that shine and glitter" (Tanizaki 1977: 14). The influences of Edgar Allan Poe and Oscar Wilde are evident in Tanizaki's work. After the woman has been inscribed with the giant spider, the symbol of evil, her beauty takes on more of a demonic, compelling power in which eroticism is combined with masochism. A femme-fatale theme is repeated in many of his works, including *Naomi*.

As a novel, *Chijin no ai* (A Fool's Love), or *Naomi,* was intended as light fare, but its cultural importance ran deeper than the first tantalizing reading and perhaps deeper than Tanizaki himself anticipated. Naomi was among the first representations of a *moga* (modern girl). This also helped to shape the concept and myth surrounding these more liberated women who were so threatening to the structure of a society in which gender was rigidly defined. Naomi's transformation is more subtle than Tanizaki's girl in the tattooer story and also more significant. She seems to grow more European. She also grows in power and corruption as she becomes more beautiful and sophisticated, and her husband, the narrator Jōji, is unable to break up with her, despite his innumerable foreign lovers. It is a tragicomedy of sexual and cultural obsession that gains its comic thrust from the ironies of misrepresentation and misperception. It is also, as Japanese critics in particular like to comment, a *fūzoku shōsetsu,* a novel of manners (Chambers 1994). It maps onto the very particular and fleeting social reality of Taisho low-*bunka.* In these two things it assumes a certain sophistication of audience, able to be amused by their own cultural misinterpretations, or of those just past, and it stresses that the moment of such cultural innocence, like the sexual innocence it also explores, is an important but also an ephemeral one.

Chijin no ai was serialized in the *Osaka asahi shinbun* from March 1924. In the years immediately preceding it and in Tanizaki's forced exile from Tokyo following the earthquake, he pursued the "West" with a singular intensity. Before moving to Kansai he had lived in the foreign settlement in Yokohama and even inherited the furniture and cook of the house from the previous British occupants. Tanizaki's life in Yokohama, with foreign friends and lifestyle, has been characterized as a certain colonial pattern of behavior in which Japanese with a taste for the foreign try to cultivate acquaintances among Westerners, who in turn seek out useful natives (Shōgo 1974). It constituted, certainly, the realization of his own obsessions with the West, which are no doubt the basis for the obsessions of Jōji in *Naomi.*

In literary terms, there is a degree to which *Naomi* can be considered a *watakushi shōsetsu,* or an "I-novel," which dominated serious fiction writing in Japan during the twenties. Inheriting the autobiographical thrust of Japanese naturalist fiction, the I-novel sought literary authority by creating the illusion of being a personal, and often sexual, confession. The genre's narrators assume a mantle of absolute sincerity, implying an impossible congruence between life and literature. *Naomi,* however, like much great fiction, transcends the genre almost to the point of parodying the feigned truthfulness and earnestness of the I-novel with its repeated and comically transparent misrepresentations and acts of bad faith by the narrator. Jōji maintains the pretence of objectivity; although obsessed and overanxious to share its thrills, the narrative is deliberately stripped of any didactic authority in the ever-widening gap between stated intent and performance. It is in this mild debasement of the I-novel's quixotic earnestness that Tanizaki is able to say more about the truths that lie behind the social structures of modern society. Furthermore, since this novel concerns subject/object relations in modern life (native/foreign, man/woman, viewer/viewed), it is even more appropriate to examine the motives and true nature of that subject, "I."

Jōji, a man from the country, represents a pattern of upward mobility common in the Taisho period, and very different from what was possible only a decade before. He is a man riding the crest of modernization; he works as an electrical engineer, a glamorous field associated with technological progress and the West. He knows nothing of Western culture outside Hollywood movies, and his self-avowed *haikara* (high-collar or up-to-date) tastes coexist with an absolute ignorance about the foreign world. His coworkers call him *kunshi,* the Confucian term for a virtuous man; he works hard, lives frugally, and for recreation occasionally goes to a café in

Asakusa. He dreams of circumventing the normal system of arranged marriages, representative also of a modern, bourgeois linkage of love and marriage, of work and self-fulfillment.

Naomi is a *jokyū* or hostess in an Asakusa café, forerunner of the modern hostess bar. The café and the *jokyū* were rapidly replacing geishas in the Taisho period as the preferred comforters of the male ego. Naomi is from Senzoku, an area made famous in Higuchi Ichiyō's story "Child's Play" (1896), in which the young heroine, Midori, and her childhood are doomed by the very strength of the institution of licensed prostitution (Ichiyō 1992). Her world of the pleasure quarter is cruel precisely because it is ordered. By Naomi's time, the old traditions have broken down; change is valued, social mobility is possible, but the economic imperatives are not much kinder. Naomi's family runs a *meishuya* or sake shop; in Taisho times such shops often offered women as a sideline, such that the term *meishuya* became a euphemism for a whorehouse of the unlicensed variety. This was prostitution at its lowest level, and Tanizaki intended these references to emphasize that the café where Naomi works represented upward mobility. Yet while she grows in sexual power and beauty, the economic power rests with men. While Jōji seems to offer her romantic and open choices, her options are stark.

Jōji reflects about Naomi's name: "Her name, written in Roman letters, it could be a Western name ... once I knew she had such a sophisticated name, she began to take on an intelligent, Western look ... Naomi resembled the motion-picture actress Mary Pickford: there was definitely something Western about her appearance ... And it's not only her face—even her body had a distinctly Western look when she's naked" (Tanizaki 1985: 3–4). These descriptions become, of course, not an objective exploration of a particular woman's beauty, but an object or canvas upon which almost any fancy can be projected. Isoda Kōichi has written that *Naomi*, with its portrayal of a rural youth who pursues his vision of the modern woman in a girl from the lower classes, testifies to the social penetration of the idea of modernity. The myth of the good Western life has taken hold at the edges of society, and Jōji, the country boy, and Naomi from the pleasure quarter both share a basic aspiration for the West.

Along with her name, one of the first items of fashion described is that of Naomi's body and the piles of clothes she puts on it. There are also her pursuits of English and the piano. The couple settles in a *bunka jūtaku* (a cultured, or Western, house) in Ōmori, with a red slate roof and a little porch. They get furniture from a secondhand shop specializing in Western furniture. On the walls they hang "photographs of Mary Pickford and several other American movie actresses" (Tanizaki (1985: 19). In defining the topography and interior spaces of the novel, Tanizaki once again sets his story squarely in Taisho culture.

The interior of Naomi's and Jōji's *bunka jū taku* has aspects that approach the camp, and to point out their superficiality or impoverishment is merely gratuitous. In Nagai Kafū's story "Fukagawa no uta," there is a picture of Wagner on the wall and an open copy of Nietzsche's *Zarathustra*, and Tanizaki gleefully notes the late-Meiji, high-culture "West," particularly European, of Kafū being transplanted by the mass-*bunka* "West" of America with its movies and fashion (Kafū 2001 [1908]). Tanizaki was one of the few Japanese writers to recognize the growing cultural influence of the United States in the years following World War I, although his choice of Mary Pickford to represent Western culture is not without a certain condescension.

Jōji feels the effects of a desire mediated by ideas and fantasies from a foreign culture, and triangular desire is the desire that transfigures its objects (Girard 1966). Jōji will transfigure Naomi not only through the gossamer filter of perception but also through a conscientious program of reconstruction. Jōji seeks to effect Naomi's transformation through piano and English lessons, precisely the kind of instruction that the upper classes might have had a few decades earlier. This, however, fails and Jōji begins to recognize the differences between a lady marked by high-*bunka* achievements and his sexual fantasy of Mary Pickford. It is through clothing and other fashions that he is able to shape her most effectively: "Do you think I look like a Westerner in this?" Naomi asks (Tanizaki 1985: 36). What is occurring is not a culturing but a fashioning. Jōji is entranced by Naomi's capacity for physical transformation, and the act of mimicry attains an erotic intensity. For both of them the sexual fantasy of the Western woman becomes an all-consuming obsession, an obsession Jōji tirelessly feeds by clothing Naomi in ever more exotic costumes and by being the audience she craves.

Jōji says; "Though I had no sense for such things, my tastes ran to the chic and up-to-date, and I imitated the Western style in everything" (Tanizaki 1985: 173). Tanizaki is capable of great vulgarity and he enjoys parodying racist sexual fantasies. There is a theme in Tanizaki, or a theory of the beautiful, an aesthetics of distance, whereby a man measures beauty by its remoteness from his own existence (Takehiko 1963). A self-reinforcing dynamic lies at the core of this aesthetic. A man's consciousness of his own unattractiveness heightens his perception of beauty, and his appreciation of beauty intensifies his feeling of inferiority. Although Tanizaki gradually ceased to articulate these aesthetics in purely racial terms, the structure of feeling that balanced an ugly self against a distant beauty remains central to his work. Perhaps this is essential to fashion also, especially fashion advertising in a modern image-heavy society. Distance also implies a kind of taboo.

There is a tragedy in this; as Naomi becomes more Westernized and beautiful, she grows progressively more aware of Jōji's Japanese ugliness. She initially makes a feeble try at improving him, but he is not malleable like her. She tries to spruce him up by ordering him to wear a navy suit and black shoes on a trip to a ballroom. But this fails, and Naomi finds lovers more in keeping with her own new self-image, first with the rich Keio University students, further up the social ladder than her country bumpkin husband. Later, Naomi graduates to affairs with men of the forbidden and mysterious white race.

Naomi's infidelity thrusts Jōji into an endless torment: "Seared indelibly on my mind was the face of a whore so loathsome that killing her wouldn't be enough ..." but later, "Little by little, the loathsomeness changed into an unfathomable beauty" (Tanizaki 1985: 173). Torn between his hatred and the allure of his fantasies brought to life, Jōji teeters on the brink of madness, and he grasps at the traditional institutions of home and family as a solution to his dilemma. This theme Tanizaki must have recognized in Japanese political life also, drawn to the West in one moment and then rejecting it the next.

Later Naomi returns to Jōji, as she always does:

> Whipping off a black garment and tossing it aside, an unfamiliar young Western woman stood there in a pale blue French crepe dress. The exposed arms and shoulders were as white as a fox. Around her fleshy nape, she wore a crystal necklace that glowed like a rainbow; and beneath a black velvet hat pulled low over her eyes, the tips of her nose and chin were visible, terrifyingly miraculously white. The raw vermilion of her lips stood out in contrast. (Tanizaki 1985: 207)

By sleeping with white men and receiving Western clothes as presents, Naomi has become what Jōji truly desires, the Westernized temptress. But Naomi the temptress will not be satisfied with anything less than Jōji's total subjugation. He must agree to his own enslavement, and Jōji commits one debasing act after another. They go to live in Yokohama, where Naomi moves in foreigners' circles, choosing lovers to her heart's content. Jōji has become a faithful slave, treated contemptuously not only by Naomi, but also by her foreign boyfriends, who call him "George" in a humiliating reference to his lost Japanese pride. This is a parallel to the transformative nature of her "modern," "Western" name that impressed him so much when they met. The novel ends with a didactic disclaimer similar to the beginning: "The record of our marriage ends here. If you think that my account is foolish, please go ahead and laugh. If you think that there's a moral in it, then, please let it serve as a lesson. For myself, it makes no difference what you think of me; I'm in love with Naomi" (Tanizaki 1985: 237).

The rapture and the intensity of Jōji's passion is impressive, and by it he lessens the experience as an admonition against sexual and cultural obsession. Jōji's masochism, the apparent determinant of his ultimate humiliation, points to deeper dynamics. Pauline Réage argues that the need to interchange the roles of slave and master for the sake of the relationship is never more clearly demonstrated than in the course of an affair. Never is the complicity between the victim and executioner more essential. A woman's power increases directly in proportion to her apparent abasement. But with a single look she can call everything to a halt. The man is only her priest, living in fear and trembling of her displeasure. His sole function is to perform the various ceremonies that center around the sacred object (Réage 1966).

The visible relationship of master and slave is only a façade; the masochist's object is not to be enslaved per se, but to make another person enslave him or her. The mechanism at work is one of dominance through submission. Tanizaki's male masochists call attention to this dynamic by actually creating their temptresses before surrendering to them.[2] Tanizaki intends this as a comment on both the relationship between Japan and the West, and the roles of looking and displaying in the modern gendering and the consumer fashion spectacle.

Nothing confirms the thesis that the masochist's only joy lies in self-contemplation as much as Jōji's eagerness to retell and relive his humiliations. What he celebrates is not so much Naomi, whose supremacy is only a precondition, but an image of himself transfigured by the power of his obsession. The modern fashion spectacle has a similar power structure—it enslaves with its drive to consume, but what is celebrated is the self-image that is transfigured by that enslavement.

The economic underpinnings of the novel reveal how the "all-powerful slave" remains in control. Only Jōji's relative affluence allows him to take Naomi into his care and remake her as he wishes. Though Jōji is careful to retain the appearance of Naomi's free will by gaining her consent to each new step in their relationship, the truth of the matter is that she never has much choice. Turning Jōji down means returning either to the quasi-whorehouse of the café or to the actual whorehouse of her family home. He is her only hope for social and economic betterment. These economic and social imperatives remain constant, no matter how slavishly Jōji eventually behaves. He may need her to realize his fantasies, but she needs him for self-preservation. The fact that she always returns reveals her weakness. If she were a true femme fatale, she would be able to gain social mobility and material comfort by using her sexual wiles on the Keio students or the Westerners, but to them she is merely a convenient woman. Naomi has sexual and social value only to the extent that Jōji assigns it to her, just as Western fashions have aesthetic value for the Japanese only to the extent that they assign it to them. It is his obsession that supports the relationship, both metaphorically and literally.

Tanizaki struggles with the central concerns of fashion: tradition and change. One side of Jōji believes that birth is destiny, and that modernity counts very little. A pessimistic view of the human capacity for change runs through Jōji's narrative, providing an insistent counterpoint to the idea of woman as a mutable creature. Is it just the clothes that change? As much as Naomi changes to become a Westernized temptress, she remains a daughter of Senzoku: a prostitute to be bought, dressed up, and used, a woman as object, the plaything of those slightly higher on the social scale.

Far from just a racy tale in a Japanese newspaper, *Naomi* is much more multifaceted. It documents a man's destruction by his passions but also insists on his ultimate mastery. He gets what he wants. Naomi may be a goddess to be worshipped, but she is also a prostitute to be used. The fashion object is assigned great power, but it is still an object. Tanaka Miyoko, in her analysis of *Naomi,* remarks that the theme of creating an ideal woman, which engaged Tanizaki throughout his long career, was synonymous with "the problem of reconstructing a culture symbolized by the woman" (Miyoko 1977). As Jōji's example shows, the Tanizaki hero's relationship with the feminine is marked by nothing less than the attempt to call into being culture itself, to possess an alternate world that satisfies fantasy. Recognizing this connection reveals the final paradox of the West in Naomi. As much as Naomi is the fable of a Japanese dominated by his obsession with the West, it is also the story of a "West" that can be manipulated, objectified, and even consumed. This is a paradox appropriate to the low-*bunka* of the Taisho period and development of the modern fashion spectacle in Japan.

–8–

Brand Storytelling: Context and Meaning for Cargo Pants

Joseph Henry Hancock II

In this chapter I consider the notions of advertising as a form of storytelling and its function to create contextual significance in order to sell products. I emphasize how advertisers make use of the postmodern condition to create new marketing strategies. The theoretical texts of Jean Hamilton (1997) and a case-study by Matthew Debord (1997) indicate how context and advertising stories play a marked role in developing associations with consumer products. The concept of "brand storytelling" developed by Klaus Fog, Christian Budtz, and Baris Yakaboylu (2005) reinforces the notion that advertising and storytelling have become normative methods for companies when creating advertising. The marketing campaign of the well-known North American brand Abercrombie & Fitch serves as my case study in describing how creating a storyline establishes meaning for fashion garments. For this analysis, I examine the "cargo shorts" and pants popularized by Abercrombie & Fitch to demonstrate how meaning is developed and created around these distinctive mass fashions. Links are made between the visual presentation of cargo styles, cultural and critical theory, and popular culture itself.

Postmodernism and Hyperreality in Advertising

During the 1960s the postmodernism of the mass media influenced consumer culture through a range of communication outlets (Baldwin, Longhurst, McCracken, Ogborn, and Smith 2000). Media outlets adopted postmodern concepts and ways of imagining the world and presented them to consumers in products including motion pictures, television, and fashion advertising. More recent examples include movies such as *Blade Runner,* the television series *Twin Peaks,* and the shopping channel QVC (Hamilton 1997).

The philosopher Jean Baudrillard's reevaluation of Marx's economic theory of the object, in which Baudrillard emphasized the "sign-value" of a commodity, was linked to his sense that contemporary society is characterized by the *re*produced object. Baudrillard's concept of simulation, in which the boundaries between what is real and what is perceived as real are conflated, challenged humanism and essentialism (Best and Kellner 1991). An individual's inability to distinguish between what is real and attainable versus fantasy is what Baudrillard calls hyperreality. Those having social standing at the macro-levels of consumer culture create the distortions between reality and hyperreality (Baudrillard 1988). Baudrillard contended that the sign (the real), or the image, is distorted by its moving through the following stages: a reflection of basic reality, the masking and perverting of a basic reality, the masking of the *absence* of a basic reality, and finally, that which bears no relation to any reality whatever, its own pure simulacrum (simulation). Television, print advertising, computers, and other forms of communication create surreal life situations but present them to consumers as real (Best and Kellner 1991). Airbrushed fashion models in magazines, bogus Internet dating services, as well as distorted lenses on television cameras alter the real appearances of their subjects while suggesting to the viewer that the subject is natural.

To Baudrillard "brands" are the principal concepts of advertising culture, and they constitute a new discourse in the order of consumption (Baudrillard 1988). According to Baudrillard, "Those of social standing have repackaged consumer products in hyperreal scenarios in order to generate continuous consumption" (19). Since those of social standing use media to create advertising and marketing to sell products, they in turn make use of postmodern popular culture and consumer lifestyles. Judith Williamson suggests that while an advertiser's main goal is to sell the products, good advertising requires the marketers to not only take into account the inherent qualities of the products, but to generate a meaning around the consumer (Williamson 2002).

Hamilton's Micro–Macro Theory

In fashion, the goal of the advertiser becomes one of not only creating a use for the garment, but also creating scenarios or stories that set the garment in a selling context. Jean Hamilton demonstrates how the macro (outside)–micro (cognitive) association of fashion forms creates meanings. Hamilton revisits the works of previous clothing and textiles researchers, noting that their investigations focus on the cognitive sciences and the analysis of individual attachment to fashion forms and appearances (Hamilton 1997). She acknowledges a lack of research on how macro forces influence the micro forces of the purchasing of fashion goods, services, and various products.

Hamilton's primary goal is the development of a model based upon the notion that macro arbiters influence the micro-level meanings that consumers associate with their personal products. Her theoretical framework illustrates the movement from (MICRO) micronegotiations with the self→to negotiations with others→to fashion system arbiters→to cultural system arbiters (MACRO; Hamilton 1997: 165).

While Hamilton recognizes the ambivalence of fashion within postmodern consumerist society, her article emphasizes the importance of decisions made by the cultural and fashion system arbiters that serve as persuasive devices for consumers when making their purchases. Since fashion garments, arguably, carry no meanings and are signifiers only of themselves, it is the arbiters who give them meaning through selling context and display. Moreover, the arbiters must always be aware of what will appeal to their consumer or risk declining sales. Hamilton cites as an example of a vehicle for retail sales the television network QVC, which creates a "selling story" about the product's function and aesthetics. The consumer listens to the selling story and begins to relate to the items. The collection of goods then serves to establish an individual's identity (Hamilton 1997).

Contextual Tyranny

In "Texture and Taboo: The Tyranny of Texture and Ease in the J. Crew Catalog," Matthew Debord discusses the relevance of J. Crew's reinvention of mail-order catalog sales in the postmodern era. By creating retail catalogs that depict hyperreal lifestyles, J. Crew purposefully entices consumers to purchase basic products that they probably already own. According to Matthew Debord, the catalog has become a work of art, creating an aura of exclusiveness that allows consumers to shop from the privacy of their own homes. The catalog creates lifestyles that are fantastical and almost surreal. What is significant about Debord's contextual analysis is his ability to recognize a retailer's talent to create meanings and fantasy associated with mass apparel for selling to consumers. Debord takes a critical view when discussing J. Crew's contextual marketing techniques. He makes no secret of his frustration with J. Crew's manipulation of what he believes to be disappointing and insignificant fashions (Debord 1997).

Branding and Storytelling

In their book *Storytelling: Branding in Practice,* Klaus Fog, Christian Budtz, and Baris Yakaboylu explain how advertising reflects the basic concept of storytelling, the means for a company to create a brand through consumption. The storytelling process relies on a company's ability to emotionally brand products and build target markets. According to the authors, a brand reaches full consumption potential when an emotional attachment to consumers is attained. These consumers (including employees of the brand) are able to understand the company's values and messages. Storytelling is the vehicle that communicates these values in a process that is easy for all to comprehend. Storytelling speaks to the emotions of the target market that in return becomes loyal to the company (Fog et al. 2005).

To Fog, Budtz, and Yakaboylu, storytelling is divided into four elements: the message, conflict, characters and plot. Advertising uses the same formula and is able to create consumer interest while building associations to its products and creating emotional meaning. New storylines encourage consumers to purchase and repurchase products that are similar. Narrative creates brand recognition and desire; the new context allows companies to reinvent products, while the actual product itself is possibly indistinguishable from other brands (Fog et al. 2005).

Abercrombie & Fitch: Reinventing Cargo

Historically, Abercrombie & Fitch were known for traditional outdoor, camping, and safari clothing for men and women. However, after being bought by The Limited Corporation in 1988, the company was reinvented. The clothing was changed to target a younger and more fashion-oriented consumer. While the company continues to sell basic items such as cargo pants, khakis, T-shirts, sweaters, peacoats, baseball caps, and various other types of active wear, the advertisements selling these products after 1988 underwent a radical change from the "old" Abercrombie & Fitch image.

Youth-obsessed marketing became a key vehicle for the new Abercrombie & Fitch to gain success in the retail market. In addition to a shift in its advertising campaign, the company redesigned the basic garments it sold. They redesigned them in worn and washed fabrications and refitted them in fashion silhouettes for a youth-oriented consumer. A T-shirt became a "muscle-fit T," while cargo pants were given the name "paratroops." Moreover, by attaching "A&F" patches on sweaters, pants, and denim garments, Abercrombie gained strong brand recognition. In 1998 Abercrombie & Fitch separated from its parent company, The Limited, to become an independent retailer. By the first quarter of 2007, the company was operating 947 stores, including its divisions. In the company's own words on its Web site (www.abercrombie.com), it is the "Creator and Operator of Aspirational Lifestyle Brands."

During the late 1990s, Abercrombie & Fitch's marketing strategy gained momentum with promotions geared toward college students, the gay community, and other Abercrombie enthusiasts. The Abercrombie "magalog" (as the *Wall Street Journal* identified it in July 1997) was popular and went beyond a mail-order catalog, evolving into a lifestyle guide for thousands of consumers (Bird 1997). Although the publication was effective as a promotional device, many conservative activist groups protested the magalog's use of group sex scenes and themes of homosexuality in order to sell Abercrombie items such as cargo pants and basic Ts. David Reines's essay "All the Nudes That's Fit to Print" reveals how the American Decency Association and other groups called for a national boycott of the retailer (Reines 2003).

Photography in the magalog features largely hyperreal WASP (white Anglo-Saxon Protestant) youth posed in suggestive positions. The whiteness of the magalog caused a stir in the national community (*60 Minutes* 2003). Dwight A. McBride, the chair of the Department of African American Studies at Northwestern University, published *Why I Hate Abercrombie & Fitch,* deploring A&F for its mostly white models and horrible treatment of minority employees. His concerns focused on young African

Americans who, he argued, experience overall rejection by the brand because they lack the social "ideal of whiteness" (McBride 2005). Perhaps as a response, A&F's hiring and marketing strategies are moving into more diversity, featuring some advertisements with people of color.

The A&F magalog offers an excellent example of postmodern techniques applied to contemporary advertising. Marketing executives are educated about cultural shifts and compose their campaigns to reflect contemporary advertisement strategies. Each advertising campaign is consciously constructed for maximum consumer impact. A&F's use of Bruce Weber to create a photographic work of art helped A&F to gain a "casual luxury" status in the retailing market. After all, by purchasing the magalog, consumers were purchasing Bruce Weber "works" by an out and proud gay photographer.

From its first publication in 1995 until it ceased in 2003, the A&F magalog featured cargo pants and shorts continuously in both photos and on models in layouts. Cargo styles were a staple in the A&F assortment, and the retailer was identified as a key player and mass distributor of cargo pants (Structure 2000). The differential form of each cargo pant and short was limited and variations in color seemed to be the major difference; however, even these became repetitive. During the late 1990s, owning a pair of A&F cargo pants or shorts was almost essential, although the truly stylish often rejected them. As Greg Lindsay stated, "The Quarterly made Abercrombie's name synonymous with a neo-preppy look found in its clothes and the all-American perfection of its models, but its edgy tone and imagery drove critics (and there were many) over the edge" (Lindsay 2003).

Interpreting the Magalog

Since Abercrombie is a key retailer responsible for the proliferation of cargo styles in mass fashion, I select two issues of the magalog here for analysis. These issues were titled "Back to School 1999: Innocents Abroad" and "A&F Quarterly Presents ... Summer 2003." I interpret associations and meanings that illustrate how Abercrombie & Fitch builds its brand using the art of storytelling to create connections to their product. By examining the visual stories of the magalog and relationships to popular culture, a generalization about each magalog's themes can possibly be determined through semiotic analysis.

Erotic Triangles, The Vampyre's Kiss, and the Male Objectified: Interpreting A&F's Visual Presentation of Cargo Styles

It is important to indicate how the cargo assortment at A&F evolved from the 1999 selling season to summer 2003. The cargo choices in the 1999 issue of A&F's magalog number thirty-one, whereas the 2003 edition offers seventy-four. The increase of more than 200 percent in the number of cargo styles from 1999 to 2003 indicates that cargo pants and shorts were a crucial product for the company's sales. The reader will note that the emphasis of cargo fashion shifts from a predominant men's range in 1999 to a women's category in 2003.

Erotic Triangles

Figure 8.1 features three individuals, two males and one female. The female sports a dark fringe top with hip-hugging cargo pants. Her stylized cargo pants, with rips on the bottom seam, complement her black, flat shoes. One of the male figures displays cargo pants with a long-sleeved T-shirt under a military-style top. His accessories are a knit cap and court sneakers. The casual appearance of both figures suggests a relaxed and casual lifestyle.

The props and setting of this photo allude to possible storylines. The former include the non-cargo male figure, the dog, and the set of headphones on the cargo male figure. The non-cargo male figure crouches on the ground with a Welsh Corgi. He appears to suggest a traditional student—the studious type with a backpack and conservative appearance. The Welsh Corgi signifies commitment and the responsibility of pet ownership. He is the "nice boy"; his counterpart wears a set of headphones. These headphones and the cargo male's general demeanor allude to fun, parties, and DJing; he is the "bad boy," who now is a conservative type of cliché himself. The female figure bridges the two male figures. She denotes a neutral zone between good student and party student. The context displays a setting for cargo pants that implies how they can be worn in an individualized manner by both male and female consumers, as well as by different archetypes of students.

Figure 8.2 features a Queen Elizabeth II impersonator and three young male figures, two of whom wear cargo pants. The other male figure is partly concealed behind the regal impersonator. The three male figures appear very casual, layered in A&F-branded ensembles. This pictorial story of a garden party then evolves into a suggestion of a rave (a dance party that frequently changes its location). Throughout this visual story, the photographs feature young men and women drinking wine, dancing, and partying. The Queen Elizabeth impersonator joins the party by holding a skateboard, dancing with the teens, and riding on the shoulders of young men. This depiction of the queen "letting it all hang out" suggests how, in reality, she is rather more uptight. By portraying the impersonator in a manner that is in opposition to that of the real queen, A&F creates a parody of Her Royal Highness.

There is more to this image. Queen Elizabeth stands in the center of the photo with a formal dress, tiara, and sash. The queen holds a skateboard in her hand. Two Welsh Corgis, one on each side of her, resemble two big, hairy balls of fur. The spatial placement of the queen and the two dogs suggests a visual phallic symbol. This visual phallus could also be viewed as homoerotic. The center of the phallus is a queen. The term "queen" being a slang term for a gay male, it marks a pun that is

Figure 8.1 "Back To School 1999," p. 320. © Bruce Weber, All Rights Reserved.

understood by homosexuals and those who understand the argot of gay culture. This double entendre creates an ironic context and yet is quite simple to read. The two male figures behind the queen, who seem to be resting upon each other, reinforce these notions of homoeroticism.

Both photos (Figures 8.1 and 8.2) present male and female models in a triangular type of relationship. Queer cultural theorist Eve Kosofsky Sedgwick argues that visual presentation of bodies in a triangular shape leads the viewer to erotic thoughts.

Figure 8.2   "Back To School 1999," p. 316. © Bruce Weber, All Rights Reserved.

According to Sedgwick, "The triangle is useful as a figure by which our 'common-sense' of intellectual tradition schematics erotic relations, allows us to condense into a juxtaposition with the folk-perception of several somewhat different streams of recent thought" (Sedgwick 1985: 21). Sedgwick believes that, culturally, we look at the triangulation of photographic images (male, female, etc.) and in so viewing, create erotic relationships. This suggests that the triangulation of individuals in these

A&F advertisements may have been carefully constructed to create a scenario in a viewer's mind.

If we examine triangulation using Jean Hamilton's study, these photos reflect her ideas of MACRO fashion context forming from the creative processes of designers and product developers. The MACRO system arbiters dictate and create the direction of the retail company's fashion, using collective data on advertising trends and the market niche. The leaders in advertising know how to create fashion marketing using industry statistics to create these campaigns. Moreover, these photographs are by the queer maestro Bruce Weber; his photos come from the perspective of the "gay's gaze" *(Mulvey 1981)*. The eroticism of his photos naturally reflects his worldview and distinctive taste. While the photographs are on one level carefully composed and almost "tasteful," allusions to homosexual eroticism are clear.

The Vampyre's Kiss

Plate 22 glamorizes the eroticism of vampires. The shirtless male vampire wears his camouflage cargo shorts accessorized with a spiked black belt. He appears to have been awakened from his coffin by the female character. She is dressed in a body suit, fishnet tights, cape, and fingerless gloves. She seductively awaits the bite of the vampire while pressing her hands against his perfect airbrushed abdominal muscles. While this photograph emphasizes the traditional eroticism between men and women, it romanticizes the ideals of male domination over female victims. The female's passive body position in comparison to the male figure is clear. He overtakes her with his muscular body, emphasized by his muscular abdominals.

However, this photo is somewhat more ambiguous. The vampire in the photo seems to be dominating his female victim; however, we (the viewers) are allowed to visually objectify the shirtless vampire. If this photo were targeted for a straight male audience, then the male vampire would appear completely clothed. The female is clothed and appears to actually be in control; she is allowing the vampire to seduce her and is not simply a victim. Bruce Weber's "gay's gaze" focus on the male physique creates desire in some readers for this A&F image for the maleness of the handsome vampire. This idea of male objectification continues in Plates 23 and 24.

The Male Objectified

In Plate 23, we view a single male figure from the A&F Summer 2003 magalog. He wears cargo shorts, a belt, and accessories suggestive of an ancient, primitive, gladiatorial and/or native context. This male is a "forbidden warrior," according to A&F, and wears leather cuffs and a shearling wrap and carries a spear. "The Forbidden Warriors" is the only example in which there is an ethnic male figure. This model appears only once again in this entire magalog, which also depicts him with a hood covering his head. By placing him in this context and dressing him in a native cargo context, A&F reinforces notions of whiteness among its target niche. E. Patrick Johnson and Mae G. Henderson, in their book *Black Queer Studies,* reveal that when black men are presented visually in the media, they are usually stereotyped or given less visual importance than their white counterparts. These authors argue that gay communities, which some might erroneously think are partial to nondiscriminatory attitudes, place visual priority on white male bodies (Johnson and Henderson 2005). The A&F summer 2003 magalog's use of predominantly white models tends to reinforce their analysis. Nonetheless, the statuesque pose might also suggest that in this man of color we have a true hero and victor.

Finally, in Plate 24, we see more overt objectification of the male figure in contemporary fashion advertising. This photograph continues to reinforce the homoerotic nature of A&F's magalog. By showing a naked male literally "coming out of the closet," the photograph reinforces the significance of "coming out," the spatial metaphor used to describe the process of gays, lesbians, bisexuals, and queers announcing their sexuality. While some consumers may not recognize the location of the male figure, others may understand this innuendo. Others may just appreciate his body and appearance. However, those who understand or enjoy the joke of "coming out" may relate to A&F and decide to purchase their cargo shorts thinking that the company is relaxed with sexual minorities.

Conclusion

As Hamilton, Debord, Fog, Budtz, and Yakaboylu discuss in their studies, a part of the fashion system concerns consumers examining a retailer's visual marketing presentation; relating to the product, context, and lifestyle presentation; and finally purchasing the product. In this study, I have highlighted a type of narrative structure used in some contemporary fashion marketing and suggesting possible readings of A&F advertising for that very simple product, cargo pants. A&F's Quarterly displays the cargo pants in various scenarios; the models and photography represent the primary points of interest. The garments seem to exist almost as theatrical props for the narrative. These "marketing narratives" create perceptions of garments' importance in the minds of consumers, who range from college students to older gay men. While the primary interest of retailers such as Abercrombie & Fitch is to make profits, its fashion advertisements are implicated in the understanding of popular and mass fashion. The "macro" arbiters of fashion decide how consumers will view garments such as cargo pants from one selling season to the next. Since 1988, A&F has associated cargo style to youth and popular culture, and also created a queer subtext that will resonate with some A&F enthusiasts for the rest of their lives.

–9–

Double Dresses for Double Brides

Catherine Harper

In post-conflict Belfast, in December 2005, the first civil partnership ceremony in the so-called United Kingdom took place. Shannon Sickles and Gráinne Close exchanged their vows at Belfast's City Hall, permitted to do so by the United Kingdom's Civil Partnership Act 2004. In that contested capital city of this contested territory, then, an alternative "Act of Union" to that of 1801, securing Britain's coupling with Ireland, legally asserted the rights and responsibilities of same-sex couples, recognizing their (our) sexual relationships, permitting social and financial equality, and, most notably, legally recognizing—more than tolerating—homosexual love rights.

Within days, civil partnerships took place in England, Scotland, and Wales, and within ten months around 16,000 such partnerships were formed in the United Kingdom, 1 percent being in Northern Ireland.[1] That the first took place in Belfast is significant. The contestations enacted passionately in this city and on this island over the preceding centuries are well known. Seamus Heaney's poetic articulations of the sexualized struggle between an "imperially Male" British colonial force and a softer, victimized, "maternal-virginal" and essentially feminine *Mise Eire* reveals, however, a singularly heterosexual frame.[2] The traumatic mono-politics of three decades of "Troubles" in the North of Ireland refused the "Alternative Ulsters"[3] of sexual and racial Otherness in a quest for "Fenian Freedom"[4] on one hand and "Loyal Union"[5] on the other. The scars on Belfast City, and its people, map those traumas, but the "peace culture" has allowed a new tentative examination—even contestation—of the politics of "sexuality difference." Since the Civil Partnership Act, where the words "never married" used to be a coded text for a homosexual (Brooke 1950: 371–72) or where coming out as lesbian meant never being a bride (Walker 2000), we cannot state that now.

The so-called "Belfast brides" (Chrisafis 2005) enacted their "marriage" at Belfast's City Hall, overlooked by the statue of Queen Victoria, imposing and imperious symbol in that city to this day. She, who famously (most probably mythically) refused to believe lesbianism existed,[6] and whose blind spot to Sapphic love supposedly excused gay women from the U.K. laws historically criminalizing homosexuality (Miller 2005). While lesbians avoided the legal persecution male homosexuals experienced, some form of erasure, whether by intention or default, from cultural and sexual history has arguably resulted in a differently styled invisibility for gay women—certainly for gay "femmes"—than for their erstwhile "criminal," and therefore more noticeable, gay male counterparts (A. Stonham, personal communication, 2007).[7]

Northern Ireland remains a closeted place for its estimated 100,000 gay men and lesbians (Chrisafis 2005, referencing British Government statistics), and even within Belfast's gay community, instances of conservative and homophobic generalizing are apparent: Aine, from Belfast, writing on the Rainbow Network's Web forum, states:

> Lesbians can be very self-righteous which, coupled with bad wedding fashion and that mawkish sentimentality that only lesbians know how to turn on to the max, makes for a somewhat queasy experience.

Aine's sentiments echo wider historical prejudices experienced by lesbians whose clothing choices did hint at, or make visible, their sexuality (Rolley 1996, Walker 2001). More than purely aesthetically meaningful, such choices are entirely concerned with "the delicate business of getting oneself across" (Bowen 1950, quoted in Wronsov 2005: n.p.), testifying to the importance of dress culture within human communication of identity and desire. Within the complexities of material culture, cultural practices, and social change lie the conventions of marriage, a social rite of passage—with its especially encoded and hetero-gendered garments—from which homosexuals in the United Kingdom have been excluded, until now. When Creed listed her lesbian bodies in 1995—"femme, vampiric, muscled, tattooed, pregnant, effete, foppish, amazonian" (86)—she left out *bride*. Yet brides as symbols of cultural acceptance of union are much represented within global gay, queer, and indeed transgender, culture. Bridal ubiquity is a hallmark of Pride marches throughout the world, reflecting a tradition of gay and transgender "mock marriages" initiated, for example, in the molly houses of eighteenth-century London (Garber 1992) and still current in trans-circles today (e.g., www.transgenderzone.com/features/weddings2. htm). And in visual art practice, Robert Gober famously let his "bride-desire" show in his tender photographic reworking of a society bridalwear advertisement, *Newspaper* (1992) and *Untitled* (1992), in which he is pictured in a traditional satin wedding dress, juxtaposed with a real-life text about the Vatican's condoning of discrimination against homosexuals (Museum of Modern Art). For this work especially, Garber's assertion is key: "What gets married *is* a dress," less a person (Garber 1992: 143).

When Garber wrote *Vested Interests: Cross-Dressing and Cultural Anxiety* in 1992, however, she carefully separated the then fantasy possibilities of queer weddings from normative conventions of actualized marriage. Since 2005, in the United Kingdom certainly, it is now possible to conflate these terms, mixing the normative (for that has been shifted) with the fantastical (for that is now possible). Whatever lesbians in civil partnership ceremonies choose to wear, their presence as same-sex protagonists and their public affirmation of sexual partnership significantly mark their self-identity, their relationship to each other and to the hetero-normative. Butler, in a discussion of queer mimicry of marriage in 1990, argued, "The replication of heterosexual constructs in non-heterosexual frames brings into relief the utterly constructed status of the so-called heterosexual original" (Garber quoting Butler 1990: 31). Butler's position is powerfully shifted now that the mimicry of the so-called "heterosexual construct" of marriage is no longer mimicry in the United Kingdom and may be as utterly constructed within a homosexual arena as within that of heterosexuals. If, then, as Wilson notes, "The role of dress in the theatre of life is extraordinarily important" (2005a: 248), and, as Steele suggests, fashion is "a symbolic system linked to the expression of sexuality—both sexual behaviours (including erotic attraction) and gender identity" (1996: 4), then the recently afforded possibility for staging of lesbian sexual identity as "married" presents a brand new opportunity and challenge to how lesbians design their public and private self-representation and identification.

Lesbians are sometimes asked the ignorant and/or impertinent question of "who's the man and who's the woman." Putting ignorance and impertinence aside, the gender references of butch and femme are important to lesbian history and culture. If the prominence of the bridal dress is related to women's long-established linkage to cloth and clothing production, their roles as childbearers and thereby their close link to family and community, and the traditionally significant change of role for women postmarriage, then in a butch–femme relationship, that must be played out as the role of the femme, to whom the butch woman acts as foil or other. In lesbian unions of this kind, we see a woman in a dress coupled with a woman in the gendered clothing of masculinity. And in queerish references to that convention, we see all kinds of alternative and variant gendered visions played out sartorially and passionately in lesbian civil unions. The focus of this research, however, is on double dresses for double brides in relation to the traditions of the singular heterosexual bride in her singular and iconic frock. It is important here to acknowledge, though, that there are already many lesbian couples for whom the femme–femme model is not relevant.

As the first women to be "married" to each other in the United Kingdom, Gráinne and Shannon selected their clothing to mark mood and moment. Both wore trouser suits, one black and one white, with dandyesque Star Lily buttonholes. As Lurie (1981: 229) points out, suits on women can and do have complex and multiple meanings—sophisticated exoticism, sex-equality casual wear, sporty tomboyism, drag king elegance—and these are further complicated in the dynamics of butch lesbian dressing and visibility, as articulated in Walker's personal testimony preface to *Looking Like What You Are* (2001: xiv):

> I remember dancing with her in a straight bar, foolishly ignoring the rules for personal safety in a homophobic culture. When the bar closed, there was a group of young men outside waiting for us. "You," they said, pointing to where I stood in a checked mini

and heels, "don't look like one." They dismissed me in an instant. I was not a real lesbian, probably just led astray, surely redeemable, all I needed was … "But you," they said, pointing to where ML stood in her jeans and button-down shirt, "we know what you are."

In choosing to wear suits for this inaugural civil partnership, this couple made an unmistakable statement, as they would have done whatever their attire. Their choice was to "queer" the institution of marriage by donning apparel that effectively separated them from its conventions. Their combined statement was, "We know you know what we are, and we are," and this had pungent political resonance. While Gráinne and Shannon sought to subvert "Brideland" (Walker 2000), I can assert that there is a different but equally potent "queering" at work in those lesbian femme pairs who have claimed the chance to both wear meringues … or the like!

Walker describes how femme identification generates its own internal cultural anxieties and marginalization. Quoting Califia's appraisal of a lesbian community where "butches think of femmes as straight girls taking a Sapphic vacation from serving the patriarchy" (Califia 1992: 10), she examines reductive readings of femmes as mere "lipstick lesbians," apolitical, ahistorical, acultural players in "lesbian chic" and "liable to run from 'the life' into the sheltering arms of normalcy at any minute" (Walker 2001: xv). Walker wrestles with notions of femme-ness as a take-on, take-off form of seasonal sexuality, less innate than its lesbian-authentic butch counterpart, whose (fixed) identity requires a different public investment and investiture. Civil partnership, however, requires public commitment, at least momentarily, to a sexual identity as essentially lesbian—butch, femme, or other—and it seems that there is a new moment in lesbian cultural history that reconfigures—or maybe just replaces—some of the anxious identity politics of previous decades. Whereas Gráinne and Shannon chose to assert their place in "the life," it has now arguably normalized them, whereas "lipstick lesbian brides" in "lesbian chic wedding dresses" perversely seem to continue the currency of corruption (Two girl-brides kissing? Where's the man? Where's even the butch?) that informed pre–civil partnership lesbian life and love.

Cole asserts the importance of oral recording of lesbian and gay histories (1999: 141), and the wider project upon which this chapter is based examines a range of enactments of style and sexuality played out between lesbian couples on their "special day." By collecting and telling personal stories, this research contributes to the growing testimonial evidence of gay and lesbian lived experience within contemporary culture. Its case studies involve women who have elected to reflect variously their similarities, their differences, the sexual politics of their unions, their conservatism or their queerness, and their determination to mobilize all the signifiers of conventional marriage or to reinvent what lesbian union means for them. Inevitably, the iconic wedding dress is present—even where it is absent—in discussion of lesbian wedding desire, and its ultra-femme hetero-symbolism—for it renders even contemporary *hetero*sexual brides as fantastically *über*-feminine, providing particular resonance and cause for reflection in lesbian "marriage."

In September 2006 my partner and I enacted our "special day" in Brighton (Plate 25). With two "brides," the "wedding dress(es)" became those material sites of self-identification and mediated contestation. I wore a pretty but anonymous store-bought silk print dress and felt like a prom queen. My proclamation of sexuality was constructed to be new, nonreferencing of my hetero-past, my hetero-culture, or my hetero-family in Northern Ireland (no Belfast bride, me!). My partner, however, put aside her store-bought frock for a bronze lamé cocktail dress owned by her mother and, as far as we can trace, worn to an aunt's wedding in 1952 (Plate 26). Both mother and aunt died some time ago, and it was important to my partner that they were present and remembered in some way via the dress:

> I wanted to wear the dress then bought the other just in case but realised in the last few days before the partnership that it was very important for me to wear it, to have my mother there with me in some way. I felt held in some way ... (A. Stonham, personal communication, June 17, 2008)

Just as the single existing photographic image of this dress in 1952 permitted my partner, as Barthes did in *Camera Lucida* (1981a), to explore and begin to understand her mother, so here the memory of that woman was reactivated through the new indexical focus of the civil partnership ceremony, the memory in/of the photograph, and the mobilization of that dress. Barthes, writing of the *punctum* of the image, describes how it punctuates the surface reading of the image: it "rises from the scene, shoots out of it like an arrow, and pierces me ... a photograph's punctum is that accident which pricks me (but also bruises me, is poignant to me)" (1981a: 26, 27). That piercing arrow punctuated my partner's enactment of this "marriage," penetrating its surface and assuring that her wedding day was essentially meaningful and communicative with her mother, loved, lost, imaged within the photograph, and present within the dress.

Thus was a maternal presence allowed at a vital and heavily loaded rite of feminine passage. And, with such emotional *in*vestment, this *vestment* referenced Kopytoff's anthropological notion of the "biography of a thing" (1986): the dress became activated, animated, and enabled, a designed object with its previous history being reinscribed by this historically significant contemporary event. Layers of meaning were opened and added to, and a series of "extra-material meaning[s]" (Vickery in Taylor 2002: 76) were powerfully created ...

During the day, however, this designed object, already over fifty years old, and selected only that morning for the ceremony, began to disintegrate. My role became that of the seamstress, charged with making good a dress falling apart at the seams. These acts of repair took place before and during the celebrations, and the dress took on a key role in marking, documenting, investigating, and explaining the significance and meaning of the day. It seemed to me, as I sewed my partner into her dress, that stitching—the textile craft previously used in my family to enact the discipline, frugality, and virtue of Northern Irish Presbyterianism and "appropriate femininity"—was used here to (re)construct a (queer) femininity that would have the righteous Old Testament women of my lineage spinning in their graves. My partner's dress, already invested with the perceived decadence of 1950s working-class London, although tempered with the respectability of her mother's successfully maternal and domestic role, was relocated on a lesbian body, thereby reconfiguring its constructed meanings of the feminine. Yet, by being configured as a bridal gown, this garment reentered the feminine normative, only to quickly skip away as the "groom" was revealed as a "second bride."

The narrative of the unraveling stitches remembers Wronsov's *Punctum* text (2005) in which a stain on a garment is the subject of consideration. "Stains are sometimes like a small wound in your dressed identity, they are a hole in your fabric-built 'armor' in a social encounter" (n.p.), asserts Wronsov, urging that the mark both reveals and "snapshots" the intricacies of the moment of staining (or in our case, of disintegrating), allowing it to reveal something of the unique vulnerability of lesbian couples entering the uncharted territory of "gay marriage." While I sewed my partner into her mother's fragile dress, I was conscious of the formal thoughtful action of sewing in a new series of complex memories, of personal poetries, retold narratives, and rituals of remembrance. An act of tenderness, working along seams holding the skin-dustings of my lover's mother, tracing the boundaries of my lover's body with the sewn edges of her mother's ... an erotics of tiny pricks and needled piercings, a poetics of talcum traces and tentative touch ...

Ingraham (1999) describes Western culture's persistent obsession with the symbolic potency of the white wedding dress, citing the wedding as "one of heterosexuality's key organizing rituals" (1999: 14) with the dress at its core. Ingraham has further critiqued the naturalizing processes by which the images or representations of "wedding culture" effectively regulated sexuality, operating an erasure of sexualities outside what she termed the culturally constructed "heterosexual imaginary" (14). That imaginary, Ingraham argued, rests upon key principles of being for a successful and above all appropriate bride: not having a (visible) colorful sexual past, exhibiting premenopausal youth, evidencing modest sexuality centered on low-maintenance femininity and potential fertility. Yet, the albeit most usually symbolic virgin status of the heterosexual bride's white wedding dress (Church 2003; Winge and Eicher 2003) is an impossible conformity for the "lesbian bride." She has arrived at her civil partnership day exactly through exploration, experiment, and experience of her sexuality. It is therefore impossible—even symbolically—for her to mobilize anything other than a fantasy of virginity (that fantasy is, of course, not the preserve only of lesbian brides-in-white). And this clearly links with another "other" in lesbian unions—the heterosexual bride has no need to "come out" as a straight woman, whereas the lesbian bride must necessarily make a formal, legal, and arguably essentialist and authoritative statement of commitment to her lesbianism (Rust 1993). The civil partnership ceremony represents another episode in the perpetual process, not fixed event, of "coming out," but its legality presents a new aspect of management and maintenance of sexual identity. While the lesbian couple is self-identified as gay, and known as such by a range of people, there may be a new tranche of disclosures attached to the ceremony. And, where the announcement of a heterosexual marriage does not forefront sexuality or sexual activity, declaring that one is to be a "lesbian bride" screams them. The lesbian bride is undoubtedly the lover of her partner, and society knows this. The tendency of my partner's dress to fall apart throughout our "marriage" day, and to require repeated mending, set up a dynamic of fixity and slippage, with sewing being the act of temporary anchorage in a field of uncertainty. The tight, white stitching taught by my puritanical grandmother (a keen homophobe within her generation and context) was reactivated in the subversive construction of a "lesbian bride." But, and to continue to trouble the normative, just as most grooms work hard to eagerly unlace the body, this female "groom" labored to sew up the erotic gaps where flesh threatened to emerge ...

However much the bride has had a mixed history in Western culture, she has always been singular, hence her iconic and symbolic status. The wedding dress has come to be her stand-in, a dress that in some way erases her as her, and makes her into "the bride," with bridesmaids, matron of honor, flower-girls, and mother of the bride forming an exclusively feminine and substantially historicized inner circle, supported traditionally by the man relinquishing the woman (the bride's father or symbolic substitute) and the man taking up ownership of the woman (the groom). The selection process of the singular wedding dress is critical to the prospective bride's social movement through a prewedding "limbo," facilitated by unwritten matrimonial law, into the circle of married women. That is, "the dress facilitates the rite of passage" (Church 2003: 18). How then to understand the mapping of such singularity and symbolic status into the "special day" of "double brides"? Doubling is already part of the tradition of wedding style. The double bride image is that of the bride gazing at her mirror reflection in admiring, pensive, or preparatory mode. Symbolic doubling also manifests in the significance of relationships between the bride and her mother, the bride and small female children—traditionally not her own—and the bride and her collective of bridesmaids rendered as one by a tradition of identical dresses echoing, but distinct from, the singular iconic bridal gown. Never previously, though, has doubling encompassed the bride and her female lover, and arguably there is a Freudian uncanny quality in the experience of traditionalists when confronted by the new phenomenon of lesbian bridal pairs ...

In preconflict Belfast, I masqueraded as a hetero-femme for thirty years, satisfying my culture and my family and coyly enacting a persuasive lie that there were, as yet, "no takers," and that my work took precedence over frivolities of the heart. Certain women made me blush, and my heart beat faster in their company, but, in that contested capital city of this still-contested territory, any alternative "Act of Union" was impossible for me. The spinster spun while passionate contestations of political and sexual borders raged around me. In 1996, just as one of the last ceasefires broke in an emergent Northern Irish peace that took an age to spawn, this spinster broke and took a night boat to England:

> Don't contact your mother, she's too upset ... how can we say that you've gone to England and become a *lesbian?* (the last word containing such a weight of disgust that it remains a word I find hard to say out loud). (personal communication from relative, 1996)

A decade after the night boat flight, the Civil Partnership Act has allowed my partner and me to stand in front of friends and family and publicly proclaim ourselves as committed to each other, romantically, sexually, financially, and legally. The dresses hardly mattered, and Garber's contention that it is the dress that gets married is countered here. Except that dress meaning is unavoidable, and while our dresses did not upstage our reason for undertaking a civil partnership, both operated differently to bring significance to the day.

The text of my partner's day is indicated above, and the strong symbolic linkages of dress and her mother were vital to her. For me, however, my dress choice allowed me to articulate solely what Steele understands as sartorial expression of sexuality and gender identity (Steele 1996: 4). It is important for me to be read and understood as female, feminine, and functional as a lesbian (the unspeakable word ...). My cultural background suggests it is impossible to pull this off, and that its possibility is an abomination. It is important to me to control the pull of history, and while I was happy to "act out" as a Presbyterian seamstress (a spinster of a kind) in sewing the transgressive body of my lover into her differently signifying dress, my dress, shoes, and all needed to be new and without traces of lineage. They represented the newness that came about in traversing the Irish Sea, reinventing myself, and surviving separate to family and culture. Further, my colorful and sequined dress, my platform heels, my bright and lipsticked smile, were markers of independence, and Pride. I may not "look like one," but I know what I am.

Notes

1. National Statistics Online, www.statistics.gov.uk/cci/nugget.asp?id=1685.
2. Seamus Heaney's poem "Act of Union," published in *North* (London: Faber & Faber, 1975).
3. The song "Alternative Ulster" featured on Stiff Little Fingers' album *Inflammable Material* (EMI UK, 1979), and it is used here to highlight the traditional refusal of "otherness" in Ulster.
4. The term "Fenian" has been used since mid-1800s to describe Irish nationalists and republicans opposing British rule in Ireland, originally and specifically Irish

Republican Brotherhood members. In contemporary usage, it is also sometimes a term of abuse.

5. In the Northern Irish context, Loyalists and Unionists are those supporting the historical union between Northern Ireland and the United Kingdom. They are loyal to the British monarchy and oppose a united Ireland.

6. The much-cited story about Queen Victoria's personal intervention to omit lesbianism from the Criminal Law Amendment Act of 1885 is most likely a myth (Hall 2000) but one that nevertheless persists in the historical narrative of lesbianism within the meta-narrative of sexuality and the law.

7. While male homosexuality was decriminalized for acts between two men (not more) over twenty-one years of age and "in private" in England and Wales through the United Kingdom's Sexual Offences Act of 1967, it was only in 1980 for Scotland and 1982 for Northern Ireland that male homosexual acts stopped being crimes.

–10–

Collection L

Maja Gunn

Collection L takes its departure from interviews and meetings with a group of homosexual women in Stockholm in 2007. Springing from questions about identity, sexuality, body, and clothes, I transformed my impression of these women into garments of my design and fabrication. The women's stories have become not only research material for the collection but also an active ingredient in using narrative to extend the concept of fashion. When I exhibited the work, their stories were displayed together with the clothes I made as well as photographs of the women wearing the clothes.[1]

Collection L is based on the lives of seven women. Over one year I conducted interviews, corresponded by e-mail and talked with the women who contributed to *Collection L*. As well as participant observation, the collection was informed by research within the history of lesbianism as well as the theories of Michel Foucault (2002 [1976]) and Judith Butler's gender analyses (2004, 2006 [1990]). From their work I was able as a designer to link the women's lives to more abstract notions of performativity. The collection includes transformations and twists of some traditionally gendered clothes such as suits and white shirts. There is a cape to hide under and a tight catsuit that highlights the body. There are family outfits with a focus on motherhood. Some outfits are made of small pieces of silk cloth sewn together, which never really fit. For one woman, who feels both ethnicity and her sexual difference very strongly, this garment, on closer inspection, is full of gaps that interpret her story. By working with their lives and their narratives I have created the sense of a private approach to the collection. Who are they? What do they feel? What are their dreams? How do they relate to fashion? To body? To identity?

By responding to questions like "How do you relate to the body?" the women were able to add their feelings and opinions about their own and others' bodies. The discussion proceeded organically over time and not through a set questionnaire. My concern has been the variations of lesbianism, the ambivalence, the level of interpretation. How much analysis can I make without posing any risk to the contributing women's feelings? This level of risk within design is important to me. It has therefore been important that I find precursors who have also worked with ambiguity. When starting to create and to style the photographic portraits, I found one inspiration in the work of Claude Cahun from the 1920s to the 1930s (Downie 2006). Cahun's admixture of femininity and androgyny provides one of the century's most complex displays of lesbian identity. The practical work is based on a handicraft knowledge of textiles. I dyed and printed the material by hand in order to keep the collection coherent. The women's identities, and my own interpretation of different lesbian life stories, were united in colors, materials, and handicraft preparation.

Lineage of the Term *lesbianism*

The word "lesbian" has historically often been used as a disparaging term (Aldrich 2006). But there have been other words for explaining the attraction between women. The identification with the word "lesbianism" for the contributors of *Collection L* was varied. For example, "Alex" (Figure 10.1) noted that women sometimes refuse the socially imposed lesbian category. Others proudly make use of the term:

> I don't identify myself as a lesbian. For me lesbian is not something negative, but it is something others are, not me. I don't see myself as a lesbian even if I live with a woman. Maybe it has to do with that I only have had boyfriends before. I think that I don't want to call myself a dyke—'cause I don't know what it means. I never called myself straight before when I was dating men. And I'm still me. I think Alex will do just fine.

The outfit made for Alex is a voluminous cape, in which she is able to hide. One of its sides is made of a mix of dark wool fabrics, to create a sculptural appearance. The other side is a form of dyed speckled greyscale with handmade prints in black, white, and neon colors. This side is more expressive, as I find Alex to be a person who wants to both blend in and stand out. The cape is a form of urban camouflage, and since both sides can be worn on the outside, Alex can show the side that suits her mood that day. Under the cape she is wearing a catsuit that highlights her thin and characteristic body. The shoes that she wore for this photo shoot are associated with sex and fetishism, since these are things that I also connect to her personality.

Connections between Fashion and Lesbianism

The connection between lesbianism and fashion is not immediately apparent to some viewers. Fashion has been an arena associated heavily with gay men, and the prevailing prejudice has instead been that dykes dress badly, that they have no style or feeling for fashion. The contributors in *Collection L* expressed varied relationships with fashion:

> I have always tried to keep myself as far away from fashion as possible. Thinking I can't wear those clothes anyway and by the way the whole industry is sick! Why should someone sit somewhere and own a horrible amount of money by just making up what should be hip for this month? And why are the garments made by almost unpaid children, and why are the clothes so small that I and many like me think that there is no possibility

Figure 10.1 *Alex.* Photograph: Hans Gedda.

to buy them? But even more people think that they have to buy the clothes anyway and modify their bodies after.

Another woman claimed, on the other hand: "I truly love fashion. I don't know why, there are of course things that could be seen as more important, but fashion is such fun!"

Many of the contributors in *Collection L* saw a difference between fashion and personal style, in that personal style is seen as something more positive. The negative aspect of fashion, according to them, is connected to an idea that fashion is something dictated from above, something that you cannot control yourself. The connection between fashion and consumption is another aspect that several of the contributors saw as negative. They saw it as an industry that produces both what we should wear and the ideal to which we should aspire. Another reason for the skepticism about fashion is connected to the contributors' feminist identity. They believed that combining fashion with feminism is problematic, that the fashion world is a world connected to antifeminism. Within contemporary feminism there is a movement that totally accepts fashion as a part of the women's rights agenda. It has become a feminist issue to be able to dress as you like. This kind of acceptance was seen during the Swedish election campaign in 2006 in which a new feminist party ran candidates for parliament. As a final effort to gain votes a few days before election day, the party invited Jane Fonda to proclaim her support for feminism. Just before the press conference and in front of all the cameras, Jane Fonda complimented the feminist leader, saying, "What beautiful legs you have"; the party leader smiled, saying, "Thank you."

Fashion and identity are frequently raised within *Collection L.* Karin, one of the contributors, said that she recently changed her style and that the way she dresses affects how people treat her:

> I am very happy with my new style. Before I was much more butch, but now I have started to elaborate with a more feminine style. I feel that I have a more ladylike body and I have girlish clothes. Like my new cute jacket with big tufts and my slightly longer hair and my new higher heels. I have recognized that women seem more interested than before but especially men. Well, a little at least. I can feel men looking at me when I'm walking down the street. That has never happened before. Now it happens every time I wear lipstick. I think it's fun! It is very small things, like lipstick or hair buckles and slides, but people treat me differently. They are much more friendly now than when I had a more butch-like style. And teenage boys—the worst person category in the world—have, since I bought this jacket, not told me once that I look weird. Before it used to happen at least once a week. It feels good. Sad that it should be like that, but that's the way it is.

Karin's dress is inspired by men's tennis shirts but transformed in a more female way. The neckline is wider, the sleeves are puffier, and the cut is more close-fitting than on men's shirts. It is still made a bit oversized, which has resulted in less focus on the feminine body; Karin is still ambivalent about her female style. The dyeing of the dress is similar to that in her girlfriend Tilda's outfit. They both contributed to *Collection L* (Figure 10.2). Their colors were faded together to strengthen their relationship. Karin also wore a tuft, a detail from her favorite woman's jacket.

Lisa (Figure 10.3) noted:

> The way we dress creates identity, at least as an outward signal about our identity to people we meet. I remember that as a teenager I had some garments that were very important for me to be able to signal who I was in the right way. But at the same time I thought: What happens if I lose those garments? If I one day wake up somewhere and have to dress in some other borrowed clothes, what will happen to my identity then? Connecting one's identity to clothes is something very risky.

Figure 10.2 *Tilda and Karin.* Photograph: Hans Gedda.

When discussing the connection between identity and clothes, questions about the lesbian dress code or "look" came up. What does a lesbian look like? The contributors identified differences between city dykes and dykes from the countryside.

During Pride, crowds of dykes arrive from the country, there are a lot of cockscombs and short vests. Like crowds of stereotyped dykes, a type I hardly see anywhere else. I would never go dressed like that.

Or:

In general, between you and me, lesbians really need to consider their cultural makeover. Tintin haircut. Cords for the younger girls, for how long have they been popular, ten years? Badly fitting jeans. Old bleached sports shirts. I don't want to think it all has to do with bad finances.

Figure 10.3 *Lisa.* Photograph: Hans Gedda.

Many of the contributors considered clothes that transform gender roles as something positive, while feminine clothes were described more negatively, or seen as a way to integrate or become accepted. Several of the women discussed the wish to feel safe in their clothes in combination with looking good as the most important aspect of clothing (Figure 10.4).

Fashion historian Katrina Rolley has written about clothes as an expression of lesbian identity in *Outlooks: Lesbian and Gay Sexualities and Visual Cultures* (Lewis and Rolley 1996). What Rolley has suggested, and what I find interesting in this context, is that there is a potential lesbian attraction in every fashion image of women. Reina Lewis argued in the same text that "lesbian responses to selected fashion images may be both objectifying and narcissistic (identificatory) ... concerned with the double movement of a lesbian visual pleasure wherein the viewer wants both to be and to *have* the object" (Lewis and Rolley 1996: 181). For all contributors in *Collection L* the attraction of fashion images was not clear. A butch lesbian, for example, found it difficult

Figure 10.4 *Anne.* Photograph: Hans Gedda.

to relate to the women in fashion magazines. Instead she found the male models more attractive. To interpret a heterosexual context (with a male photographer photographing a woman) within a lesbian context was sometimes seen with skepticism:

> I don't like it that lesbianism always has to be something mysterious or unspoken. Like something unable to be mentioned. Something dangerous. Horrible. When lesbians and lesbian cultures are so veiled and marginalized it feels like I have to defend things that I don't necessarily like. I like to see lesbians becoming more visible, that there is security and not so much shame. That it has become played down, that you don't become happy over small possible hints or signals in a picture.

And as Karin said: "I can absolutely interpret fashion images as erotic. I can interpret all images, of all kind of people, as erotic."

The eroticism is also considered in the design of the clothes, and what the women became excited about. For example: "I get excited dressing like a man," or "I like wearing a dildo when I go out," or "I wear a special T-shirt with the Argentinian pop star Rodrigo on the front," or "For me the most important thing is that my body is fit. If I am fit I can wear anything."

The differentiation between men and women was also discussed, as was the sexual attraction to men. Karin explained:

> I often think that men are very sexy. Even more often than I think women are. But it's only in theory. All men are like posters for me. It has very little to do with who they are, and so on. They are just something to look at …

Karin's view of men as something only to look at becomes, in a way, an inversion of gender roles. For Karin, men become objectified, and only that. The relation between men and women is discussed in the collection, as is the exclusion of men from daily life. Lawen commented:

> There are lesbian codes. The most obvious one is not to dress or behave to suit the male gaze. There is something honest, straightforward, in the lesbian gaze.

The relation to men, or the lack of men, becomes clear when lesbians want to have children. Lisa was photographed with her daughter Siri. Several of the contributors discussed the problem for lesbians in having children, but for Lisa her role as a parent became central for the collection. Lisa wanted to live as an "ordinary family" and felt that the skepticism about homosexual families was problematic. A few weeks before her daughter was born she said:

> Together we have planned this child. We have been talking for hours and thousands of years about how we should do it. We have discussed over and over whether it should be me or my girlfriend who would get pregnant and I was the one that inseminated her. So, where in all this am I not part of it? In biology, oh yes. I am missing there. And because of that I have to fight all the time, create myself as a parent over and over again.

Lisa's outfit was inspired by the image of a stereotypical family: the type that goes on camping vacations dressed in the same jogging suits. But Lisa is also an old friend of mine, and I have known her since we were teenagers. We were then dressed in more punk-style clothes, with batik. I wanted to add that as well. Lisa also told me that she didn't like clothes that were too tight, and that she preferred outfits with a mix of volume and tightness. It was important, she said, that she be able to walk or move in them. She felt ridiculous when wearing clothes that restricted her way of acting. Therefore, I created a mixture of those elements: the family look in jersey material and the batik style with tight leggings and oversized jacket. Under the jacket Lisa is wearing what I call a *mother-tee,* a T-shirt that highlights or constructs the symbol of the mother: breasts. On the mother-tee they are draped in a silky material. The T-shirt is decorative as well as symbolic of something that Lisa wished to be.

While Lisa considered the family structure with children as something desirable, some of the contributors have instead made clear choices not to have children or get married because, as they put it, that would be copying a heterosexual structure. The French philosopher Pierre Bourdieu (2001) argued that the queer family becomes normal when it reproduces heterosexual gender roles. Bourdieu claimed that the queer reproduction of gender roles is built upon masculine dominance, but according to many queer theorists, gender and sexuality, such as, for example, the butch/femme, are examples of traditions in which the relation between gender and power is questioned. In the queer community, masculinity does not necessarily have to be the same as power. The butch woman can, for example, have the role of fulfilling the wishes of the femme. Erica, who changed from being a heterosexual man to being

Figure 10.5 *Erica.* Photograph: Hans Gedda.

a lesbian woman, also changed her traditional family structure. For an outsider the change might seem very radical, but for the people close to her the change might not have been as great as expected (Figure 10.5).

> As a dad I think I am basically the same as I have always been, even if it is with a more feminine approach.

Conclusion

The matter of normative gender in *Collection L* is questioned through the transformation of sex-typed garments. The process continued with the contributors during the photography session. They dressed to my interpretation, were styled by me, and then re-presented the image, enacting a form of performance. The performative, which is an essential part of the queer community, became the final result in *Collection L*. What distinguishes the performance in *Collection L* from other performative expressions, such as drag and some lesbian cross-dressing, is that in *Collection L* the contributors do not express their personal identity, but instead they perform my interpretation of them. In the same way that costumes can be seen as narrative tools in film or theater, the clothes in *Collection L* become a tool for displaying lesbian stories. Later on, when the clothes enter the customer's wardrobe, they might not only remind the wearer about aspects of lesbianism, but also help to create new stories, depending on the context and wearer. I hope that they keep on transforming.

Note

1. My earlier collections also explored the connection between clothes and identity. In MajaGunn2005 I created a series made from clothes that I had been wearing myself from childhood. In work for the theater and for film I have created homosexual characters, but this is the first time I have worked with homosexuality as a theme for a fashion collection.

Part 3
The Pleasures of the Text

11

Fashion Reform: Aesthetic Movement in Dress and Interiors

Marilyn Casto

Emerging from the late nineteenth-century welter of reform efforts that addressed everything from social ills to fashion and home décor, the Aesthetic Movement took as its central tenet the importance of the visual as a guiding component of the well-lived life. Supporters perceived a positive effect in that conscious awareness of design would add an extra dimension to life. Detractors declared aesthetes guilty of selfish posturing and an alienating tendency to set themselves above others (Dowling 1996: 75). To some observers the aesthetes created a separate world as a writer envisions a fictional world and lived in it divorced from the reality or understanding of average people. Focused on tangible objects, the Aesthetic Movement sought through celebrating good design to rise above the very materials that they used as tools to improve lives. Like other reform movements with which it overlapped, aestheticism sought to integrate all arts, elevating the design of everyday objects and tying the material to the verbal. All life experiences, whether sartorial or mental, could theoretically be improved by casting them as art.

Words had helped to form and characterize aesthetes. Researchers have frequently cited Walter Pater's work as inspiring the fascination with art that lay at the core of the movement (Dowling 1996: xi). John Ruskin, while not an aesthete, provided underpinning to the movement by his body of literature that stressed visual experience as necessary to an educated person aware of the world by which he or she was surrounded (Schaffer and Psomiades 1999: 2). As the Aesthetic Movement solidified into easily recognizable motifs such as lilies, sunflowers, peacocks, and blue and white china adorning spaces decorated in subdued colors and occupied by people wearing unfashionably flowing garments, poets and fiction writers picked up their pens in support or caricature. Both clothing and dress were mentally constructed as analogous to paintings that could be described in words (Haweis 1879: 15). Rosamund Marriott Watson, poet, editor, and writer on interior design and fashion, drew a straightforward analogy between the arts of assembling words and furnishings (Schaffer 2000: 88). A vast range of literature portrayed characters involved with or observing Aesthetic Movement spaces and costume that had developed into an archetype identifiable through particular symbols. That "types" existed was recognized by the movement's defenders, and fiction writers eagerly exploited them (Hamilton 1882: 24). Authors' approaches encompassed sarcasm, comedy, approval, and condemnation, reflecting contemporary public opinions. Cohesive use of motifs, colors, and forms that helped to position individuals as aesthetes and declaimed their group membership also separated them from the main population and made them an easy target for people who disagreed with aesthetic aims or found them amusing. To some it was a frivolous trend best treated as comical entertainment. Some saw the designs as charmingly divergent from mainstream culture. To others, the movement's methodology threatened the social order or demonstrated a demoralizing superficiality that needed to be rooted out. Whatever the individual author's aims, Aesthetic Movement literature linked fashion in interior design and clothing, portraying interrelationships sometimes positive, but often negative. Writers evoked dress and interior design as a means of commenting on characters' attitudes and beliefs. Both, as highly visible choices, put the owner's taste on display. As they walked about in public, aesthetes' clothing provided an obvious sign of their beliefs and values. Similarly, interiors laid out occupants' preferences and were read as either positive or negative commentaries on character. The Aesthetic Movement particularly entwined clothing and interiors, rendering all material culture as reflections of the owner's aspirations or lack of them and making the person inseparable from owned objects. Many notable authors published on both dress and interior decoration, including Charles Eastlake and Mary Eliza Haweis (Schaffer 2000: 102). The verbal and the visual were closely linked, as poets and writers such as Dante Gabriel Rossetti, Oscar Wilde, and Algernon Charles Swinburne frequently associated with designers, each group influencing the other. Georgiana Burne-Jones remarked, "Think what it is, to see a poem lived" (quoted in Stewart 2007: 94).

Many authors and artists cared greatly about the design of books and thus bound literature tightly to the visual image (Plate 27). Aestheticism proponents linked all material culture as expressions of personality, but also of a progressive attitude and a lifestyle that diverged from the mainstream. Decisions to wear aesthetic-inspired clothing or decorate in that style were highly conscious choices. Inanimate design was closely linked to the people who wore the costumes and inhabited the interiors. They set the individual apart from the mainstream and drew attention. For participants in the Aesthetic Movement, possessions defined people to an extraordinary degree, extending from the spaces they occupied to what they put on their bodies. Oscar Wilde's Lord Henry in *The Picture of Dorian Gray* decrees, "It is only shallow people who do not judge by appearances" (Wilde 2007 [1891]: 22). Aesthetes shaped their own story, scripted a performance, by offering an image to be read.

Literature of the period is quite diverse in the manner of Aesthetic Movement presentation. For some it was a superficial matter best suited to comedy, although even comedic portrayals could include sharply pointed remarks. For others, the familiar images of aestheticism were surface manifestations of a deeper and disturbing tendency to privilege things over people. As Henry James phrases it, "He judges and measures, approves and condemns, altogether by [taste]" (James 1908: 71). In a lighter vein, the style filtered into children's literature separate from aspects of the style that some regarded as degenerate. Kate Greenaway's portrayal of aesthetic costume is quite different from that of such authors as Henry James. In Greenaway children who just happen to be dressed in a fashion that diverged from the norm, favored a décor of lilies and peacock feathers, and lived in red-brick Queen Anne houses present an image of charm and innocence, at odds with authors who describe aesthetes as sinister. Children in Greenaway illustrations march sedately across the pages, oblivious to anyone or anything outside their world.

Reformers sought through the medium of distinct fashion in furnishings and dress to declaim membership in a group of reform-minded individuals while separating themselves from the larger body of fashion, their self-worth expressed not through belonging, but through intentionally failing to belong, while simultaneously denying that it was fashion at all (Plates 28 and 29). This attitude can be seen in the Gilbert and Sullivan operetta *Patience* when the soldiers sing, "A year ago they [their uniforms] were very well in our eyes, but since then our tastes have been etherealized, our perceptions exalted" (Gilbert 1881: 146). Badges of belonging operate in two ways—denoting membership and "others." In a paradoxical situation, reformers wanted to set themselves apart as better than the larger culture, while simultaneously reforming the larger world of design, which would have removed the exclusivity. Furnishings and dress became expressions of both rejection and of inclusion. Like teenagers, aesthetes separated from the larger culture by paradoxically forming another type of conformity. The individuality that might at first glance characterize people whose design choices diverged so markedly from the mainstream was actually submerged in a tide of conformity within their own group. A children's book pointed to this uniformity in a description of girls (clearly of the Kate Greenaway type) who were "of about the same height, and went to school in pink dresses, white aprons, and white sun-bonnets, and these were so large that they looked for all the world like *bonnets* out for a walk ... and they all looked so exactly alike" (Haile 1879: 15–16).

Fashion in clothing and interiors were presented as something handed to outsiders as an improving gift. In *Patience* it is said of Bunthorne that "he has come among us, and he has idealized us" (Gilbert 1881: 148). This desire to improve others by example, which Gilbert and Sullivan treat lightheartedly, was more sharply critiqued by William Dean Howells in *A Woman's Reason,* when a character says of a comfortable house that it is nice not to have to "admire the aesthetic sentiment, and where every wretched little aesthetic prig of a table or a chair isn't asserting a principle or teaching a lesson" (Howells 1882: 28). There was power in the ability to command attention, even if the viewer did not choose to adopt the proffered designs, and setting up design as a moral message implies criticism of those who do not embrace it.

For some authors the superiority aesthetes felt and displayed through possessions was foolish determination to be merely different, the actions of superficial people who thought very well of themselves but who dressed and lived in willfully bizarre ways, living in "grim, smut-engrained houses in Bloomsbury … with just the same sort of weird furniture, partly Japanese, partly Queen Anne, partly medieval; with blue-and-white china and embroidered chasubles stuck upon the walls if they were rich, and twopenny screens and ninepenny pots if they were poor, but with no further difference" (Lee 1884: 298). Women "with hair cut like medieval pages, or tousled like moenads, or tucked away under caps like eighteenth-century housekeepers, habited in limp and stayless garments, picturesque and economical, with Japanese chintzes for brocade, and flannel instead of stamped velvets—all of whom, when not poets or painters themselves, were the belongings of some such" were equally identifiable as a subset of the population (300). In their uniformity, they were less original than they thought themselves to be.

The hallmarks of Aesthetic Movement interiors defined a group clearly identifiable by its possessions. Lee described an aesthetic painter's studio "with its curious carved furniture, its Japanese screens, its bits of brocade and tapestry (rubbish which Hamlin would have blushed at in London), its shelves of books and chipped majolica and glass" (Lee 1884: 131). Making a link to aesthetic illustration and literature, the author described another space full of embroidery and oriental objects as "like the rooms in Walter Crane's fairy books, with their inlaid chests and brocade couches, and majolica vases full of peacock's feathers" (267). From sartorial decisions to interior decoration, aesthetes used artifacts for self-definition.

Obsession with material culture seemed to some viewers a superficial matter that screened lack of application to deeper matters of the mind. In a Henry James novel, when a character remarks of another that he "must be very clever," another responds, "He has a genius for upholstery" (James 1908: 131). Aesthetic Movement sensitivity to possessions was seen by some as a false sensitivity, a life of consumption, albeit consumption of particular, not random, items, designed to be carefully composed into an overall image, "only for the selfish enjoyment of beauty" (Lee 1884: 133, Book 4). One character listens to "strictures on modern costumes, on stays, and heels, and tight waists and full skirts; and she immediately set to work untrimming her frocks and making them up into wondrous garments, not at all like what any aesthetic woman had ever worn in her life, but queer, fantastic, delightful … individual and quaint and fascinating" (250, Book 4). This point of view, celebrating the unique, was cited by Wilde, who wrote of "fashion, by which what is really fantastic becomes for a moment universal" (Wilde 2007 [1891]: 107). For others, aestheticism was the mark of the intellectual, in *Dorian Gray* the desire "to combine something of the real culture of the scholar with all the grace and distinction and perfect manner of a citizen of the world" (107). For Walter Hamilton, "Chippendale furniture, dadoes, old-fashioned brass and wrought iron work, mediaeval lamps, stained glass in small squares, and old china are all held to be the outward and visible signs of an inward and spiritual grace and intensity" (Hamilton 1882: 34).

The very concept of fashion had been brought into question by design reformers, who presented it as ephemeral, silly, superficial, and potentially a danger to morals because it encouraged obsession with the trivial. When the uncle of Louisa May Alcott's heroine, Rose, in *Eight Cousins* seeks to inspire her to embrace a healthier lifestyle, he simplifies her clothing and her room, redoing both in a style that at first both appalls and amuses her and later convinces her that rejection of the status quo is not to be feared. Rose moves away from fashion plates toward what has been presented to her as a more individualistic lifestyle expressed in both her space and her dress. Her new sensible approach to life is contrasted with a silly fashionable girl who stumbles about in heels and tries to draw Rose into her thoughtless world. Notably, the book's target audience was youthful and theoretically impressionable.

As demonstrated through Rose's reconstituted dress and room, fashion and interiors were seen as an integrated package, like a story in which the lines of a plot weave together. Like the pre-Raphaelite painters with whom some aesthetes associated, interiors and clothing were laden with symbolism to be read by initiates. Charlotte Yonge speaks of a young man "absolutely beautiful, through perfection of polish, finish, applicability ... deserving to be cherished in a velvet case. The case might be the pretty drawing-room, full of the choice artistic curiosities of a man of cultivation" (Yonge 1879: 3).

Women, fashion, clothes, and interiors had long been linked. Connections of gender and consumption made women seem natural parts of a movement so focused on material culture. As feminist scholars have pointed out, the entrenched association of women and design made them natural components of the Aesthetic Movement, but the professionalization of the arts diminished anything seen as amateur. A complicating factor has been the association of aestheticism with effeminacy and the many implications of that connection (Schaffer and Psomiades 1999: 1, 6). Developing late nineteenth-century criticism of women as consumers often guilty of faulty judgment raised questions about their parts in aesthetic promotion of objects. Women's roles were changing, as they began to move to the forefront of decorative arts professions, participating as pottery designers and as interior decorators, and those shifting roles provoked mixed responses. Literature related to the aesthetic movement often places women as central characters around whom men's actions revolve, either drawing them toward aestheticism or being pulled by them into its orbit. In the latter instances women's influence sometimes reads as negative. *The Colonel* features a mother and daughter who made the daughter's husband miserable through surrounding him with unsympathetic people, inadequate food, and strange décor (Burnand 1881). In *Patience* an officer remarks to a soldier attempting to convert to aesthetic dress, "My good friend, the question is not whether we like it, but whether they [women] do. They understand these things; we don't. Now I shouldn't be surprised if this is aesthetic enough—at a distance" (Gilbert 1881: 161). A core character of Vernon Lee's anti-Aesthetic Movement novel, *Miss Brown,* who is an unsympathetic individual viewed as corrupting, is described with "her almost amorous admiration, the limp gown" (Lee 1884: 10). It is that character who remarks, in a point of view meant to read as bizarrely superficial, that "I always make it a rule to engage only handsome servants, because it spiritualizes the minds of our children to be brought up constantly surrounded by beautiful human forms" (41). Such treatment of people as inanimate objects to be observed like attractive vases is reflected in literature that positions aesthetes as insensitive users. In *Miss Brown* a woman pulled into aestheticism by a man is told by another person that he "drags you down, freezes all your best aspirations" (65, Book 7).

In fiction critical of the movement, people, and women in particular, were objectified, "all of whom, when not poets or painters themselves, were the belongings of some such" (Lee 1884: 300). Henry James composed numerous such analogies. In *The Portrait of a Lady* a woman is viewed by an aesthetic man as a suitable acquisition for his collection, and she later sees herself as "like some curious piece in an antiquary's collection" (James 1908: 42). The latter statement suggests the degree to which authors writing of aesthetic men attempting to form aesthetic women portrayed the results as divergent from the mainstream and to the detriment of the women. Pansy in *The Portrait of a Lady* is viewed by an admirer as "absolutely unique," the sort of comment a collector might make about a suitable acquisition (107). James has a male character compare a woman to a china Dresden shepherdess and remark that he is always kind to people who have "good Louis Quatorze," thus making the individual less important than his or her possessions, a point of view made explicit when an individual says he was told his possessions were the best thing about him (90, 92). The character's "admiration of [a child] ... was based partly on his eye for decorative character" (105). A woman abandons the décor of her home to her husband, giving over a dimension of expressed personality to another, who, despite questionable taste, has convinced her of his superiority (110). Popular novelist Ouida cited a man's attitude toward a woman as similar to a collector's relationship to china (Ouida 1883).

Health reform emerged in the latter years of the nineteenth century in both dress and interiors. Clothing promoted freer movement and more exercise, as women involved themselves in outdoor activities such as collecting natural materials and gardening. The movements to a healthier lifestyle expressed through house ventilation, removal of dust-catching accessories, and looser clothing existed contemporaneously with aesthetic fashion. While Aesthetic Movement clothing, being looser and uncorseted, looks on the surface like a healthier alternative and Aesthetic interiors often featured less clutter than earlier nineteenth-century spaces, individuals associated with aestheticism were often portrayed as unhealthy people living in unhealthily constrained spaces. An old lady remarks in *Miss Brown*, "I'm thankful at least that Walter has not brought home a bag of bones like the other beauties of his set. *Loveliness in decay*, that's what I call their style; but you look a good flesh-and-blood girl" (Lee 1884: 269). She indicates that while she likes the fashionable dress her visitor wears, Walter would not like it, that he prefers the mediaeval look: "no stays, and no petticoats, and slashings, and tags and boot-laces in the sleeves, and a yard of draggled train" (270). For authors such as Vernon Lee, who questioned the aesthetic movement, there was a strong association with decay and decadence that reflected "artifice, intense experience, the mixing of beauty and strangeness" (Schaffer and Psomiades 1999: 3). Drawings in a room might be described as portraying "strange, beautiful, emaciated, cruel-looking creatures, ... with wicked lips and combed-out locks" (Lee 1884: 268), a description in which it is not difficult to recognize such drawings as those by Aubrey Beardsley or more languid portrayals by du Maurier. By contrast, James states that a girl ought to be "fresh and fair; she should be innocent and gentle," attributes certainly not associated with his Aesthetic Movement characters (James 1908: 347). Similarly, *The Colonel,* in comic mode, contrasts mainstream décor and dress with the aesthetic, suggesting that the aesthetic is less physically and emotionally satisfying and, in the eyes of a normal person, peculiar. When a man flees his aesthetic home in *The Colonel,* a friend says he is now "where there is lightness, movement ... music, and life, instead of die-away languor ... sickly lilies, and the beauty of decay" (Burnand 1881: 44). Clearly, the implication was that departure from the aesthetic house represented a life-saving flight to a better existence. Certainly, this is an ironic point of view since aesthetes perceived their actions as an improving immersion in life through making design integral to daily activities.

Both aesthetic dress and aesthetic interior design were famously mocked, especially by cartoonists and playwrights. George du Maurier's *Punch* illustrations particularly targeted aesthetic fashion. The play *The Colonel* by Francis Burnand, an editor of *Punch,* focused on the extremes of Aestheticism. Gilbert and Sullivan took solid aim at aestheticism in *Patience.* As a defender and explicator of aestheticism, Walter Hamilton sharply criticized du Maurier's caricatures as unfair and mean-spirited and *The Colonel* as an inferior, superficial, and unoriginal play, claiming, "Some of us, *Mr. Punch* amongst the number, would be better and wiser not to ridicule intellectual aims we do not understand" (Hamilton 1882: 82, 91, 109, 137, 143). Hamilton took a kinder view of *Patience* as genuinely entertaining, allowing that even as *Patience* satirized the aesthetic, it identified the movement's key points. Bunthorne speaks of the "wail of a poet's heart on discovery that everything is commonplace," a point he echoed later to another aesthetic character whom he advises, "Your conversation must henceforth by perfectly matter-of-fact. You must cut your hair. In appearance and costume you must be absolutely commonplace" (Gilbert 1881: 149, 163). Commonplace was a condemnation of the unimaginative by aesthetic movement adherents, but normalcy for those who opposed it. Hence the character in *Miss Brown* who, finding "a spontaneity, an aristocratic fibre, sort of free-borness, which he missed among the clique-and-shop shoddy aestheticism," decided he would "have his coats made by less romantic tailors, and cut his hair and beard in less pictorial style" (Lee 1884: 7).

Press comments on *Patience* suggest the degree to which the outward design presentation of aestheticism was viewed as self-conscious posturing. The London *Daily News* commented that the characters were "dressed and made up in the aesthetic style, looking like figures cut out of a Pre-Raphaelite picture and vivified. The constrained attitudes, distorted positions, and grotesque gestures of the three, and the quaint music which they sing, produced a richly humorous effect" (quoted in Allen 1975: 141). A character in *Miss Brown* is appalled to discover that her clinging dress, which she finds very strange, has been made by a theater dressmaker and questions why the donor cares that she wear it and whether it makes her "a sort of live picture" (Lee 1884: 307, 309). Later she compares herself to "a piece of artistic embroidery, or a Japanese cup, or a green tree" (230, Book 4). Similarly, Lee, leaving the impression of a group posed for a portrait, wrote of "a quaint little assembly of ladies in peacock-blue and dull sage and Japanese dragooned … gowns …—of men got up to look like Frenchmen or Germans, or Renaissance creatures" (73, Book 4). Henry James quite bluntly wrote of a man eternally posing, with regard to both his person and his surroundings, who "always had an eye to effect, and his effects were deeply calculated … the motive was as vulgar as the art was great." He viewed what he did as a picture to be admired by others. The same individual is described as striving "to tantalize society with a sense of exclusion, to make people believe his house was different from every other, to impart to the face that he presented to the world a cold originality … not to please the world, but to please himself by exciting the world's curiosity" (James 1908: 144).

The aesthetics set themselves apart by a type of design they saw as more literate, grounded in the past rather than the present, and more tastefully subtle than most Victorian design, a denial of the present and a disassociation with contemporary design. One might legitimately question how refusal to connect with the present could result in reform and exactly how that tendency projected the goals of the movement. "Rickety eighteenth-century chairs and tables marshaled around the walls" (Lee 1884: 11) is a setting meant to read as distinct from normal. Hence a character in *Patience* could say, "You are not even Early English. Oh, to be Early English ere it is too late!" (Gilbert 1881: 149), and Bunthorne says, "Of course you will pooh-pooh whatever's fresh and new, and declare it's crude and mean …" (150). One of the more famous passages from that play tells of "a cobwebby grey velvet, with a tender bloom like cold gravy, which, made Florentine fourteenth century, trimmed with Venetian leather and Spanish alter lace, and surmounted with something Japanese—it matters not what—would at least be Early English" (149). This suggests, of course, that proponents of the Aesthetic Movement were less than historically accurate in their borrowing from the past. The whole matter of sourcing the past for clothing and interiors was questioned. *Miss Brown,* having mistakenly assumed that the eighteenth-century-style furnishings around her are all truly old, is set straight, that they are imitations because present "life is trivial and aimless and hideous. We can only pick up the broken fragments of the past and blunderingly set them together" (Lee 1884: 273).

Margaret Oliphant, author, literary critic, and no admirer of the aesthetes, who seemed to her to be artificial and turned inward, presents a self-deluded character who believes her actually minor artistic talent to be something on which her life should center and, indeed, something that should be acknowledged by others. Rose, the daughter of a drawing master and the product of one of the schools of design, obsesses with the design of thistles, musing over exactly how they should be portrayed while ignoring the actions of other characters. Oliphant offers a sarcastic portrayal of Rose's self-absorption with a superficial matter of visual impressions. Disdain for those fixed on material goods echoes in Oliphant's pointed remark that "everybody knows that hanging pictures is just the thing of all others that requires a person of taste" (Oliphant 1866: 127). In the end, Rose must give up art to run her father's house and, abandoning her belief in the importance of artistic matters, along with her faith in schools of design, says that she is no longer so certain about the "moral influence of Art" (Vol. III: 176). Rose exemplified people so focused on the visual that they became deficient in the realities of existence and failed to deal well with genuine life, as opposed to illusion.

Literature of the aesthetic movement, as it linked home and personal dress fashion concepts, brought the very question of fashion into question. The logic in selection of furnishings and dress was presented as a sensible reflection of decisions to follow a path to reform in opposition to fashion. Ironically, even as the Aesthetic Movement adherents derided mainstream fashion, they were themselves mocked as eccentric adherents to a decidedly nonfashionable style. As a result, "fashion," even as it flourished, became a term of derision. That condemnation of fashion would be seen through the twentieth century as modernism took hold and designers sought to avoid "mere" fashion. Professions such as interior design that were perceived as providing ephemeral fashionable style that changed as quickly as clothing styles suffered from the connection with fashion. The Aesthetic Movement and its designs came to be regarded as an inconsequential frivolous diversion from the march toward modernism. Only in the late twentieth century did researchers turn serious attention toward aesthetic writers and designers, recognizing their centrality to shifting late nineteenth-century attitudes and their formative influence on later developments in the arts and literature.

Much nineteenth-century nonfiction prose was written on the Aesthetic Movement, a portion of it praising and some of condemning its precepts. But fiction may, in some ways, have been more important than the nonfiction accounts of dress and interiors. Fiction can present art in integral association with characters, personalizing abstract concepts and allowing a reader to envision an artistic movement as real people might react to it. All aspects of attitudes toward the Aesthetic Movement played out in the literature of the time. For some writers, privileging the visual detracted from the necessities of living and from genuine feeling. In one way or another, authors who favored the Aesthetic Movement and its goals shared Oscar Wilde's belief that "life itself was the first, the greatest, of the arts, and for it all the other arts seemed to be but a preparation" (Wilde 2007 [1891]: 107).

12

Holly Golightly and the Fashioning
of the Waif

Gabrielle Finnane

Two Tramps in Lost Time

In Christopher Isherwood's 1939 novel *Goodbye to Berlin,* Sally Bowles is a creature of color whose clothing, which can be grubby, always has something eye-catching: "She was dressed in black silk, with a small cape over her shoulders and a little cap like a page boy's stuck jauntily on one side of her head." As the narrator, also called Christopher Isherwood, watches her dial a phone number he notices "her fingernails were painted emerald green, a colour unfortunately chosen for it called attention to her hands, which were much stained by cigarette-smoking and as dirty as a little girl's" (2003: 34–35). In a later scene in the Wittenbergplatz, Sally revels in her appearance: "Everybody stared at Sally, in her canary yellow beret and shabby fur coat, like the skin of a mangy old dog. "I wonder," she was fond of remarking, "what they'd say if they knew that we two old tramps were going to be the most marvellous novelist and the greatest actress in the world" (60).

Sally's mention of the "two old tramps" alludes to *Modern Times,*[1] a Charlie Chaplin film released two years earlier that examined modern life from the perspective of a vagabond odd couple. In his last screen appearance as the Tramp, Chaplin for the first time had a companion, a barefoot, rebellious, and insouciant street waif called, according to the credits, the Gamine. The Gamine character was scripted for the actress who played her on-screen, Paulette Goddard. Sally's remark now reads as anticipating a cycle of novels, stage plays, films, and even real-life careers that did indeed link tramping with aspiring actresses and writers. It is with Isherwood's Sally Bowles that the outsider status of the street waif merged with the existential restlessness of the upper-class waif. In her blend of glamour with childish grubbiness and a notable lack of possessions, Sally Bowles foreshadows her American descendant, the character Holly Golightly from Truman Capote's novel *Breakfast at Tiffany's,* although Sally was flamboyant and Holly was given to Chanel-like elegance.

Goodbye to Berlin is generally agreed to have been the model for *Breakfast at Tiffany's,* published twenty years later.[2] In both novels a series of vignettes is narrated several years after the event by a writer who lived, along with other transients, in the same building as the principal woman character. In both, the woman is a muse to the aspiring writer, and both heroines leave the city, Berlin and New York, respectively, after a brush with the law. The heroines of the two novels, Sally Bowles and Holly Golightly, came to be viewed as archetypes of the waif through stage and film adaptations, respectively, in the late 1950s and early 1960s. There were in fact a plethora of waifs on the screen, beginning in the early 1950s and always associated as much with particular stars as with the characters they played. Among the better known ones were Giulietta Masina in Fellini's *La Strada* (1954) and *Nights of Cabiria* (1957), Shirley MacLaine in *Some Came Running* (1959) and *The Apartment* (1960), Julie Harris in *I Am a Camera* (1955), and Leslie Caron in *Daddy Long Legs* (1955).[3] In the 1960s these waif girls evolved into the "kooky girl," typified early on by the filmic Holly Golightly and culminating, through a cycle of films, late in the decade with the character Pookie Adams (Liza Minnelli) in *The Sterile Cuckoo* (1969) and Shirley MacLaine in *Sweet Charity* (1969).[4]

Unlike Holly Golightly, however, Isherwood's Sally Bowles never acquired a fixed association with a particular star. Several actresses of varying physical dimensions and personalities have portrayed Sally Bowles on stage and screen in the last five decades.[5] Even the popular rendition of Sally by Liza Minnelli in *Cabaret*[6] served only to inspire a fresh round of stage musical adaptations. Holly Golightly, however, is singularly identified with an incarnation of Capote's heroine by Audrey Hepburn in the 1961 film adaptation of *Breakfast at Tiffany's.* Although both Sally Bowles and Holly Golightly were definitive waifs in both psychological and existential terms, only Holly Golightly evolved into a film/fashion icon.

Holly is an orphan, a child bride, and has escaped a poor white backwoods past, in sharp contrast to Sally's wealthy one. As her name suggests, Holly is elusive, whereas Sally Bowles, as her name suggests, is unstoppable. After gazing at an exotic birdcage in a shop window and noting the price ($350), the narrator in *Breakfast at Tiffany's* sees "a happy group of whisky-eyed Australian army officers baritoning 'Waltzing Matilda.' As they sang they took turns spin-dancing a girl over the cobbles under the El; and the girl, Miss Golightly, to be sure, floated round in their arms light as a scarf" (Capote 1961: 20). Holly is like a scarf—an object that is tied and yet flying free. Her clothing suggests an effacement of physical presence and a translucency allying her to the ephemeral and eternal simultaneously. Similarly the lightness written into her name makes Capote's character more evanescent and insubstantial than Sally Bowles.[7] Later plot developments involving the birdcage ally her with imagery of a trapped, fluttering bird, while the repeated references to wild things underscore her desire to be free. Not coincidentally the song "Waltzing Matilda" is about another wandering spirit—a vagabond, rogue, and fugitive from the law. Its mention here provides a myth for a flighty modern girl. The film adaptation is remembered, however, for another song, Audrey Hepburn's rendition of Henry

Mancini's "Moon River," with its explicit reference to "my huckleberry friend," al-luding to Huckleberry Finn, the quintessential fictional American vagabond.

Just as song and scarf provide both ballad and visual trope suggestive of the vaga-bond or hobo desire for journeying forth, so the waif story dovetails into the gamine look of the single urban girl of the late 1950s. The waif had a long history before Capote and even Isherwood as a social type and fictional character type.[8] Capote's *Breakfast at Tiffany's,* and the 1961 film adaptation that cast Hepburn in the role, cre-ated an identification of the waif with a certain look—a 1950s gamine variation on the waif, a variation with which Hepburn was dominantly associated (Plate 30). The film adaptation of *Breakfast at Tiffany's* transposed the Second World War setting of the novel to an urbane lounge culture of the late 1950s, a modernist comic abstrac-tion, obscuring what Elizabeth Wilson calls "a genuine Greenwich Village bohemia, and … the squalor and humiliation of Holly's life" (1993: 36). Yet, like the casting of Hepburn herself, this transposition introduced an intertextual set of style references, which also conflated elements of the waif narrative with certain looks. The conflation between "action and appearance" in the portrayal of Holly Golightly (D'Arcy 1996: 376) is an operation intrinsic to fictional characterizations, which build on the image-repertoire of a society. Analyzing the promotion of the "new look" modern girl of 1920s France, Mary Louise Roberts describes how the "visual" became entwined with the "behavioral":

> First, they associated the new styles with the aesthetic of modern consumer culture, de-fined in terms of mobility and speed. Second, they conflated physical and psychological qualities in their logic of human behaviours: how one dressed encouraged behaviours analogous to the visual image produced. This confusion of the visual and the behavioural was key to the politics of fashion in the postwar era (1994: 77).

A rhetorical confusion of the visual and the behavioral is evident in the way the term "waif" is used in the press and in fiction to suggest both a character type—a young woman who is "forlorn," "lost," "friendless," "childlike," "plucky"—and a phys-ical type—a woman who is "slight," "thin," and "fragile" and has cropped, wispy-fringed, uncared-for hair and raggedy clothes.[9] The core elements of this fusion, which converge in Holly Golightly, are exemplified in the complex descriptions of Holly's looks and clothing in Capote's novel. We can see all these elements adum-brated in the narrator's first direct view of Holly.

> She was still on the stairs, now she reached the landing, and the ragbag colors of her boy's hair, tawny streaks, strands of albino-blond and yellow, caught the hall light. It was a warm evening, nearly summer, and she wore a slim cool black dress, black sandals, a pearl choker. For all her chic thinness, she had an almost breakfast-cereal air of health, soap and lemon cleanness, a rough pink darkening of the cheeks. Her mouth was large,

her nose upturned. A pair of dark glasses blotted out her eyes. It was a face beyond child-hood, yet this side of belonging to a woman. (Capote 1961: 17)

Five aspects of the waif look resonate in this description: the pink-cheeked ingé-nue with her "breakfast-cereal air of health," the gamine with "ragbag colors," the child-woman, the Beat Girl in dark glasses, and the androgyny of a thin young thing with "boy's hair." When it comes to dress, however, a different woman emerges: the "slim cool black dress, black sandals, a pearl choker" suggest a mature self-containment, or an attempt at it, lifting the waif or gamine from her tramp ancestry and turning her into an image of free-floating unparented, unmarried glamour.[10] Ihab Hassan has remarked that Holly Golightly "approaches the ideal of the new pica-resque, the free-wheeling hero who insists on the freedom to experience" (1999: 110). Rather than being on her way to maternal womanhood, she is an emblem of permanent liminality.

The Ingénue, the Gamine, the Child-Woman, the Beat-Girl, the Androgyne

The Ingénue

The waif is an ingénue, and the ingénue is an innocent. The innocence of typical waifs is often due to their being country girls who have come to the big city. Holly Golightly, for example, is from Kansas, like Dorothy in the *Wizard of Oz*. When Holly-wood adapted *Breakfast at Tiffany's* to the screen in 1961, Capote objected to the casting of Audrey Hepburn in the film. He wanted Marilyn Monroe.[11] Monroe's per-sona, like Golightly's, was a mix of the shrewd and the naïve. On the screen Monroe was one of the actresses whose style and look created a bridge between the youthful innocence of the 1950s and the modern girl of the 1960s. The film historian James Harvey describes the 1950s version thus: "The fifties woman star was nicer, simpler, younger (at least in spirit), more girlish than womanly, whether the style was baby doll (Marilyn Monroe), or butch (Doris Day), sophisticate (Grace Kelly) or gamine (Audrey Hepburn)" (2001: 45).[12]

The film *Breakfast at Tiffany's* is a paradigm of what Robert Stam calls "transtext-uality": "the pressures of artistic biographies, cultural historical events and artistic and extra-artistic or paratextual elements, in a film/novel pairing" (2004: 15).[13] Al-ready a complex intertextual figure in the novel, the cinematic Holly Golightly pro-moted a popular investment of 1950s ingénue and gamine styles in portrayals of the single urban girl who has not settled down. Initially, the ingénue was emphasized in Audrey Hepburn's waifish persona. In the Broadway production of *Gigi,* the 1950s musical based on the 1944 novel by Colette, Hepburn played Gigi, cast as an in-génue. The French writer had glimpsed Hepburn being filmed in a minor role on the

Riviera. Colette, working at the time with Anita Loos on the Broadway adaptation of *Gigi,* immediately proposed Hepburn for the Broadway play. It was to jump-start Hepburn's Hollywood career. She was summoned to meet Loos. Anita Loos was with her traveling companion at the time, Paulette Goddard, who had played the character called the Gamine in Chaplin's film *Modern Times:* "When Audrey came to see Loos ... [b]oth women were entranced by this delicate, gazelle-like creature, simply and stunningly dressed in a black skirt and flat shoes, with a man's shirt tied around the waist" (Karney 1993: 41).

Many elements of the cinematic Holly Golightly tie her to the Cinderella persona with which Hepburn had become associated because of her first two Hollywood movies, *Roman Holiday* and *Sabrina.* In the first, the princess dresses down to experience life as a commoner and falls in love, a reversal of the Cinderella tale, and in the second, the servant's daughter returns from Paris transformed into an elegantly dressed woman: in both films, changes of character are indicated by changes in clothing. The Givenchy design Golightly wears in the early morning trip to the Tiffany's window that opens the film *Breakfast at Tiffany's* evokes the earlier films. The diamonds, pearls, long black evening dress, and gloves are suitable for a midnight ball.[14] The story of Cinderella is like something a waif might dream: it is being able to afford Tiffany's.

The Gamine[15]

Hepburn's film roles in the 1950s/early 1960s can be seen as variations on the theme of the picaresque heroine—from the Cinderella roles to the "gypsy" style of the Indian girl in *Unforgiven* (John Huston, 1960) and the sprite of *Green Mansions* (Mel Ferrer, 1959). All these variations played on the gamine look. The gamine look in the 1950s was primarily associated with a style of haircut. Even today *The Thames and Hudson Dictionary of Fashion and Fashion Designers* defines the gamine look in fashion as exemplified by Hepburn's and French dancer Zizi Jeanmaire's "short haircuts that framed their elfin faces" (Callan 1998: 108).[16] Early in the 1950s Beaton claimed it as the hallmark of the Hepburn image. "Nobody ever looked like her before World War II ... now thousands of imitations have appeared. The woods are full of young ladies with rat-nibbled hair and moon-pale faces" (Drake 1987: 10). Beaton correctly identified it as postwar, but Hepburn's gamine look was shared with certain European stars. In the late 1950s Madge Garland's compendium *The Changing Face of Beauty* identified the "short nibbled fringe" with the gamine, offering as an example a picture of Elsa Martinelli sporting a single dark lock of hair over one shoulder and a choppy fringe: "with her expressive dark eyes, [Martinelli] is typical of the unkempt *gamines* who have been a recent Italian export" (1957: 208).

The fringe and the straggling locks seem to have been the defining features of waif hair. Until the fifties, waif hair was long and straggling. De Beauvoir, unpacking the image of Bardot in 1959, described her look in terms reminiscent of Garland's description of Martinelli. "The long voluptuous tresses of Melisande flow down to her shoulders, but her hair-do is that of a negligent waif" (de Beauvoir 1972: 11). The long-haired look of the waif girl had its genesis in the silent cinema's orphan girls, such as those played by the Gish sisters, with their extravagant Victorian tresses. The postwar waif was a transnational abstraction, often iconically marked by gypsy traits, in some films literally a gypsy girl. A related aspect of the waif look was inflected with associations with clowns and traveling players, notably influenced by Fellini's early films with Giulietta Masina, whose clownlike looks and gestures earned her the epithet "a female Chaplin." Giulietta Masina's international popularity in her role as a vagabond child bride in *La Strada* (1954) culminated in the film's U.S. release and an Oscar award in 1957. Like the nineteenth-century illustrations of Gavroche, the *Les Misérables* gamin character invented by Victor Hugo, Masina's hair in *La Strada* was a tousled, outgrown, multicolored thatch.

Throughout the 1950s film and fashion literature, then, "waif" hair and even "gamine" looks might refer to either the long straggling hair of the waif and gypsy girl or undercut, unevenly cut, or wispily cut hair. The visible scruffiness of these hairdos seems to be an integral part of their appeal. As well as signifying social waywardness or poverty, the exaggerated dishevelment adds to the childlike aspect of the characters, the equivalent of rumpled hair in cartoon drawings of boys. We feel some tenderness for them on this count alone. There is too an implied flightiness in that disordered hair, a signal of a desire to escape.

Hepburn's persona was a Euro-American variation, sleek and modern, of such gamines and shared with actresses such as Leslie Caron in *Daddy Long Legs* (1957) and Jean Seberg in Preminger's *Bonjour Tristesse* and Godard's *Breathless* (1959).[17] The modernity was achieved through a metonymy of gamine disorder: the "short, nibbled fringe," as Garland described it, influenced by the flapper's bobbed hair. Rachel Moseley traces Hepburn's own gamine look—"a small, neat, head shape"—to a Paris style fashion for the small head in 1949 (2002: 57). The "small head" fashion endured. As late as 1987 *Vogue International* defined gamine glamour as "a small head, strong swept brows, brightly lipsticked mouth, small waist and coltish limbs," displaying pictures of Audrey Hepburn, Jean Seberg, and Shirley MacLaine as examples. On first meeting Audrey Hepburn in 1953 Cecil Beaton had called this look a "coconut coiffure" (1979: 262). This reminds us that Sally Bowles also had a "little dark head," due in part to her bobbed hair (Isherwood 2003: 40).[18]

The fusion of an updated flapper's bob with the hairstyle of a street waif not only was a matter of fashion but drew its inspiration in an increasingly common identification, in narrative fiction and film, of modern girl with an antibourgeois vagabond ethos such as that exemplified by Holly Golightly. Written in the same period as *Breakfast at Tiffany's,* Garland's book *The Changing Face of Beauty* articulates the way the visual consciousness of the late 1950s equated a gamine appearance with rebellious behavior. In one photo spread titled "Airs without Artifice," showing a page of young women with tumbled hair and variously styled fringes, she writes: "The new young beauties of the late fifties are not in bondage to the past but live uncluttered by contrivance, unfettered by tradition." She concludes her historical survey with the caption: "Where do we go from here? Will the gamine continue on her free and easy way? Or will a change of fashion make ladies of us all?" (1957: 216–18).

The gamine is always a figure of rebellion, a female trickster. Just as Garland referred to Martinelli's "carefree and spirited acting," *Vogue* in the fifties referred to the "impish Shirley MacLaine," while Leslie Caron's look was "rather like that of a pixie with a Sorbonne degree" (Drake 1987: 96–97) or an "impish schoolgirl" (Garland 1957: 202). The impishness and carefreeness signal a desire to live at an angle to convention. Holly Golightly's hair in the novel is boyish and has ragbag colors, gamine hair. Audrey Hepburn's hair, however, in *Breakfast at Tiffany's* was long, unlike her hair in her earlier films. Arguably, the beehive bun she wears with the evening ball gown and the tall Givenchy fur helmet she wears in the Tiffany's store have the exaggerated style of outfits donned for a masquerade, suggesting the high jinks of a child mimicking the adult world.

The Child-Woman

The waif girl is something of a child-woman. The child-woman, in our iconography, is changeless, indifferent, and forgetful. In this the child-woman is reminiscent of the indifferent narcissism of the "eternal feminine." "The adult woman now inhabits the same world as the man, but the child-woman moves in a universe which he cannot enter" wrote de Beauvoir in 1959 (1972:10).[19]

De Beauvoir saw the child-woman phenomenon as a postwar attempt to revive erotic mystery in films in an era when "social differences between the two sexes diminished" (1972: 8). She argued similar trends in theater and novels, mentioning Arthur Miller's *View from the Bridge* and Nabokov's *Lolita*. For Capote, on the other hand, writing *Breakfast at Tiffany's* in the same era, the child-woman was associated with Marilyn in his mind, as his 1979 retrospective portrait "A Beautiful Child" showed. In it he describes the all-black clothing Monroe wore to Constance Collier's funeral. Wearing an "obscuring head scarf ... With her tresses invisible, and her complexion cleared of all cosmetics, she looked twelve years old, a pubescent virgin who has just been admitted to an orphanage and is grieving over her plight" (Capote 1987: 280). Holly Golightly also looks "not quite twelve years" without makeup, "her eyes, for once minus their dark glasses, clear as rain water" (Capote 1961: 89).

The child-woman approaches the adult world as a dress-up game. Her childlikeness is reinforced by her infertility: whereas Sally Bowles won't have a child (and aborts one), Holly can't carry a child (and miscarries). Her childlikeness confers on her a spiritual eroticism, a quality that was part of Audrey Hepburn's own appeal.

The child-woman is changeless, or, as I said earlier, permanently liminal. After Doc Barnes has revealed her early rural life as Lulamae, an orphan girl with a brother, and as a child bride, Holly says, "I'm not fourteen anymore and I'm not Lulamae. But the terrible part is (and I realized it while we were standing there) I am. I'm still stealing turkey eggs and running through a briar patch. Only now I call it having the mean reds" (Capote 1961: 69). The other side of Holly's and the waif's permanent liminality is a desire to constantly re-create herself, and the threat of failure.

The Beat Girl

As early as 1954 Cecil Beaton observed:

> Stars such as Audrey Hepburn, a troubled sprite in blue dungarees, a citizen Puck; or Renee Jeanmarie, with her air of existential suffering, her peasant-cropped hair and pale-faced intensity … are living embodiments of those ideals of physique or personality that must eternally recreate themselves … Who is to say that a neurotic gamine in Hamlet black is not as authentic as a lady in a picture hat and yards of crinoline? (1954: 337)

What was "neurotic" about the gamine and how did she come to be associated with "Hamlet black"? A certain kind of gamine called the Beat Girl in the movies had a predilection for black, a cinematic fashion partly due to the influence of pop existentialism.[20] The "gamine" type in Hollywood movies about city life, whether playgirl or single working girl, was a special case of the urban waif. In American fiction, the waif was a descendant of Theodore Dreiser's *Sister Carrie,* the aspiring provincial girl newly arrived in the great city. In American social history she was described as a type of woman "adrift" in American cities of the late nineteenth century and compared to the roaming tramps of that era. The bachelor girl of the 1950s was a later enhanced version. Like the male hobo, she was in a flight from being bonded, committed, tied down to marriage and conventional life, although her flight took her less to the road and more often to an existence as a single working girl without permanent relationships. Holly Golightly thus speaks to a modern conflict between individuality and attachment, characteristic, as Barbara Ehrenreich showed in *The Hearts of Men* (1983), of early-1960s bachelorhood but equally characteristic of the young modern girl in fiction of the same period.

Cecil Beaton, in "The Changing Venus," also described Audrey Hepburn as one of several "existentialist gamines [who] whirled out of Europe like wild leaves in the wind," among them Juliette Greco and Leslie Caron, whom he saw as "undisguised reincarnations of the revolutionary sprites who unfurled the banners and strode through the France of 1789" (Moseley 2002: 189). Anne Hollander connects the black dresses of the French revolutionary period with an avant-garde vogue for the look of poverty (1993: 385). A cycle of films and stage plays about Joan of Arc, including even a revival of the severe Joan haircut, provided additional inspiration to

an emerging culture of rebellious femininity in the mid 1950s. Like their revolutionary and bohemian ancestors, the Beat girls who wore black rejected a certain kind
of life.

In a 1962 response to the film of *Breakfast at Tiffany's,* the critic Herbert Feinstein
compared Hepburn's character to one played by Brigitte Bardot in Clouzot's *The
Truth.* Feinstein noted the way the girls in the two films, whom he called Beat girls,
engaged in "gaminship: in a pinch they make love for a living." Pregnancy, he noted,
was no longer a problem for unwed screen mothers, and he mourned the procession
of stories appearing on the screen devoted to nonvirginal Beat girls. "Black angels,"
Feinstein called them. "After a time, nobody wants them. Nobody gets them: there is
no need: they get themselves" (1962: 65–66).

The films Feinstein was reacting to had appeared at the end of the 1950s and in
the early1960s, films about single girls in the cities who were struggling and adrift
in a quest to escape suburban marriage. Betsy Israel, in *Bachelor Girl,* remarks on
the large number of young women from about 1953 who, fleeing their "domestic
destiny," settled in New York City (2002: 186–87). Capote had remarked on a similar phenomenon as being the inspiration for *Breakfast at Tiffany's:* he observed the
influx of large numbers of unmarried young women to New York City during the
Second World War and he set his novella in 1943 because of it. By the mid-1950s
34 percent of young American women were reaching the age of twenty-four without
marrying. In the same period the motives of young single women, as Elizabeth Wilson points out, were the subject of speculation in the press: "In 1955, an article in
Twentieth Century wondered at the way young women dressed like their boyfriends,
in jeans and duffle coats, yet appeared uninterested in feminism or careers. Even
when they rebelled, young women seemed more likely to be rebelling for artistic
than for feminist reasons" (1993: 38).

In some quarters, the lack of feminism was viewed with alarm. In most quarters,
the association of rebellious young women in black clothing with art and artists was
viewed as troublingly undirected toward a clear goal. The ambiguous position of the
rebellious young woman is captured in a memoir of the period:

> I see the girl Joyce Glassman, twenty-two, with her hair hanging down below her
> shoulders, all in black like Masha in *The Seagull*—black stockings, black skirt, black
> sweater—but, unlike Masha, she's not in mourning for her life. How could she have
> been, with her seat at the table in the exact center of the universe, that midnight place
> where so much is converging, the only place in America that's alive? As a female, she's
> not quite part of this convergence. (Johnson 1983: 237)

The view of the Beat girl's life as morally ambiguous is suggested by Holly Golightly's dark glasses with their connotations of concealment, "the price of unortho-
doxy, the intensity of her involvement with life," writes Hassan in *Birth of a Heroine*
(1999: 82). Hassan sees the dark glasses as the badge of the hipster. But, like gamine

hair and Hamlet black, the dark glasses are emblems of paradox: the young woman is ascetic and a sexualized "tramp," a free spirit and a lost soul.[21] Holly's dark glasses and long cigarette holder, like a conductor's baton or wand, suggest her to be a master of ceremonies, a trickster figure. The waif as Beat girl is a 1950s version of the fin de siècle New Woman and created similar consternation. "Politically, the New Woman was an anarchic figure who threatened to turn the world upside down and to be on top in a wild carnival of social and sexual misrule" (Dowling 1979: 442).

The Androgyne

The moral alarm about Golightly's courtesan way of life masked a deeper discomfort with the homosexual subtext of the novel, the chief reason for the "scandal" of its canceled publication by *Harper's Bazaar* in 1958. In addition to Holly's joking references to "bull-dykes" and the "Lone Ranger" (1961: 25), there are many allusions to the homosexual scene by way of puns, comic dialogue, and place names, as Tilson Pugh has pointed out (2002: 51–54). In *Breakfast at Tiffany's,* the demimonde of urban single women finds a parallel in the homosexual underworld.

Like Colette's 1941 novel *The Pure and the Impure,* Capote's *Breakfast at Tiffany's* portrays a world of shifting sexualities and liaisons in elegiac terms. There is something sexually indeterminate in Holly Golightly's looks as described. Her paradoxical shape-shifting can take an androgynous form. We see her playing the innocent in the newspaper reports after her arrests: "Miss Golightly, a fragile eyeful, even though attired like a tomboy in slacks and leather jacket" (Capote 1961: 84). After she has gone, when the novel opens, a photograph taken in Africa of a wood carving of a girl's head reminds her acquaintances irresistibly of her: "her hair sleek and short as a young man's, her face, her mouth wide, not unlike clown lips" (12). Waifs are often, in film and literature, androgynous figures. When they are, their androgyny is usually a trope for their desire for independence. Boyishness is a recurring characteristic of the waif, a characteristic that suggests a refusal to close off possibilities that aren't conventionally feminine, and skepticism about the usual expectations of what woman can and can't do. The negligent, underplayed, or offhand aspects of androgynous appearance only underline the lightness with which she treats these social norms and expectations. Holly "isn't a phony, because she's a real phony" (32).

Notes

1. Charles Chaplin (dir.), *Modern Times* (United Artists, 1936).
2. Hardwick (1998: 257–60) draws some textual comparisons. See also Wilson (1993: 36) and Hassan (1999: 10). Katherine Bucknell comments on the influence and cites Edmund White doing the same in Bucknell (2000: 6).

3. Federico Fellini (dir.), *La Strada* (Ponti-de Laurentis, Italy, 1954) and *Nights of Cabiria* (Ponti-de Laurentis, Italy, 1957); Vincente Minnelli (dir.), *Some Came Running* (USA, 1959); Billy Wilder (dir.), *The Apartment* (USA, 1960); Henry Cornelius (dir.), *I Am a Camera* (USA, 1955); Jean Negulesco (dir.), *Daddy Long Legs* (USA, 1955).

4. Alan J. Pakula (dir.), *The Sterile Cuckoo* (Paramount, 1969); Bob Fosse (dir.), *Sweet Charity* (1969).

5. The many versions of Sally Bowles are analyzed in Mizejewski (1992). The provenance and various metamorphoses of Holly Golightly prior to the film adaptation are discussed by Kramer (2004).

6. Bob Fosse (dir.) *Cabaret* (1971).

7. It is the narrator and other characters who perceive Holly as lost; she resists this view.

8. The significant aspects of that history for understanding the genesis of the female waif are the expanding numbers of the real-life homeless, particularly orphans and street women, in the nineteenth-century industrial city; the evolution of the music hall tramp from the "tramp scare" of the American civil war; and, in fiction, Charlotte Bronte's 1847 novel *Jane Eyre*, which employed an introspective female voice to narrate a story of an orphaned young woman. Significantly, Jane Eyre wears mainly unadorned dark, black, or "governess grey" and, in a pivotal episode in the story, becomes a homeless beggar woman wandering alone through the stormy countryside.

9. These terms are from a variety of sources including dictionary definitions, newspaper book reviews, and film reviews. A 1998 theater review describes Sam Mendes's "revisionist" production of *Cabaret* as turning the "gamine Sally Bowles into a desperate and self-deluded waif" (http://www.britannica.com/eb/article-232133/Performing-Arts). An article on Kate Moss by Peter Conrad (2005) borrows many descriptors from waif fictions, borrowing its title from Rhoda Broughton's late nineteenth-century novel *A Waif's Progress*.

10. Chanel is credited with originating this idea of an elegant black that concealed its expense in a look marked by simplicity and austerity and, sometimes, by little signs of poverty.

11. Monroe is said to have declined the role when offered it. In interviews in the 1980s Capote suggested Jodie Foster for the part if there was a remake.

12. He continues, "The trend was apparent not only in the abundance of starlet stars—Debbie Reynolds, Shirley MacLaine, Janet Leigh, Mitzi Gaynor, Shirley Jones *et al.*—and in the popularity of recent child stars like Elizabeth Taylor and Natalie Wood, but in the changes that came over some of the older stars who were still around."

13. For example, Australian expatriate writer Sumner Locke Elliott wrote the first screenplay for the film adaptation. His biographer reports him withdrawing over studio pressure to change the homosexual narrator of the novel to the

heterosexual gigolo played by George Peppard on screen. See Clarke (1996: 212). Gore Vidal worked briefly on the screenplay before it was passed, to Capote's dismay, to George Axelrod, writer of *The Seven Year Itch.* A studio letter rejecting the Sumner Locke Elliott draft for lack of warmth and effeminacy is discussed in Kramer (2004: 62).

14. The film's opening scene showing Holly wearing her ball gown at sunrise echoes Elaine Landy's popular 1958 novel, *The Dud Avocado,* whose heroine walks in Paris in the morning in her ball gown.

15. The feminine form "gamine" is still commonly used to refer to the "gamine" fashion look and the gamine characters and stars portrayed in films and fashion spreads. The female "gamine" is not always distinguished from the masculine form, "gamin," in nineteenth- and early twentieth-century literature.

16. The other defining gamine look, a tomboy style of clothing made popular, according to Callan, by Jeanne Moreau's tweed cap, layered pullover, and knickerbockers in *Jules and Jim* (1961), has strong cinematic antecedents in *La Strada* and earlier films about girls on the road.

17. Jean Seberg's "waif" haircut in *Breathless,* which "became the uniform of bohemianism," is a key example of the influence of films on fashion, according to Breward (2003: 136).

18. There is also an implied association with Jewishness, as when Isherwood (2003: 35) remarks, "She was dark enough to be Fritz's sister." Hepburn is described as having a "huge mouth and flat Mongolian features" in Beaton (1979: 262). Audrey Hepburn always refused to dye her hair blonde.

19. This essay was first published in 1959 in *Esquire* (de Beauvoir wrote it in English), the same magazine that published *Breakfast at Tiffany's* the year before.

20. And "dancer's black." See Moseley (2002: 43) and Smith (2002: 40).

21. The paradoxical connotations of Hamlet's black clothing are discussed in Harvey (1995: 97).

13

Becoming Neo: Costume and Transforming Masculinity in the *Matrix* Films

Sarah Gilligan

Contemporary Hollywood action and sci-fi cinema offer a multiplicity of images of self-consciously stylish, cool masculinity to the spectator. Films such as the *Matrix* trilogy (1999, 2003, 2003), *Minority Report* (2002), the *Mission Impossible* trilogy (1996, 2000, 2006), *I Robot* (2004), *Constantine* (2005), and *V for Vendetta* (2005) use costume as a spectacular intervention, by providing the spectator with numerous opportunities to gaze at the suited, leather-clad, or trench-coated hero as he attempts to save the day from the latest threat to humanity. Through lingering close-ups and slow-motion sequences, a visual narrative discourse is created in which even the most sartorially uninterested spectator is almost forced to notice the clothes, such is the overt spectacle of fabric, movement, and the body through the display of cool shades, wafting coats, and well-toned bodies encased in tight-fitting T-shirts.

Through an analysis of the representation of Neo in the *Matrix* trilogy, one will argue that a radical shift has taken place in the representation of masculine identities within recent sci-fi and action cinema. Central to this shift is the displacement of the construction and performance of identity from the body onto clothes and gadgets. Through costume, the male hero is able to undergo a seemingly effortless trans-formation from the ordinary to the extraordinary male, in an image that rejects the hysterical phallocentric appropriation of muscularity (see Tasker 1993, Dyer 1982, Neale 1983), in favor of a look that blurs gender boundaries through the perfor-mance of identity and self-consciously offers the sexualized pleasures of costume as spectacle to the spectator. Thus gendered identity is not only inscribed through costume but becomes dominated by a spectacle of surfaces that is raised to the level of fetish. While such representations can be seen to eroticize the male hero and cre-ate crossover appeal for the straight female and gay male spectator, such gender ambiguity and eroticism needs to be made safe from the "threat" of homoeroticism for the straight male spectator. As Steve Neale (1983) and Richard Dyer (1982) have both argued, the homoerotic threat within representations of masculinity is often displaced through the use of action, spectacle, sadomasochism, and phallic props, while our rugged, frequently monosyllabic hero avoids engaging our gaze, such is his preoccupation with important events or falling for the charms of the female love interest. Within the *Matrix* films gadgets such as mobile phones and sunglasses function not only as narrative devices, but also as phallic and techno-fetish props (see Gilligan 2009), together with a hysterical excess of weaponry in order to attempt to disavow the potential feminization of the male hero and reassert heterosexual masculine power.

Two significant shifts within the action/sci-fi genre are embodied through the representation of Neo in the *Matrix* films. First, a more slender, fluid, mobile, clothed hero has replaced the hysterical muscular excess of the male action hero embodied by stars such as Arnold Schwarzenegger, Sylvester Stallone, and Jean-Claude Van Damme. Such heroes, as Yvonne Tasker discusses, were characterized as "top heavy, almost statuesque" males who essentially strike "poses within an action narrative" (1993: 73). In contrast, the representation of Neo is marked by a fluid kineticism, which enables the spectator to revel in both the spectacle and eroticism of the combination of clothes and the body in motion. Second, the *Matrix* films can also be seen to be part of a wider millennial cultural preoccupation with a questioning of the real and identity. This preoccupation is evident in a number of sci-fi and action films so seemingly broad ranging as *Twelve Monkeys* (1995), *Strange Days* (1995), *Face/Off* (1997), *Gattaca* (1997), *Mission Impossible 2* (2000), *Minority Report* (2002), *Cypher* (2002), *Paycheck* (2003), *Sky Captain and the World of Tomorrow* (2004), and *Constantine* (2005). Within each of these films, masculine identity is the subject of transformation, performance, or a fluidity between the real and the imagined, past, present, and future. Such a preoccupation with transformation and identity is also evident in the surge of comic-book adaptations of "ordinary" men with either a secret identity and/or super powers such as *Superman Returns* (2006), the *Spiderman* trilogy (2002, 2004, 2007), the *X-Men* trilogy (2000, 2003, 2006), and the *Fantastic Four* (2005) and its sequel, *Fantastic Four and the Silver Surfer* (2007).

The digital revolution is central to both the thematic concerns and the shifting representation of the male hero within contemporary action/sci-fi cinema. In the knowledge economy of the digital age, the nature of work and labor is ever-changing and no longer demands the same physicality as it did twenty years ago. The new heroes of postindustrial culture are those with the technical skills in digital information, manipulation, and programming rather than physical strength and power. Thus, rather than the statuesque, unattainable ideal of the muscular male hero being both "a triumphal assertion of a traditional masculinity" (Tasker 1993: 109) and offered to the spectator as a figure for idolization and aspiration, Neo, as a new postmillennial hero, is characterized by his androgyny, beauty, and fluidity within the worlds he inhabits. Masculinity become represented no longer through a hysterical excessive image, but through a combination of feminized beauty and phallic masculinity; he blurs not only gendered boundaries (between masculinity and femininity), but also multiple images of masculinity. Neo is thus the product of the hybrid evolution of two decades of changing masculinity in the digital age, in which a third space is created, that of the metrosexual male, placed between the binary oppositions of the bubbling homo-eroticism of the New Man and heterosexism of New Lad culture,[1] to represent multiple masculinities as points of identification and aspiration for the style-conscious, intelligent, and technologically savvy male.

Regardless of the era of masculinity under discussion, I would agree with Rosalind Gill that in analyzing media (and cinematic) texts the "one-size-fits-all notion of masculinity" is problematic, and that rather than thinking in terms of "fixed identity positions or essences" one needs to see the different images of masculinity as discourses that can be performed" (2003: 39). Thus contemporary masculinity will be used within this chapter in a similar way as it is by Jonathan Rutherford as a means to "describe, define and problematise performances, representations and discourses of ways of doing and being a man." Masculinity thus enables men to shift from being an "unquestioned norm" governed by the obligations of manliness, to a "new type of gendered subjecthood" that is "open to self reflection, criticism, analysis and debate" (Rutherford 2003: 1).

In turn, the *Matrix* films in their representation of masculinity are clearly informed by a cultural moment of production in which gendered identities and our future selves are in a moment of transition. Amanda Fernbach argues that contemporary Western culture is currently marked by a "plethora of evolutionary fantasies that imagine and invent our future selves and their forms of embodiment" (2002: 3). Whether it is in the appropriation of nanotechnology to create a cyborg self or in the capacity of the Web environments such as chat rooms to enable identity morphing, "fantasies of transformation run rife" (3). Central to the emergence of such fantasies is a cultural preoccupation with the future of the body in the age of technology. One can argue that the "hybrid technologised body" may "indicate the physical and conceptual end to the body" (3). Through the revealing of "real life" to be a computer simulation and its representation of characters "jacking in," the *Matrix* films can be seen to demonstrate a clear thematic preoccupation with the loss of the natural body within the digital world. While such representations are both integral to the narrative and interesting subjects of analysis, what for me is of particular interest is the ways in which such representations of the body and technology are constructed and performed through costume and gadgets. Although the material body may still be biologically defined as male or female, it is no longer the site at which masculinity and femininity becomes constructed. Thus, rather than the excesses of muscularity or the hyperfeminine body, gendered identity becomes constructed at the level of performance.

As Peter X. Feng argues, *The Matrix* is structured around the "the consequences of failed passing" (2002: 154). If one unplugs from the Matrix the body dies, and death in one world leads to the death of the self. Thus, despite the posthuman fantasy of "jacking in" enabling an escape from the confines of the material body, *The Matrix* can be seen to highlight the notion that we cannot truly separate our performed identities (me) from "the meat" of the internal sense of self, the "I." The text can thus be seen to explore the relationship and potential conflict between external and internal identities. The mission to "free your mind" and fight against the dominant structures of power (symbolized by the machines) in the pursuit of a liberated, collective identity on Zion can in turn be read as a discourse in identity politics. While Zion promises to bring individuals together in a utopian community devoid of gender, class, racial, or sexual boundaries, it does not eradicate or problematize identity at the level of "being." As Edwards argues, the "display of artifice and performance of masculinity" within contemporary culture can be seen to both deconstruct and reinforce the "distinction between 'real' and 'unreal' masculinity," or between "doing" and "being" masculine (2006: 113). In turn, while identity is rendered as a construction that with knowledge can be played with, the characters within the narrative are never given the opportunity to wholly escape, manipulate, or subvert their identities. As Feng argues, the imagery of the Matrix is "reliant on the world we live in: The Matrix is thoroughly implicated in our bodily materiality" (2002: 154). In turn, while the text offers a more fluid and multiple set of gendered identities, the characters are still confined to their sexed and raced bodies. Despite the confines of the material body that are represented within the text, if identity becomes reduced to a level of surface appearances, then it can more easily be the subject of transformation and the boundaries between reality and illusion can be manipulated. Identity, one can argue, within such a framework becomes about "doing" rather than "being." In turn, costume enables a transformation of Neo's identity from the ordinary to the extraordinary, in which masculinity is dominated by performance, ambiguity, spectacle, and fetishism. Subsequently masculine identities become the subject of transformation, rather than crisis, through which masculinity emerges as self-aware, skilled, stylish, and considerably more interesting. Though coded as heterosexual, gendered identity becomes somewhat more ambiguous, creating a space where the spectator is encouraged to gaze, aspire, and desire the extraordinary, active, and yet often beautiful male.

From the opening scenes of the first *Matrix* film, masculine identity is represented as dominated by a fracturing of subjectivity between the real and the performed. As Morpheus guides Neo from the confines of his corporate cubical into a realization of his place within the world of the Matrix, he undergoes a sartorial transformation from hacker "geek" to a millennial hero as "The One."[2] Through the fragmentation of his identity and his seemingly superhuman capabilities as "The One," Neo can be read as a "superhero." But unlike the superheroes of films such as *Fantastic Four,* the *X-Men* trilogy and the *Spiderman* trilogy, Neo's hero costuming within *The Matrix* following his "rebirth" is represented as possessing considerably more sartorial sophistication and style than that of the Lycra-clad comic-book heroes. Within the superhero genre, costume functions as a means of differentiating the heroes and villains as "superbeings" from those who reside within the "noncostumed ordinary world." Through color, pattern, and cut the superhero's costume becomes a marker of "individual identity—a new identity as the alter ego has been shed, if not actually hidden behind a mask" (Reynolds 1994: 26). In turn, for the comic-book superhero, as Vicki Karaminas discusses, costume functions as "a conductor for channeling powers" (2005: 5). In the case of the male superhero, the costume both highlights the muscularity of the torso and shoulders while also constraining the excesses of the body to construct the ideal hypermasculine physique (see Karaminas 2005: 13). The hypermuscular body in turn functions as a stable signifier of gendered identity. For instance, as Antony Easthope discusses, stories such as Superman "force a boy to choose between a better self that is masculine and another everyday self that seems feminine" (1992: 29). In rejecting the image of the bespectacled, everyday Clark Kent, Superman is offered up as a "super masculine ideal" (Easthope 1992: 29) in which changing "into costume" functions as a "sign of inner change" from wimp to superhero (Reynolds 1994: 32). Rather than the hero attempting to create a disguise to mask the "real" self, identity within the virtual world of the Matrix becomes rendered as a transformative performance.

The costumes within the Matrix films lend themselves to either traditional mise-en-scène analysis or more recent methodologies of reading the costumes as constructing a visual narrative discourse of their own (Church Gibson 2005: 115). This chapter will appropriate both strategies, exploring both their relationship to character and also their fetishistic visual spectacle. Taking a "traditional approach" to costume analysis, Craig Batty (2007) argues that within cinematic narratives there are two separate but intertwining threads, that of the physical (external thread) and that of the emotional journey (internal thread). Thus costume has the potential to set the plot in motion as a marker of narrative intention and development. In turn, the character's emotional transformation is externalized via the use of costume. To Batty, costumed excess functions as a departure from the ordinary to an extraordinary world. One can apply Batty's approach to costuming to an analysis of Neo's physical and emotional journey within *The Matrix*. His journey, though, is not simply one where dressing up functions as a marker of narrative intention; rather, there is a self-conscious representation of both dressing up and stripping his existing identity away through the process of a graphic, painful physical "rebirth" so that he can undergo his passage of emotional transformation and understanding of what the matrix is. Thus costuming functions as a way of signifying emotional growth and in turn costume becomes a stage in itself (see Batty 2007). While the process of rebirth marks the most obvious visual representation of the fracturing of Neo's subjectivity, masculine identity is represented from the opening scenes as the subject of performance. Neo's hacker identity is represented as seemingly more authentic and real than his "real-life" corporate persona of Thomas Anderson. Rather than successfully passing in his "suit of power," his ill-fitting, crumpled suit, coupled with late-night bleary eyes and nonchalant appearance, act as slippage. Such slippage is made explicit not only when he is disciplined by his boss, but also when he is placed in opposition to the sharply dressed Agents, adorned in their black slim-cut, retro sixties suits and sunglasses. Whereas in their uniformity the agents initially appear to signify conformity and a seemingly fixed and stable identity, Neo's/Thomas's identity is marked as performative from the start. His costuming separates him from both his former identity of Thomas Anderson, his new "real-world" self on board the ship, and that of the mere unknowing mortals trapped within the inauthentic world of the Matrix.

As Pamela Church Gibson discusses, costume functions within the *Matrix* films to support a visual narrative in which a series of binary oppositions are created between the "real and the unreal," the "inauthentic" and the "authentic." This division between the authentic and the inauthentic can be read as one of the central tensions within the *Matrix* films. Through the crew's drab, color-coded, oversized grunge sweaters, the postapocalyptic murky real world on board the ship is represented as infinitely less attractive than the "glossy, gleaming, slick and stylish" computer-simulated world of the Matrix (2005: 116). In turn, as Claudia Springer discusses, The Matrix "not only looks cool, it is also about the attainment of cool, about the transformation of a geek into an icon of incomparable cool" (2005: 89). As the narrative of the first film progresses, Neo's costuming becomes ever more spectacular, as seemingly ordinary clothing is transformed into an extraordinary style. Neo's clothing shifts from casual jackets and black suits to the flowing excesses of the trench coat. In alluding to (and further fashioning) cyberpunk style, the costume functions to mark Neo's difference from the agents, adorned in their anonymous suits, and signals his increasing power and status within the narrative. Yet he is not simply constructed as the hypervirile, hysterically phallic male, but rather as an image that can be read as blurring gender boundaries. Through the appropriation of codes of femininity, his image is both softened and eroticized, marking his representation as a radical shift in the dominant codes of masculine representation.

In her analysis of costuming within *The Matrix,* Sarah Street argues that the "dark trenchcoats, thick, heavy boots and shotgun armoury" worn within the final scenes of *The Matrix* "suggest an uncomfortable allusion to fascist iconography" (Street 2001: 93). She argues that it is as though the "rebels must outclass their enemies in their adoption of militaristic costume in the final shootout" (93). In acknowledging the "spectacular display of warrior imagery" in relation to the "masculinist imagery" of Neo's clothing, she argues that the heavy black clothing, combined with the saturation of phallic imagery, creates connotations of "regimentation, discipline and power" (96). While Street's analysis is both valid and interesting, Neo's costuming also creates a spectacular intervention within the narrative, which both highlights the visual pleasures of spectacle and action and blurs gender boundaries in the fashioning of a new image of the male hero. What Street does not acknowledge (or perhaps does not even see) in her analysis is the degree of erotic charge in the costuming of Neo in the iconic lobby and rooftop sequences of the film.

While Trinity's shiny PVC and rubber outfits may offer the most obvious appropriation of "fetish wear" to create an eroticized spectacular intervention within the narrative, Neo's costuming also appropriates such a high degree of eroticism that it is raised to the level of fetish for the spectator. His costuming draws attention to the physicality and movement of the character/star while also offering a displacement of desire onto the clothes themselves through the "bliss" of the textile. In the lobby scene, as Neo strides through the lobby, the camera cuts to reveal a swath of dark fabric floating behind him. As Neo moves, the texture, movement, and noise (if only in the imagination) of the flowing fabric can be seen to be highly alluring. As the camera draws closer in to a close-up, the spectator is forced to notice the juxtaposition of soft fabric against the hardness of his boots as the details of costuming fill the frame. While the close-up draws the spectator in to survey the details, the moment is only brief as the camera pulls away, leaving us behind in turn, revealing the beauty of silhouette. In battle with his encroaching enemy, Neo twists, turns, and cartwheels, his coat swirling around and behind him, falling into place as he stands rigid—the fabric falling behind him revealing a hard but slender body.

Later, as Neo battles the agents on the rooftop, he once again twists, turns, and bends, this time leaning back, the fabric falling toward the ground, exposing the arch of his back, the precarious balancing act as his body seemingly defies gravity, hovering without falling. The camera forces the spectator to gaze at his body, hard and toned but devoid of the excessive muscularity that so frequently dominates action cinema. The camera circles around him, revealing another view, another glance at the body while he is preoccupied with the business of action. Through the use of the innovative "bullet time" technique, time is slowed down, almost frozen, enabling the opportunity to survey the body, linger, disappear into a daydream—a combination of action, movement, sensuality, eroticism, rigidity, and fluidity. Contradictory elements combine to create an arresting visual yet visceral cinematic experience. Action and music combine to raise the spectator's heartbeat to such an extent that it is virtually in time with the pounding dance-music soundtrack. While action, spectacle, and soundtrack combine to create an adrenaline-pumping sequence, the fluidity of the fabric and movement creates another, different spectacular intervention. The sequence leaves the spectator gasping, breathless with an unexpected engagement and arousal as the camera forces the gaze to linger on every last detail of both the spectacular excess and the movement of both the body in motion and the fabric as it swells, floats, and twists, both connected and almost devoid of the body, seeming to possess a life of its own.

Such a self-consciously explicit, alluring, and erotic use of flowing swaths of fabric was prior to *The Matrix* largely unseen within representations of the male action/sci-fi hero. While the trench coat could be read as alluding to the hero's duster coat in the western, Neo's coat does not protect and conceal in the same way as the coat of the unpredictable, inscrutable westerner whose coat binds him to the wilderness that surrounds him. Instead, Neo's coat is dominated by its capacity for display, for aesthetics over functionality. As the coat flows, the spectator is still able to read the movements of the body and the weapons he carries.[3] In turn, rather than desire being centered upon either the revealing of flesh, or the boundaries between fabric and flesh, in which the flesh threatens to "spill out" from the clothes, the very excess of the fabric itself becomes the focus of attention. Yet to theorize such eroticism of clothes on the male body, which verges upon the fetishistic, is fraught with tensions and difficulties.

Classical fetish theory drawn from Freud's interpretation of fetishism does not fully account for the ways in which Neo's costuming is raised to the level of fetish in the latter scenes of *The Matrix* (and also within the action scenes of *Matrix Reloaded* and *Matrix Revolutions*). The fetish, according to Freud, stands in "for the mother's missing phallus and masks her sexual difference" (Fernbach 2002: 4). Sexual stimulation is achieved by the fetishist via the fetish object via "a fantasy of phallic sameness and the disavowal of sexual difference" (6). Thus the fetishized position within such a framework is gendered feminine and associated with lack and needs to be phallicized by the controlling (male) subject (Fernbach 2002). Thus, if applying such a framework, Neo's coat comes to function as a fetish object, and in turn sexual desire becomes displaced onto a sexual substitute. To Freud, fur and velvet have the capacity to function as fetish objects, due to their capacity to "recall the sight of pubic hair at the moment of undressing," a moment at which the woman "could still be regarded as phallic" (Freud in Fernbach 2002: 7). In addition, modern techno-fabrics such as PVC and rubber offer new possibilities to function as fetish objects when worn on the fetishized female body (Fernbach 2002; Steele 1996). Yet when the male adorned in the flowing swaths of the trench coat is offered up in the position of the fetishized object for the female and/or male spectator, such a framework becomes more problematic. While the sheen of Trinity's PVC clothing reflects our gaze and creates hard, phallic armor, the soft, ornamental, voluptuous, excessive spectacle of fluid surfaces of the coat in motion is feminized, thus blurring the boundaries of both real and imagined sexual difference.

In addition to the fabric fetishism drawing upon the cultural coding of the eroticized feminine,[4] one can also argue that the coat appropriates sexual symbolism in order to both eroticize and feminize the representation of Neo. In her analysis of the Gainsborough melodrama *The Wicked Lady* (1945), Sue Harper argues that Barbara's costuming makes an "extended play with sexual symbolism" (1994: 130), with the multitude of folds, pleats, and whorls symbolizing the labia, vagina, and clitoris. One can argue that Neo's coat can be seen to function in a similar way. Yet in its appropriation of sexual symbolism, Neo's coat can be seen to mix vulval and phallic imagery, as the layers of fabric reveal not a vortex, but a hard phallic body. Anne Hamlyn (in a different context) argues that "fabric acts to conceal and cover object and persons while, at the same time, disclosing them—hinting at their presence" (2003: 11). The wrapping gives the object "a certain mystery, vitality, and seductiveness. Fabric is malleable. It lends itself to wrapping, draping, and swathing." It restricts direct access to the naked object, but it also has the ability to suggest, enhance, and draw attention to what it covers over and adorns (11).

Thus Neo is represented as an image that can be read as blurring gender boundaries through the appropriation of both male and female signifiers. Through the appropriation of codes of femininity, his image is both softened and eroticized, marking his representation as a radical shift in the dominant codes of masculine representation. Rather than inscribing masculinity through the display of muscularity (see Tasker 1993), the representation of Neo adheres to Edwards' discussion of images of the New Man, which center upon seeing his physicality via clothes—in turn creating "intensely phallocentric" representations in the peek show of "now you see it, now you don't [… of] his manhood" (Edwards 1997: 42). As Edwards notes, while performativity is supposedly all about the breaking down of sex/gender boundaries, performativity repeatedly "reveals the body beneath the performance" (2006: 114). As Easthope argues, "Images of the perfect male body return to the masculine gaze a flattering reflection of how he would like to see himself" (Easthope 1992: 53). With its lack of fat, tensed muscle, "Flesh and bone can pass itself off as a kind of armour" (Easthope 1992: 52). In turn, the male body creates a defense between the inside and outside in which, through the hardness of the body, the male is constructed as wholly masculine, rather than possessing the softness attributed to femininity. The hard, muscular, but lean body is coupled with a hysterical excess of phallic props to attempt to remasculinize Neo as a phallic male. The guns frame his groin as he is preoccupied with fighting and the business of action. If, as Steele proposes, "fetishism involves phallic symbolism" (1996: 15), then the hard body of Neo, coupled with the use mobile phones (see Gilligan 2009) and the excess of weapons can be clearly seen to function as phallic props. While drawing upon the iconography of the western gunfight sequence, the scene self-consciously reveals masculinity as a performative drag, in which in order to become the action hero, Neo must be adorned in the appropriate excess of phallic weapons.

Yet the visual spectacle of the clothing, coupled with the star presence, further undermines the attempt to represent the performance of phallic masculinity. Throughout the scene Neo is offered up as the object of the gaze. In addition to the use of movement, the black coat, dark sunglasses, and star presence function to further eroticize and objectify Neo. As John Harvey discusses, the cultural associations of wearing black are multiple, functioning as a "power colour" that "is associated at once with intensity […] and with importance, and with the putting on of impersonality" (1995: 257). Anne Hollander argues that black carries not only symbolic but also optical power in which it functions as an "enhancement to the individual qualities of the human face" (1993: 366). It is "a beautiful foil for the face" in which features are both enhanced and given authority (390). Thus when the coat is coupled with the dark sunglasses, a dramatic emphasis of the face is created that is enhanced by the fabric itself. Unlike Trinity's shiny PVC catsuit, Neo's coat absorbs the light, drawing us in to gaze at the chiseled features of both Neo and Keanu Reeves, the star (Church Gibson 2005: 117).

While the representation of Neo can be seen to strive to adhere to the dominant conventions of the male pinup through the use of action, phallic props, and a framing of the groin, the casting of Keanu Reeves disrupts the attempts by the text to construct a wholly active, powerful phallic male. As Charles Taylor proposes, as

Neo, Keanu Reeves allows us to "revel in his physicality" (Taylor 1999: 1), which, as with so many of Reeves' other films, emphasizes "a kind of fluid kineticism over character depth, over any fixed notion of identity" (Rutsky 2001: 192). In turn, both the text and surrounding intertextual discourses create a fluid representation of gendered identity that both masculinizes and feminizes Neo/Reeves, in turn increasing the potential for crossover appeal for both the straight/gay and male/female spectator. In his analysis of the male as erotic object, Kenneth MacKinnon proposes that costuming, the use of close-up, "ethnic otherness," and "unexpected gentleness" all contribute to the feminizing of the male star (1997: 79). Despite his playing the action hero in films such as *The Matrix, Speed* (1994), and *Point Break* (1991), the star presence of Keanu Reeves is repeatedly characterized by such feminizing strategies. Dyer (1982) argues that on the occasions when the male pinup does look back at the spectator, he stares at the viewer, lacking the accompanying smile that dominates representations of women, whereas in the case of Keanu Reeves, the focus in the visual intertextual discourses that surround his films repeatedly draws attention to his beauty, representing him-to-be-looked-at, often engaging the spectators' gaze. For instance, in the huge array of images collated by loyal fans on the "Keanu Connection" Web site, he is repeatedly shown with a beaming smile, head tilted, and floppy hair, in poses dominated by their movement and playfulness—in turn subverting the dominant representations of the male pinup.[5]

Through the processes of feminizing Reeves, not only does he become desired, but there is also a desire for him to be silenced. In turn, he comes to exist as an objectified image, raised to the level of fetish for the female/nonmasculine spectator who has no desire to hear him speak, but instead exists at the level of fantasy where his purpose is to be looked at and desired. The spectator is able to revel in his physicality and the cinematic eroticism of his movement (also see Rutsky 2001: 192). We are enabled a direct gaze, which is unmediated by other characters. While the gunfight, action, rapid editing, and dance soundtrack can be seen as an attempt to remasculinize and render the gaze safe, Neo's balletic movements and cartwheels repeatedly undercut the dominant reading and further draw attention to the clothes and the physicality of the character/star.

Yet despite the numerous fantastic moments of action and spectacle within all of the *Matrix* films (for me at least), Neo and his trench coat in the lobby and rooftop sequences remain a spectacular, intensely erotic and haunting intervention that is raised to the level of fetish. If the coat can be read as a feminine signifier, then placing that upon the beautiful, androgynous figure of Keanu Reeves becomes an act of not only gender blurring but perhaps even cross-dressing. Thus the image may exist within a third space, beyond masculinity and femininity but also between fetishism and eroticism. While to analyze the coat and the representation of Neo in terms of classical fetishism is by no means straightforward, one must remember that fetishism, as Valerie Steele discusses, has "acquired an expanding repertoire of meanings" and that in turn the once separate discourses have come to intersect (1996: 5). Thus, while fetishism is frequently about sexuality, power, and perception, it is also increasingly not connected only to the abnormal, sensational, kinky, or deviant. Fetishism has become an increasingly integral part of mainstream fashion (Steele 1996).

Perhaps, therefore, the appeal resides more in the ability for cinema to bring otherwise "dead clothes" to life. Rather than the latest fashion and subcultural styles existing as frozen fashion frames or empty and lifeless upon a clothes hanger, film enables us to lose ourselves in the sensory pleasures of the movement of fabric. As Steven Shaviro discusses, the experience of film viewing is one that "offers an immediacy and violence of sensation that powerfully engages the eye and the body of the spectator" (Shaviro 1993: 25–26). "Images confront the viewer directly, without mediation. […] We respond viscerally to visual forms, before having the leisure to read or interpret them as symbols" (26). While the spectator may not be able to touch the cinematic image, the "tactile convergence" is both alluring and present in its visceral impact upon the spectator, luring the spectator into "excessive intimacy" with the image (54). Thus, while a representation such as that of Neo can be analyzed in terms of signaling a shift in cinematic representations of the male hero, in addition by juxtaposing fashion, action, and the body, spectators, whether male, female, gay, or straight, are able at the cinema or on DVD to temporarily lose themselves in the highly visceral, sometimes seemingly unexplainable, sublime pleasures of both clothing and cinema.

Notes

1. For further discussion of the New Man and New Lad culture in the United Kingdom in the 1980s and 1990s, see (among others) Benwell (2003), Edwards (2006), Nixon (1996), and Simpson (1994a). For further discussion of the metrosexual male, see Simpson 1994b.
2. For further discussion of issues of performativity and gender passing, see Butler (1993, 1999).
3. See Gaines and Herzog's (1998) discussion of the duster jacket. M. R. Haweis in *The Art of Dress* (1879) argued that there are three "great requirements of dress […] 1) to protect, 2) to conceal, 3) to display" (Laver 1952: 8).
4. Also see Kenneth MacKinnon's analysis of the eroticizing of Rudolph Valentino through costume (1997: 79).
5. For instance, in the huge array of magazine images collated by loyal fans on the "Keanu Connection" Web site (http://keanuconnection.com), he is repeatedly shown with beaming smile, head tilted, and floppy hair, in poses dominated by their movement and playfulness—in turn subverting the dominant representations of the male pinup.

–14–

Signs of Bliss in Textures and Textiles

Dagmar Venohr

Textile and vestimentary words can be seen as textual indications in an implicit sense. Therefore, the use of *signs* in the title does not refer to a somehow determined relation between an exterior symbol and an inner sense. This semiological perspective on the use of vestimentary or textile metaphors in written texts, in literature, is sufficiently known[1] and will not be the subject of this article. Rather, these signs will be taken as symptoms, perhaps somewhat medical in meaning, or as indicators of something subtle and not obvious, like an attempt to trace vestiges. The textile and vestimentary words will be considered as material signatures (Derrida 2004: 101) with their own textual quality. The garment is not a symbol or a metaphor for something, but the textile is a structural indication for another text level. This level, the texture per se, is found not under or behind the obvious, but within. Therefore this text is not a semiotic or any other theoretical examination, but a blissful reading of Friedrich Nietzsche's *Unfashionable Observation:* "Utility and Liability of History for Life" (Nietzsche 1995) with a sensual relationship to the use of textile words within the text (Plate 31).

But what is "text" and "textual"? According to Barthes, "text is language without its image reservoir" (1995: 33), and "textual" means, in this sense, the structure and material of this specified kind of language. So what does "texture" mean? The texture is the tissue of the text. It means focusing on a special kind of textual level. Here it means to look at the textile words and allow them to leave an impression on the reader, to see or to feel how and in which way they weave their inner sense. As Barthes says, no thesis is possible here (Barthes 1995: 34). No theory can or should be constructed. The only opportunity to point it out comes from looking at one's own ability to perceive bliss. So, when I talk about the "bliss concept" in the title, I am thinking of an open space, an individual wideness and freedom of scope. "Bliss" can be understood here as a disclosing, a discovering of another textual coating, the woven tissue, the textile's texture.

Nietzsche's influence on the work of Barthes is already well documented (Mortimer 1989). There also seem to be many concrete references between the second piece of *Unfashionable Observations* and *The Pleasure of the Text* (Ette 1998: 361–68). Conversely, it is possible to find a way to read Nietzsche with Barthes.

Therefore some historical facts about the essay "Utility and Liability of History for Life" are useful. Friedrich Nietzsche wrote the second piece of *Unfashionable Observations* in 1873 and it was published the following year. Like the first and the following two observations in the years between 1873 and 1876, this piece, about the predominant historical cultivation of the times and its vehement critique, is not really unfashionable. Actually, it is very fashionable. More than this, it is both, namely in a dialectical sense, which means the impossibility of saying one thing without referring to its opposite. In this sense the *Unfashionable Observations* really start a motion between these two polarities: fashion and the unfashionable, surface and an inner sense. This intellectual movement between the contradiction of content and form takes place with all the consequences of ambiguity, inconsistency, and the impression of paradox.

The reactions to the second observation of close friends, like Cosima and Richard Wagner, were cool and polite but not really positive. Nietzsche generally received no enthusiastic feedback about this piece (Nietzsche 2003). On the contrary, he received a lot of critical annotations concerning his rhetorical style. However, unlike Cosima Wagner, Erwin Rohde, another close friend, made a lot of suggestions for corrections and improvements. But he was still critical of the curious use of metaphors, the strange mosaiclike texture, and the incoherent string of fragments, which seemed to be stitched together without internal logic or causal continuity. All these criticisms from his closest friends led Nietzsche to doubt his own abilities as a writer, a critic, and a self-reflective thinker. But it was precisely the most criticized points that made the second piece in *Unfashionable Observations* one of his most interesting essays. It is interesting because the style and texture that express the contrast of interior and exterior take place not only in the content but also in the specific form of his writing, and also because Nietzsche expressed one of his main theses by using vestimentary metaphors (Venohr 2002)—for example: "Historical cultivation and the bourgeois cloak of universality rule simultaneously" (Nietzsche 1995: 117). Many textile words without an explicit metaphorical meaning, but with an implicit figurative textual value, could be found. Therefore, looking at the form, the "*figure*," as Barthes (1995: 56) says, it is possible to see that textile texture is an appearance of the topic itself.

Roland Barthes's disquisition, *The Pleasure of the Text,* from 1973 (Barthes 1995) was written exactly one hundred years after Nietzsche's observation. It can be seen as a turning and pivotal point of Barthes's work. It is the first text in which he combines a philosophical and theoretical approach in an experimentally literary way. Written in fragments, it can be described as a frictional writing model (Ette 1998: 360). "Friction" should be understood here as a motion that provokes bliss, as a frictional relationship between text and recipient.[2] To distinguish "bliss" from "pleasure" we need to take pleasure as a steady comfort, as a consistency of selfhood, and bliss as a celebration of form, the loss of selfhood as an inner worth. So bliss challenges pleasure. This challenge means the interdependence of both: pleasure as one step into the text and bliss as another, as a step into the texture. It is not possible to distinguish clearly between the two perspectives. There always remains an open space for a permanent oscillating motion. To accept this means going ahead, finding out more about bliss and being prepared to bear it.

Reading the textile words with bliss starts a process of motion between the poles: the interior and exterior senses move and undermine the obvious. By demonstrating the meaningful consistency of the red thread of textile words in Nietzsche's text, this specific understanding of "bliss" concerning the textual level of the observation becomes evident. The use of "to spin," or better: "to overspin," of "to weave," "to envelop," "to conceal," and "to disguise" occurs throughout the whole argumentation of the main topics. Besides expressing certain content, the very appearance of these words presents something else: an inexpressible, an unutterable impression (Wittgenstein 1963: 115)—perceptible not in a cognitive but in only an aisthetical way (Böhme 2001). Besides the process of signification, this use signifies a material quality that lies in the texture, in the tissue of the text itself. Like a net, a web, a veil, or a particular texture, the textile is knitting this text together. The kind of use and choice of textile words make bliss perceptible. The bliss with and within the text (Kolesch 1997: 87) becomes visible in the special kind of textile texture. This kind of reading and perceiving of Nietzsche's text has an effect similar to a "subtle subversion" (Barthes 1995: 55) of dualism. The opposites seem to come to nothing. A third term between the poles of inner sense and exterior form, namely, *the other,* and therefore *something between,* becomes obvious. Nietzsche calls it "the ravingly unreflective splintering[3] and defibration[4] of all foundations, their disintegration into a fluid, dispersing becoming, the tireless unraveling and historicizing by the modern human being—this great spider at the center of the cosmic web" (Nietzsche 1995: 147–48). And, like a reply, the following is found in Barthes's *The Pleasure of the Text:*

> *Text* means *Tissue;* but whereas hitherto we have always taken this tissue as a product, a ready-made veil, behind which lies, more or less hidden, meaning (truth), we are now emphasizing, in the tissue, the generative idea that the text is made, is worked out in a perpetual interweaving; lost in this tissue—this texture—the subject unmakes himself, like a spider dissolving in the constructive secretions of its web. (Barthes 1995: 64)

The subtle subversion of the textual structure by the use of textiles is paradigmatic for Nietzsche's negative diagnosis of the German cultural condition caused by the overkill of monumental, antiquarian, and critical history. This condition[5] is no longer of strong value but merely an emotion of something interior, perhaps only a feeling. It is a mental collection of knowledge, a historical science of conservation. This special kind of practicing historical science, of writing history, produces an inner value, called "inwardness" (Nietzsche 1995: 110). This is the "secret of modern cultivation that is so painstakingly concealed" (110). The "concealed" secret is that there might be nothing inside. Nietzsche finds no evidence of any condition, because there is nothing shown, but always something purported. There is no analogy between inside and outside, between thinking and acting. There is no form that could be an expression of this much-lauded German inwardness: "We Germans commonly regard form as a convention, as a disguise and deception, and for this reason among us form, if not actually hated, is at any rate not loved" (112). Therefore the German national dress is nothing but "something borrowed from a foreign country and carelessly copied" (112). Also, the modern values of identity and personality are not noticeable for Nietzsche through observing the German culture. Throughout his searching he discovers only "anxiously disguised universal human beings" (117). Here Nietzsche reproaches the refined, modern German for his or her arrogance. Besides his critique of the overemphasized and blind collection of historical facts, he also criticizes the permanent modern critical, scientific dissociation from the past. Therefore he argues that "the heightened historical need to sit in judgment [is] nothing but the same conception dressed up differently" (139). The surfeit of history causes the human being's inadequate disguise, the contradiction between content and form and finally a form that no longer expresses an adequate content. The inwardness is concealed by costume. The individual masquerades[6] itself with a "piece of clothing whose invention does not require any ingenuity and whose design does not cost any time" (113). Everybody tries to dress up—without any effect.

Nietzsche sees a possible mode to escape this unfulfilled inwardness in realizing a certain dose of ahistorical and aesthetical thinking and acting. The human being needs, as Nietzsche proclaims, "that mantle of the ahistorical" (1995: 91) to begin a creative and self-dependent way of living. Without this mantle, to use as a protective cover, people will never have the courage to start risking anything. Such a mantle could be something like an envelope or an atmosphere, something like a sphere of mania. He is convinced that "every human being who wants to become *mature* needs such an enveloping illusion, such a protecting and enveloping cloud" (134). It seems to be a covering atmosphere, perhaps a textile, a tissue with a special texture. It should be tight enough to protect and transparent enough to become active, perhaps like a veil. The ahistorical condition causes a special disposition, not of arrogance or objective criticism but of distance. This distant attitude is, as Nietzsche says, necessary to create something new with the knowledge of the old. Not least, the artist needs such a mindset toward history "to think of all things as interrelated, [and] to weave events into a totality" (126). He postulates that a "unity of plan must be inserted into the things if it is not already inherent in them" (126). Content and form should be interwoven into one structure of tissue, a unique texture.

Nietzsche advises the modern bourgeois of his time to model themselves on the Greek citizens and their aesthetic culture. By doing this, the real meaning and effective force of genuine culture will unveil itself. When the disclosed, the naked[7] kind of "*true* cultivation" (Nietzsche 1995: 167) is to be seen, the modern "will begin to grasp that culture can be something other than the *decoration of life*" (167). Hence modern people will discover that content needs an adequate form to be recognized and finally to exist, because such a culture of decoration and surface is "at bottom always only mere dissimulation and disguise, for all ornaments have the purpose of concealing what they adorn" (167). Therefore, the act of disclosing, unveiling, and undressing could be seen as a step toward truthfulness.

In the described motion of the enveloping and weaving over the concealing and disguising toward an unveiling of something within, something inner, we can see Nietzsche's attempt to combine the contradictions in a literal way. It is, in a way, the appearance of a textual level that is not obvious at first sight. It becomes apparent if we look at the textile words, on the specific kind of texture—the tissue, as Barthes says. If he is asking, then it means nothing more than that the seam, the void between an inner and an outer worth, is not annullable, but it is both, something like an oscillation. And this means that the textile texture of the written language interweaves the contradictions and overspins the gap.

The supported intention is to face a text with regard to its textile texture, its specific tissue. The underlying conviction is that by doing this it is possible to sense pleasure and perceive bliss. The reader's relationship to the texture could and should be sensual, because of his or her playing with the blissful motion of veiling and unveiling, or he or she feels mantled by textual tissue, like Nietzsche's atmosphere, which should mantle the modern people. The use of textiles in language is of great value, because it always offers more than just a metaphorical content; it offers a blissful form of textual materiality (Plate 32).

The aim is to claim more bliss on the subtle textile in written texts, or, as Nietzsche says, "This is why we should no longer allow ourselves to be deceived, why we should demand of them: 'Either take off your jackets or be what you seem'" (Nietzsche 1995: 117).

Notes

1. See all the vestimentary examinations in the semiotic tradition from Lurie (1981) to Barnard (1996).
2. Referring to the Latin origin meaning of *recipere* as "to recapture."
3. The German word *zersplittern* is translated as "shattering" (see Nietzsche 1988: 313).
4. The German word *zerfasern* is translated as "destruction" (see Nietzsche 1988: 313).
5. See the relationship between fashion and modernity within the works of other famous modern thinkers in Lehmann (2000).
6. See Nietzsche's use of "costume" and "to masquerade" (Nietzsche 1995: 102).
7. See "the honest, naked goddess Philosophy" (Nietzsche 1995: 118).

Bibliography

Abercrombie & Fitch. 1999. "Innocents abroad." *A&F Quarterly,* back-to-school 1999.

Abercrombie & Fitch. 2003. "A&F Quarterly presents ... summer 2003." *A&F Quarterly,* summer 2003.

Abercrombie & Fitch. n.d. Available at: http://www.abercrombie.com.

Aine. Belfast Rainbow Network. www.rainbownetwork.com/UserPortal/Article/Detail.aspx?ID=17980&sid=95. Accessed November 16, 2007.

Aldrich, Robert, ed. 2006. *Gay life and culture. A world history.* London: Thames & Hudson.

Alhoy, M. 1841. *Physiologie de la lorette, vignettes de Gavarny.* Paris: Aubert.

Allen, R. 1975. *The first night Gilbert and Sullivan.* London: Chappell.

Alvarado, M. 2001. "Photography and narrativity (1979–80)," in *Representation and photography: A screen reader,* ed. M. Alvarado, E. Buscombe, and R. Collins. Basingstoke, Hampshire: Houndsmills; New York: Palgrave.

Anonymous.?1853. *The habits of good society. A handbook of etiquette for ladies and gentlemen.* London: James Hogg.

Anonymous. 1887. "Servants and household management." *Lady's World,* May.

Aspers, P. 2006. *Markets in fashion: A phenomenological approach.* London: Routledge.

Avgikos, J. 1994. "Andrea Zittel—Andrea Rosen Gallery, New York, New York." *Artforum International* 32: 88.

Baldwin, Elaine, Brian Longhurst, Scott McCracken, Miles Ogborn, and Greg Smith. 2000. *Introducing cultural studies.* Athens: University of Georgia Press.

Balzac, Honoré de. 1998 [1830]. *Traité de la vie elégante.* Paris: Arléa.

Balzac, Honoré de. 1971 [1837]. *Lost illusions,* trans. H. J. Hunt. London: Penguin.

Barnard, Malcolm. 1996. *Fashion as communication.* London: Routledge.

Barthel, Diane. 1992. "When men put on appearances: Advertising and the social construction of masculinity." In *Men, masculinity and the media,* ed. Steve Craig. Oxford, England: Sage Publications.

Barthes, R. 1961. "From gemstones to jewellery." In *The Language of Fashion,* ed. Andy Stafford and Michael Carter, trans. Andy Stafford, 59–64. Power Publications/Berg.

Barthes, R. 1985 [1967]. *The fashion system,* trans. Matthew Ward and Richard Howard. London: Jonathan Cape [Paris: Editions du Seuil].

Barthes, R. 1981a. *Camera lucida: Reflections on photography,* New York: Hill and Wang.

Barthes, R. 1981b. *Le Grain de la voix.* Paris: Seuil.

Barthes, R. 1983. *The fashion system.* New York: Hill.

Barthes, R. 1995. *The pleasure of the text.* Oxford, England: Blackwell.

Barthes, R. 2002. *Œuvres completes I–V.* Paris: Éditions du Seuil.

Batty, Craig. 2007. "You are what you wear: Clothes as a means of understanding character." Paper presented at Fashion in Fiction: An International Transdisciplinary Conference. University of Technology, Sydney, Australia. May 26–27, 2007.

Baudrillard, Jean. 1988. "The system of objects." In *Jean Baudrillard selected writings,* ed. Mark Poster. Stanford, Calif.: Stanford University Press.

Baumann, A. 1888. "Possible remedies for the sweating system." *National Review* 69 (November): 289–307.

Baxter, D. 2007. "Fashions of sociability in Jean-François de Troy's *tableaux de mode, 1725–1738.*" In *Performing the "everyday": The culture of genre in the eighteenth century,* ed. A. Cavanaugh. Newark: University of Delaware Press.

Bayuk Rosenmann, E. 2002). "More stories about clothing and furniture: Realism and bad commodities." In *Functions of Victorian culture at the present time,* ed. C. L. Krueger. Athens: Ohio University Press.

BBC News. 2001. "Church brands line-dancing 'sinful.'" Available at: http://news.bbc.co.uk/1/hi/northern_ireland/1336157.stm. Accessed February 10, 2008.

Beaton, C. 1954. *The glass of fashion.* London: Weidenfeld and Nicholson.

Beaton, C. 1979. "The beginning of a new reign: 1952–3." In *Self-portrait with friends: The selected diaries of Cecil Beaton 1926–1974,* ed. Richard Buckle. London: Weidenfeld and Nicholson.

Beauvoir, S. de. 1972 [1959]. *Brigitte Bardot and the Lolita syndrome.* New York: Arno Press and the *New York Times.*

Beetham, M., and K. Boardman. 2001. *Victorian women's magazines: An anthology.* Manchester, England: Manchester University Press.

Benhamou, R. 1997. "Fashion in the *Mercure:* From human foible to female failing." *Eighteenth-Century Studies* 31 (1): 27–43.

Benson, John, and Gareth Shaw. 1992. *The evolution of retail systems 1800–1914.* London. Leicester University Press.

Benwell, Bethan, ed. 2003. *Masculinity and men's magazines.* Oxford, England: Blackwell.

Berger, Arthur Asa. 2003. *The portable postmodernist.* Walnut Creek, Calif.: AltaMira Press, 2003.

Best, Steven, and Douglas Kellner. 1991. *Postmodern theory: Critical interrogations.* New York: The Guilford Press.

Bigg, A. H. 1893. "What is fashion?" *Nineteenth Century* 33 (February): 235–48.

Bird, Laura. 1997. "Beyond mail order: Catalogs now selling image, advice." *Wall Street Journal* (July 29): sec. 1B.

Böhme, Gernot. 2001. *Aisthetik. Vorlesungen über Ästhetik als allgemeine Wahrneh-mungslehre.* München: Fink.

Bourdieu, Pierre. 2001. *Masculine domination.* Cambridge, England: Polity Press.

Bourriaud, N. 2002. *Relational aesthetics.* Paris: Les presses du réel.

Bowen, E. 1950. *Collected impressions.* New York: Knopf.

Bowie, M. 2001. "Barthes on Proust." *Yale Journal of Criticism* 14 (2): 513–18.

Braun, S. D. 1946. "The courtesan in French theater (1831–1880): An attempt at classification." *French Review* 20 (2): 161–66.

Breward, C. 1999. *The hidden consumer: Masculinities, fashion and city life 1860–1914.* Manchester, England: Manchester University Press.

Breward, C. 2003. *Fashion: Oxford history of art.* Oxford, England: Oxford University Press.

Brooke, J. 1950. *Orchid trilogy.* London: Penguin Books.

Brooks, P. 1993. *Body work: Objects of desire in modern narrative.* Cambridge, Mass.: Harvard University Press.

Bruzzi, Stella. 1997. *Undressing cinema: Costume and identity in the movies.* London: Routledge.

Bucknell, K. 2000. "Who is Christopher Isherwood?" In *The Isherwood century: Essays on the life and work of Christopher Isherwood,* ed. James J. Berg and Chris Freeman. Madison, Wisc.: University of Wisconsin Press.

Burnand, F. C. (1881). *The colonel.* Available at: http://www.xix-e.pierre-marteau.com/ed/colonel/transcript.html.

Butler, Judith. 1990. *Gender trouble: Feminism and the subversion of identity.* New York: Routledge.

Butler, Judith. 1993. *Bodies that matter: On the discursive limits of sex.* London: Routledge.

Butler, Judith. 1999 edition. *Gender trouble: Feminism and the subversion of identity.* London: Routledge.

Butler, Judith. 2004. *Undoing gender.* New York: Routledge.

Butler, Judith. 2006 [1990]. *Gender trouble: Feminism and the subversion of identity.* New York: Routledge.

Califia, P. 1992. "Clit culture: Cherchez la femme …" *On Our Backs* 8 (4): 10–11.

Callan, G. O. 1998. *The Thames and Hudson dictionary of fashion and fashion designers.* London: Thames and Hudson.

Capote, T. 1961 [1958]. *Breakfast at Tiffany's.* Middlesex, England: Penguin Books.

Capote, T. 1987. "A beautiful child." In *A Capote reader.* London: Hamish Hamilton.

Carlyle, Lucy. 2006. Review of *Dressed in Fiction,* by Clair Hughes (Berg, 2006). *Fashion Theory* 11 (2–3): 361.

Carruthers, A. E. 1999. *La mode chez Proust—réalité et imagination.* Doctor of modern languages thesis, Middlebury College, Middlebury, Vermont.

Carter, M. 2003. *Fashion classics from Carlyle to Barthes.* Oxford: Berg.

Cavanaugh, A., ed. 2007. *Performing the "everyday": The culture of genre in the eighteenth century.* Newark: University of Delaware Press.

Chambers, Anthony. 1994. *The secret window: Ideal worlds in Tanizaki's fiction.* Cambridge, Mass.: Harvard University Asia Center.

Champfleury. 1879. *Henry Monnier, sa vie, son oeuvre.* Paris: E. Dentu.

Chansons de Béranger. 1875. Vol. 1. Paris: Garnier frères.

Chrisafis, A. 2005. "Champagne, pedicures, and a place in history for the Belfast brides: Same-sex couple take first plunge in last place in UK to decriminalise homosexuality." *The Guardian* (December 19): 9.

Church, K. *Fabrications: Stitching Ourselves Together.* Available at: http://womenspace.ca/Fabrications/.

Church, K. 2003. "Something plain and simple? Unpacking custom-made wedding dresses from Western Canada (1950–1995)." In *Wedding dress across cultures,* ed. Bradley Foster, H. Clay, and D. Johnson. Oxford, England: Berg.

Church Gibson, Pamela. 2005. "Fashion, fetish and spectacle: The Matrix dressing up and down." In *The Matrix Trilogy: Cyberpunk reloaded,* ed. Stacy Gillis. London: Wallflower.

Clark, J. 2001. "A note: Getting the invitation." *Fashion Theory* 5 (3): 343–53.

Clark, J. 2004. *Spectres: When fashion turns back.* Victoria and Albert Museum/Modemuseum, Antwerp. London: V&A.

Clarke, S. 1996. *Sumner Locke Elliott: Writing life.* St. Leonards, New South Wales, Australia: Allen & Unwin.

Cole, S. 1999. "Invisible men: Gay men's dress in Britain, 1950–70." In *Defining dress: Dress as object, meaning and identity,* ed. E. Wilson and A. de la Haye, 141–54. Manchester, England: Manchester University Press.

Cole, S. 2000. *Don we now our gay apparel.* Oxford, England: Berg.

Colette. 1971 [1941]. *The pure and the impure,* trans. Herma Briffault. Harmondsworth, Middlesex, England: Penguin Books.

Colomina, B., M. Wigley, and A. Zittel. 2005. "A–Z drive through conversation." In *Andrea Zittel: Critical Space* [exhibition catalogue]. New York: Prestel Verlag.

Connelly, J. 2000. "A corporate affair." *Surface* 24 (Summer): 88–91.

Conrad, P. 2005. "A waif's progress." *Observer* (January 30).

Crane, D. 2000. *Fashion and its social agendas: Class, gender and identity in clothing.* Chicago: University of Chicago Press.

Creed, B. 1995. "Lesbian bodies: Tribades, tomboys and tarts." In *Sexy Bodies: The Strange Carnalities of Feminism,* ed. E. Grosz and E. Probyn. London: Routledge.

Czyba, L. 1984. "Paris et la Lorette." In *Paris au XIXe siècle. Aspects d'un mythe littéraire,* ed. Roger Bellet, 107–22. Lyon: Presses Universitaires de Lyon.

D'Arcy, C. C-G. 1996. "Who's afraid of the femme fatale in Breakfast at Tiffany's? Exposure and implications of a myth." In *Gender, I-Deology: Essays on theory, fiction and film,* ed. Chantal Cornut-Gentille Darcy and Jose Angel Garcia Landa. Amsterdam, The Netherlands: Rodopi.

Davidson, D. Z. 2005. "Making society 'legible': People-watching in Paris after the revolution." *French Historical Studies* 28 (2): 265–96.

Debord, Matthew. 1997. "Texture and taboo: The tyranny of texture and ease in the J. Crew catalog." *Fashion Theory* 1 (3): 261–78.

de Langlade, Jacques, ed. 2007. *Oscar Wilde, Stéphane Mallarmé, noblesse de la robe*. Paris: Les Belles Lettres.

de Lauretis, Teresa. 1987. *Technologies of gender: Essays on theory, film, and fiction*. Bloomington: Indiana University Press.

Derrida, Jacques. 1995. "Choreographies." In *Points ... Interviews 1974–1994* (orig. *Points du suspension, Entretiens*, 1992), ed. Elisabeth Weber, trans. Peggy Kamuf and others. Stanford, Calif.: Stanford University Press.

Derrida, Jacques. 2004. "Signatur ereignis kontext." In *Die différance. Ausgewählte texte*. Stuttgart: Reclam.

Desprez, E. 1832. "Les grisettes à Paris." In *Paris, ou le livre des cent-et-un*. Paris: Librairie Ladvocat.

Dictionnaire de l'Académie française. 1694. 1st edition. Available at: http://humanities.uchicago.edu/orgs/ARTFL.

Dingemans, J. 1999. *Mastering fashion styling*. London: Macmillan Press Macmillan Master Series.

Dior Ready-to-Wear Spring/Summer 2007. Available at: http://www.style.com/fashionshows/collections/S2007RTW/review/CDIOR.

Dior Haute Couture Spring/Summer 2007. Available at: http://www.style.com/fashionshows/collections/S2007CTR/review/CDIOR.

Dior Autumn/Winter 2007/8. Available at: http://www.style.com/fashionshows/collections/F2007RTW/review/CDIOR.

Dolan, T. 1981. *Gavarni and the critics*. Ann Arbor, Mich.: UMI Research Press.

Dowling, L. 1979. "The decadent and the New Woman." *Nineteenth Century Fiction* 33: 440–41.

Dowling, L. 1996. *The vulgarization of art: The Victorians and aesthetic democracy*. Charlottesville: University Press of Virginia.

Downie, Louise. 2006. *Don't kiss me—The art of Claude Cahun and Marcel Moore*. London: Tate.

Drake, A. 2006. *The beautiful fall: Fashion, genius and glorious excess in 1970s Paris*. London: Bloomsbury.

Drake, N. 1987. *The fifties in Vogue*. New York: Holt.

Duggan, G. G. 2001. "The greatest show on Earth: A look at contemporary fashion shows and their relationship to performance art." *Fashion Theory* 5 (3): 243–70.

Duggan, L. 2000. *Sapphic slashers: Sex, violence, and American modernity*. Durham, N.C.: Duke University Press.

Dyer, G. 1982. *Advertising as communication*. London: Methuen.

Dyer, Richard. 1982. "Don't look now: The male pin-up." In *Screen* (1992), *The sexual subject: A screen reader in sexuality*. London: Routledge.

Easthope, Anthony. 1992. *What a man's gotta do: The masculine myth in popular culture.* London: Routledge.

Edwards, Tim. 1997. *Men in the mirror: Men's fashion, masculinity and consumer society.* London: Continuum.

Edwards, Tim. 2006. *Cultures of masculinity,* London: Routledge.

Ehrenreich, B. 1983. *The hearts of men: American dreams and the flight from commitment.* London: Pluto Press.

Eicher, J., and L. Ling. 2006. *Mother, daughter, sister, bride: Rituals of womanhood.* Washington, D.C.: National Geographic.

Entwistle, J. 2000. *The fashioned body: Fashion, dress and modern social theory.* Cambridge, England: Polity Press.

Ette, Ottmar. 1998. *Roland Barthes: Eine intellektuelle biographie.* Frankfurt am Main: Suhrkamp.

Evans, C. 2000. "Yesterday's emblems and tomorrow's commodities." In *Fashion Culture. Theories, Explorations and Analysis,* ed. S. Bruzzi and P. Gibson, chapter 6. London: Routledge.

Evans, C. 2001. "The enchanted spectacle." *Fashion Theory* 5 (3): 271–310.

Evans, C. 2003. *Fashion at the edge.* New Haven: Yale University Press.

Exhibitions of Romantic Art. 1981 [1885]. New York: Garland.

Farwell, B. 1977. *Cult of images.* Santa Barbara: University Art Museum, University of California, Santa Barbara.

Farwell, B. 1989. *The charged image: French lithographic caricature, 1816–1848.* Santa Barbara, Calif.: Santa Barbara Museum of Art.

Farwell, B. 1994. *The image of desire: Femininity, modernity, and the birth of mass culture in 19th-century France.* Santa Barbara: University Art Museum, University of California, Santa Barbara.

Farwell, B. 1981–1998. *French popular lithographic imagery, 1815–1870.* Chicago: University of Chicago Press.

Fashioning fiction in photography since 1990 (exhibition). 2004. New York: Museum of Modern Art.

Feinstein, H. 1962. "My gorgeous darling sweetheart angels: Brigitte Bardot and Audrey Hepburn." *Film Quarterly* Special Issue on Hollywood, 15 (3): 65–68.

Feng, Peter X. 2002. "False and double consciousness: Race, virtual reality and the assimilation of Hong Kong cinema in *The Matrix.*" In *Aliens R Us: The Other in Science Fiction Cinema,* ed. Ziasuddin Sarder and Sean Cubitt. London: Pluto.

Fernbach, Amanda. 2000. "The fetishization of masculinity in science fiction: The cyborg and the console cowboy." *Science Fiction Studies* 81 (27): Available online at: http://www.depauw.edu/sfs/backissues/81/fernbach81art.htm.

Fernbach, Amanda. 2002. *Fantasies of fetishism: From decadence to the post-human.* Edinburgh: Edinburgh University Press.

Festa-McCormick, D. 1984. *Proustian optics of clothes: Mirrors, masks, mores.* Stanford French and Italian Studies, volume 29. Saratoga, Calif.: Anma Libri.

Flügel, J. C. 1930. *The psychology of clothes.* London: Hogarth Press.

Fog, Klaus, Christian Dudtz, and Baris Yakaboylu. 2005. *Storytelling: Branding in practice.* Copenhagen: Springer-Verlag.

Fortassier, Rose. 1988. *Les écrivains français et la mode. De Balzac à nos jours.* Paris: PUF/écriture.

Foster, V. 1984. *A visual history of costume: The nineteenth century.* London: Batsford.

Foucault, Michel. 2002. *Sexualitetens historia 1—Viljan att veta* (orig. *La Volonté de savoir 1976*). Göteborg, Sweden: Daidalos.

Fraser, W. H. 1981. *The coming of the mass market 1850–1914.* London: Macmillan.

Freadman, A., and A. MacDonald. 1992. *What is this thing called "genre"?: Four essays in the semiotics of genre.* Mt. Nebo, Queensland, Australia: Boombana.

Friese, S. 1997. "A consumer good in the ritual process: The case of the wedding dress." *Journal of Ritual Studies* 11 (2): 51–62.

Furbank, P. N., and Alex Cain. 2004. *Mallarmé on fashion: A translation of the fashion magazine "La Dernière Mode," with commentary.* Oxford, England: Berg.

Gaines, Jane Marie, and Charlotte Cornelia Herzog. 1998. "The fantasy of authenticity in Western Costume." In *Back in the saddle again: New essays on the Western,* ed. Edward Buscombe. London: British Film Institute.

Galliano Autumn/Winter 2007/8. Available at: http://www.style.com/fashionshows/collections/F2007RTW/review/JNGALLNO.

Garber, M. 1992. *Vested interests: Cross-dressing and cultural anxiety.* New York: Routledge.

Garland, M. 1957. *The changing face of beauty.* London: Weidenfeld and Nicolson.

Gerould, D. 1981. "Henry Monnier and the Erotikon Theatron: The pornography of realism." *Drama Review* 25 (1): 17–20.

Giddens, Anthony. 1991. *The consequences of modernity.* Cambridge, England: Polity Press.

Gilbert, W. S. (1881), *Patience.* In Reginald Allen, 1975, *The first night Gilbert and Sullivan.* London: Chappell.

Gill, Rosalind. 2003. "Power and the production of subjects: A genealogy of the New Man and the New Lad." In *Masculinity and men's magazines,* ed. Bethan Benwell. Oxford, England: Blackwell.

Gilligan, Sarah. 2009, forthcoming. "Get me an exit: Mobile phones and transforming masculinity in *The Matrix* trilogy." In *Cinema, identities and beyond,* ed. Ruby Cheung et al. Newcastle-upon-Tyne, England: Cambridge Scholars Publishing.

Ginsburg, M. 1981. *Victoria and Albert Museum: Wedding dress 1740–1970.* London: Her Majesty's Stationery Office.

Girard, René. 1966. *Deceit, desire and the novel: Self and others in literary structure.* Baltimore: John Hopkins University Press.

Gissing, G. 1894. *In the year of Jubilee.* London: Lawrence and Bullen.

Gluck, M. 2005. *Popular Bohemia: Modernism and urban culture in nineteenth-century Paris.* Cambridge, Mass.: Harvard University Press.

Goethe, Johann Wolfgang von. 1989 [1774]. *The sorrows of young Werther,* trans. Michael Hulse. London: Penguin: 134, 135.

Goethe, Johann Wolfgang von. 1994 [1786]. *Wilhelm Meister's apprenticeship,* trans. E. A. Blackall. Princeton, N.J.: Princeton University Press.

Goncourt, E., and, J. de Goncourt de. 1925. *Gavarni: L'homme et l'oeuvre.* Paris: E. Fasquelle.

Gougenheim, G. 1946. "Le féminins diminutifs en français moderne." *Modern Language Notes* 61 (6): 416–19.

Grant, L. 2004. "Clothes lines." *Vogue UK* (October): 135–36.

Gunn, Maja. 2005. *MajaGunn2005* (exhibition). Stockholm: Maja Gunn.

Gunn, Maja. 2007. *Collection L* (unpublished paper). Stockholm: Stockholm University.

Haile, E. 1879. *Three brown boys and other happy children.* New York: Cassell.

Hall, L. A. 2000. *Sex, gender and social change in Britain since 1880.* Basingstoke, Hampshire, England: Palgrave MacMillan.

Hamilton, Jean A. "The macro-micro interface in the construction of individual fashion forms and meaning." *Clothing and Textiles Research Journal* 15 (3): 165–71.

Hamilton, W. 1882. *The aesthetic movement in England.* London: Reeves and Turner.

Hamlyn, Anne. 2003. "Freud, fabric, fetish." *Textile: The Journal of Cloth and Culture* 1 (1): 9–27.

Hardwick, E. 1998. "Tru confessions." In *Sight-Readings: American Fictions,* ed. Elizabeth Hardwick. New York: Random House.

Hardy, T. 1876. *The hand of Ethelberta: A Comedy in Chapters.* 2 vols. London: Smith Elder.

Hardy, T. 1896. *Jude the obscure.* London: Osgood McIlvaine.

Harper, Sue. 1994. *Picturing the past: The rise and fall of the British costume film.* London: British Film Institute.

Harvey, J. 1995. *Men in black.* Chicago: University of Chicago Press.

Harvey, J. 2001. *Movie love in the fifties.* New York: Knopf.

Hassan, I. 1999 [1960]. "Birth of a heroine." In *The critical response to Truman Capote,* ed. Joseph J. Waldmeir and John C. Waldmeir. Westport, Conn.: Greenwood.

Haweis, M. E. 1879. *The art of dress.* London: Chatto and Windus.

Hebdige, Dick. 1989. *Subculture: The meaning of style.* London: Routledge.

Hiroshi, Minami. 1959. "Bosei kara no tōsō—Tanizaki bungaku no shinriteki haikei." In *Tanizaki Jun'ichirō,* ed. Yoshida Sei'ichi. Vol. 9 of *Kindai bungaku kanshō kōza.* Tokyo: Kodaokawa Shoten.

Hollander, A. 1978., *Seeing through clothes.* New York: Avon.

Hollander, A. 1991. "Fashion art." In *The idealizing vision: The art of fashion photography,* ed. A. Wilkes. New York: Aperture Foundation.

Hollander, A. 1993 [1978]. *Seeing through clothes.* Berkeley: University of California Press.

Hollander, A. 2002. *The fabric of vision.* London: National Gallery: 128.

Horne, Peter, and Raina Lewis. 1996. *Outlooks—Lesbian and gays: Sexualities and visual cultures.* London: Routledge.

Horyn, C. 2007. "Does the shoe fit?" *New York Times* (February 25). Available at: http://www.nytimes.com/2007/02/25/style/tmagazine/25tshoe.html. Accessed March 1, 2007.

Howells, W. D. 1882. *A woman's reason.* Boston: Houghton Mifflin.

Huart, L. 1979 [1841]. *Physiologie de la grisette, vignettes de Gavarni.* Reprint edition. Geneva: Slatkine Reprints.

Hughes, A., and Al Nobel, eds. 2003. *Phototextualities: Intersections of photography and narrative.* Albuquerque: University of New Mexico Press.

Hughes, Clair. 2005. *Dressed in fiction,* London: Berg.

Hughes, George. 2002. *Reading novels.* Nashville, Tenn.: Vanderbilt University Press.

Ichiyō, Higuchi. 1992. "Child's play." In *In the shade of spring leaves: The life of Higuchi Ichiyō, with nine of her best short stories,* ed. Robert Lyons Danly. New York: Norton.

Ingraham, C. 1999. *White weddings: Romancing heterosexuality in popular culture.* New York: Routledge.

Isherwood, C. 2003 [1939]. *Goodbye to Berlin.* London: Vintage.

Israel, B. 2002. *Bachelor girl: The secret history of single women in the twentieth century.* New York: William Morrow.

Jacobs, Jane. 2003. Introduction to Mark Twain, *The Innocents Abroad.* New York: Modern Library.

James, H. 1908. *Portrait of a lady.* New York: Charles Scribner's Sons. Reprinted in 1970.

James, H. 1909. *The ambassadors.* New York: Charles Scribner's Sons. Reprinted by Augustus M. Kelley in 1971.

James, H. 1984. *Literary criticism.* 2 vols. New York: Library of America.

Janin, J. 1862 [1840]. "La Grisette." In *Les français peints par eux-mêmes: Encyclopédie morale du dix-neuvième siècle,* vol. 5. Paris: L. Curmer.

Jansen, Marius B. 2002. *The making of modern Japan.* Cambridge, Mass.: Harvard University Press.

Jencks, C. 1973. *Modern movements in architecture.* London: Penguin.

Johnson, E. Patrick, and Mae G. Henderson. 2005. *Black queer studies.* Durham, N.C.: Duke University Press.

Johnson, J. 1983. *Minor characters.* London: Picador.

Jones, Ann Rosalind, and Peter Stallybrass. 2000. *Renaissance clothing and the materials of memory.* Cambridge, England: Cambridge University Press.

Jones, J. 1996. "*Coquettes* and *grisettes:* Women buying and selling in ancien régime Paris." In *The Sex of things: Gender and consumption in historical perspective,* ed. Victoria de Grazia with Ellen Furlough, 25–53. Berkeley: University of California Press.

Jones, J. 2004. *Sexing "La Mode": Gender, fashion, and commercial culture in old regime France,* Oxford: Berg.

Kafū, Nagai. 2001 [1908]. "Fukagawa no uta" (A song of Fukagawa). In *Meiji no bungaku (Meiji literature).* Vol. 25. *Nagai Kafū and tanizaki Jun'chirō.* Tokyo: Chikuma Shobō.

Kafū, Nagai. 1994. *During the rains and Flowers in the shade: Two novellas,* trans. Lane Dunlop. Stanford, Calif.: Stanford University Press.

Kaplan, J. H., and S. Stowell. 1994. *Theatre and fashion: Oscar Wilde to the suffragettes.* Cambridge, England: Cambridge University Press.

Karalis, Vrasidas. 2008. *Recollections of Mr. Manoly Lascaris.* Blackheath: Brandl & Schlesinger.

Karaminas, Vicki. 2005. "No capes! Über fashion and how luck favours the prepared. Constructing contemporary superhero identities in American popular culture." Research paper presented at the Imaginary Worlds Image and Space International Symposium (University of Technology, Sydney). October 14, 2005. Paper available online at: http://mams.rmit.edu.au/y5ulbhd5fr4z.pdf.

Karimzadeh, M., and M. Socha. 2006. "System analysis." *WWD The Magazine* (Spring): 106–9.

Karney, R. 1993. *A star danced: The life of Audrey Hepburn.* London: Bloomsbury.

Khan, N. 2000. "Catwalk politics." In *Fashion culture. theories, explorations and analysis,* ed. S. Bruzzi and P. Gibson, chapter 7. London: Routledge.

Kift, D. 1996. *The Victorian music hall: Culture, class and conflict.* Cambridge, England: Cambridge University Press.

Kismaric, S., and E. Respini, eds. 2004. *Fashioning fiction in photography since 1990* [exhibition catalog]. New York: Museum of Modern Art.

Kolesch, Doris. 1997. *Roland Barthes.* Frankfurt am Main: Campus.

Kopytoff, I. 1986. "The cultural biology of things: Commoditization as process." In *The social life of things: Commodities in cultural perspective,* ed. A. Appadurai. Cambridge, England: Cambridge University Press.

Kosinski, D. 1988. "Gustave Courbet's *The Sleepers:* The lesbian image in nineteenth-century French art and literature." *Artibus et Historiae* 18: 187–99.

Kramer, P. 2004. "The many faces of Holly Golightly: Truman Capote, *Breakfast at Tiffany's* and Hollywood." *Film Studies: An International Review* 5: 58–64.

Kuhn, Cynthia, and Cindy Carlson, eds. 2007. *Styling texts. Dress and fashion in literature.* Youngstown, N.Y.: Cambria Press.

Lansdell, A. 1983. *Wedding fashions 1860–1980.* Aylesbury, Bucks, England: Shire.

Laver, James. 1952. *Costume and fashion.* London: Thames and Hudson.

Lee, V. 1884. *Miss Brown.* Edinburgh: William Blackwood and Sons.

Le Guen, M. 1997. "Une acquisition du musée de la vie romantique de Paris: *La porte fermée* (1855) par Octave Tassaert." *Revue du Louvre* 1: 59–63.

Le Guen, M. 1998. "Octave Tassaert (1800–1874), peintre des larmes et de la bonne fortune." *Bulletin de la Société de l'Histoire de l'Art Français:* 273–86.

Le Guen, M. 2000. "Un nouveau regard sur les dessins d'Octave Tassaert (1800–1874), du Musée Léon Bonnat à Bayonne." *Revue du Louvre* 2: 77–84.

Lehmann, U. 2000. *Tigersprung: Fashion in modernity.* Cambridge, Mass.: MIT Press.

Leitch, Vincent. 1996. "Costly compensations: Postmodern fashion, politics, identity." *Modern Fiction Studies* 42 (1): 111–28.

Lemoisne, P.-A., 1924. *Gavarni: Peintre et lithographe.* Paris: H. Floury.

Lemon, A. 1987. Introduction to R. Clark. *Hatches, matches and dispatches: Christening, bridal and mourning fashions.* Melbourne, Australia: National Gallery of Victoria.

Leribault, C. 2002. *Jean-François de Troy, 1679–1752.* Paris: Arthena.

Lewis, Reina, and Katrina Rolley. 1996. "Ad(dressing) the dyke: Lesbian looks and lesbians looking." In *Outlooks: Lesbian and gay sexualities and visual cultures,* ed. Peter Horne and Reina Lewis, 178–90. New York: Routledge.

Liebowitz, A. 2007. "The big shoot." *Vanity Fair* (March): 150, 165, 168.

Lindsay, Greg. 2003. "Death of A&F's Quarterly: Problem wasn't sex but brand's loss of cool." *Women's Wear Daily* (December 11): 1–3.

Lipovetsky, G. 1994 [1987]. *The empire of fashion: Dressing modern democracy,* trans. Catherine Porter. Princeton, N.J.: Princeton University Press.

Lipovetsky, G. 2002. "More than fashion." In *Chic clicks: Creativity and commerce in contemporary fashion photography.* Institute of Contemporary Art Boston in association with Hatje Cantz. New York: Distributed Art Publishers.

Lurie, A. 1981. *The Language of clothes.* London: Bloomsbury.

Mackinnon, Kenneth. 1997. *Uneasy pleasures: The male as erotic object.* Lond, N.J.: Cyrus Arts and Fairleigh Dickinson University Press.

Mag Lochlainn, P. A. n.d. *Dealing with difference—sexuality.* Available at: http://www.bbc.co.uk/northernireland/learning/eyewitness/difference/sexuality/maglochlainn.shtml.

Mahérault, M.J.F. 2004. *Gavarni: Catalogue raisonné of the graphic work.* San Francisco: Alan Wolfsy Fine Art.

Mahuzier, B. 1999. "Unbuttoning Proust." *Modern Language Studies* 29 (1): 49–59.

Marash, J. G. (1951). *Henry Monnier: Chronicler of the bourgeoisie.* London: Harrap.

Marie, A. 1931. *Henry Monnier 1799–1877.* Paris: Floury.

Marsh, A. 2003. *The darkroom: Photography and the theatre of desire.* South Yarra, Victoria: Macmillan.

Matthews, A. V. 1999. "Aestheticism's true colours: The politics of pigment in Victorian art, criticism and fashion." In *Women and British aestheticism,* ed. T. Schaffer and K. A. Psomiades. London: University of Virginia Press.

Maynard, P. 1997. *The Engine of visualization: Thinking through photography.* Ithaca, N.Y.: Cornell University Press.

McBride, Dwight. 2005. *Why I hate Abercrombie & Fitch.* New York: New York University Press.

McCollum, A., and A. Zittel. 2002. "Talking with Allan McCollum." In *Andrea Zittel: Diary #01,* ed. S. Vendrame. Milan: Tema Celeste Editions.

McCracken, E. 1993. *Decoding women's magazines: From Mademoiselle to Ms.* New York: St. Martin's Press.

McDowell, C. 1997. *Galliano.* Great Britain: Weidenfeld and Nicholson.

McKenzie, J. 1998. *The best in bridalwear design.* London: B. T. Batsford.

Melcher, E. 1950. *The life and times of Henry Monnier, 1799–1877.* Cambridge, Mass.: Harvard University Press.

Mendelsohn, Daniel. 2006. "Lost in Versailles." *New York Review of Books* 53 (19) (November 30): 22.

Mercier, L. S. 1994 [1782]. *Tableau de Paris.* Reprint edition. Paris: Mercure de France.

Meyer, Katrin. 1998. *Ästhetik der historie. Friedrich Nietzsche, Vom Nutzen und Nachteil der historie für das leben.* Würzburg: Königshausen und Neumann.

Miller, N. 2005. *Out of the past: Gay and lesbian history from 1869 to the present.* New York: Alyson.

Mirecourt, E. de. 1857. *Henry Monnier.* Paris: G. Harvard.

Mitchell, W.T.J. 1994. *Picture theory: Essays on verbal and visual representation.* Chicago: University of Chicago Press.

Miyoko, Tanaka. 1977. "Kami ni natta onna." *Umi* 9 (7): 214–31.

Mizejewski, L. 1992. *Divine decadence: Fascism, female spectacle, and the makings of Sally Bowles.* Princeton, N.J.: Princeton University Press.

Moers, Ellen. 1960. *The dandy.* London: Secker and Warburg.

Moretti, Franco. 2000 [1987]. *The way of the world.* London: Verso: vii.

Morrison, A. 1894. *Tales of mean streets: Lizerunt, Squire Napper, Without Visible Means, Three Rounds and Others.* London: Methuen.

Morsiani, P., and T. Smith, eds. 2005. *Andrea Zittel: Critical space* (exhibition catalogue). New York: Prestel Verlag.

Mortimer, Armine Kotin. 1989. *The gentlest law: Roland Barthes's "The Pleasure of the Text,"* New York: Lang.

Moseley, R. 2002. *Growing up with Audrey Hepburn,* Manchester, England: Manchester University Press.

Mulvey, Laura. 1975. "Visual pleasure and narrative cinema." Reprinted in Sue Thornham. 1999. *Feminist film theory: A reader.* Edinburgh: Edinburgh University Press.

Mulvey, Laura. 1981. "Visual pleasure and narrative cinema." In *Popular Television and Film,* ed. T. Bennett, S. Boyd-Bowman, C. Mercer, and J. Woollacott. London: British Film Institute.

Neale, Steve. 1983. "Masculinity as spectacle." In *Screen.* 1992. *The sexual subject: A Screen reader in sexuality.* London: Routledge.

Nietzsche, Friedrich. 1988. *Unzeitgemäße Betrachtungen,* Zweites Stück: "Vom Nutzen und Nachtheil der Historie für das Leben." In *Kritische Studienausgabe Bd. I* (KSA I), ed. G. Colli and M.:Montinari. München: dtv and de Gruyter.

Nietzsche, Friedrich. 1995. "On the utility and liability of history for life," Second Piece. In *Unfashionable observations,* trans. R. Gray. Stanford, Calif.: Stanford University Press.

Nietzsche, Friedrich. 2003. *Sämtliche Briefe.* In *Kritische Studienausgabe Bd. 4* (KSA IV), ed. G. Colli and M. Montinari. München: dtv and de Gruyter.

Nixon, Sean. 1996. *Hard look—Masculinities, spectatorship and contemporary consumption.* New York: Palgrave Macmillan.

North, M. 2005. *Camera works: Photography and the twentieth-century word.* New York: Oxford University Press.

Oliphant, M.O.W. 1866. *Miss Marjoribanks.* Edinburgh: W. Blackwood. Reprinted by Garland, 1976.

Ouida. 1883. "Afternoon." In *Frescoes and other stories.* Leipzig: Bernard Tauchnitz.

Paisley, I.R.K. 2001. "More sex we are liberal minded." *European Institute of Protestant Studies* 7 (October). Available at: www.ianpaisley.org/article.asp?ArtKey= sexmad.

Palmer, J. 1991. *Potboilers: Methods, concepts and case studies in popular fiction.* London: Routledge.

Pillement, G. 1974. "Decouvrons le xixe siècle: Les vrais précurseurs de l'impressionisme." *Galerie-jardin des arts* 136: 56–59.

Praz, Mario. 1969. *The hero in eclipse.* Oxford, England: Oxford University Press.

Probert, C. 1984. *Brides in Vogue since 1910.* London: Thames and Hudson.

Prost, B. 1886. *Octave Tassaert: Notice sur la vie et catalogue de son œuvre.* Paris: L. Baschet.

Proust, M. 1999. *À la recherche du temps perdu. (Texte établi sous la direction de Jean-Yves Tadié).* Ringwood, Victoria: Éditions Gallimard Quarto. All translations from this volume in the text of chapter 4 are by Sophia Errey, 2007.

Pugh, T. 2002. "Capote's Breakfast at Tiffany's." *The Explicator* 61 (1): 51–54.

Radnor, H. 1995. *Shopping around: Feminine culture and the pursuit of pleasure.* New York: Routledge.

Razek, Rula. 1999. *Dress codes: Reading nineteenth-century fashion.* Stanford, Calif.: Stanford University Press.

Réage, Pauline. 1966. Preface to Jean de Berg, *The Image,* trans. Patsy Southgate. New York: Grove Press.

Reckermann, Alfons. 2003. *Lesarten der philosophie Nietzsches.* Berlin: de Gruyter.

Reines, Dan. 2003. "All the nudes that's fit to print." Available at: http://www.nerve.com. Accessed May 26, 2006.

Relihan, C. C., and G. V. Stanivukovic, eds. 2003. *Prose fiction and early modern sexualities in England, 1570–1640.* Basingstoke, Hampshire, England: Palgrave.

Reynolds, Richard. 1994. *Superheroes: A modern mythology.* Jackson: University Press of Mississippi.

Ribeiro, Aileen. 2005. *Fashion and fiction: Dress in art and literature in Stuart England.* New Haven: Yale University Press.

Richard, Jean-Pierre. 1954. *Littérature et sensation: Stendhal et Flaubert.* Paris: Editions du Seuil.

Richardson, B. 2000. "Recent concepts of narrative and narratives of narrative theory." *Style* 34: 168–75.

Roberts, M. L. 1994. *Civilization without sexes: Reconstructing gender in postwar France, 1917–1927.* Chicago: University of Chicago Press.

Robbins, M. 2000. "Mighty real." In *Against design* (exhibition catalogue). Philadelphia: Institute of Contemporary Art, University of Pennsylvania.

Rolley, K. 1996. *The lesbian dandy: The role of dress and appearance in the formation of lesbian identities.* London: Cassell.

Ross, N. 1982. *Manet's "Bar at the Folies-Bergère" and the myths of popular illustration.* Ann Arbor: UMI Research Press.

Rust, P. C. 1993. "'Coming out' in the age of social constructionism: Sexual identity formation among lesbian and bisexual women." *Gender and Society* 7 (1): 50–77.

Rutherford, Jonathan 2003. Preface to Bethan Benwell, ed. *Masculinity and men's magazines.* Oxford: Blackwell.

Rutsky, R. L. 2001. "Being Keanu." In *The end of cinema as we know it: American film in the nineties,* ed. Jon Lewis. 185–94. London: Pluto Press.

Saltz, J. 1994. "Review of Purity Exhibition at Andrea Rosen gallery." *Art in America* 82: 100–101.

Salaquarda, Jörg. 1984. "Studien zur zweiten Unzeitgemässen Betrachtung." In *Grundfragen der Nietzscheforschung,* ed. M. Montinari and B. Hillebrand. Berlin: de Gruyter.

Sanders, J., ed. 1996. *Stud: Architectures of masculinity.* New York: Princeton Architectural Press.

Schaffer, T. 2000. *The forgotten Aesthetes: Literary culture in late-Victorian England.* Charlottesville: University Press of Virginia.

Schaffer, T., and K. A. Psomiades, eds. 1999. *Women and British Aestheticism.* Charlottesville: University Press of Virginia.

Schumacher, R. 2003. "How do I get inside a Trojan horse?" In *Andrea Zittel,* ed. R. Schumacher. Munchen: Ingvild Goetz and Rainald Schumacher.

Scott, C. 1999. *The spoken image: Photography and language.* London: Reaktion.

Sedgwick, Eve Kosofsky. 1985. *Between men: English literature and male homosexual desire.* New York: Columbia University Press.

Seidensticker, Edward. 1991. *Tokyo rising: The city since the Great Earthquake.* Cambridge, Mass.: Harvard University Press.

Seigel, J. 1986. *Bohemian Paris: Culture, politics, and the boundaries of bourgeois life, 1830–1930.* New York: Penguin.

Shaviro, Steven. 1993. *The cinematic body: Theory out of bounds.* Minneapolis: University of Minnesota Press.

Shaw, G. 1992. "The economic and social context of retail revolution." In *The Evolution of Retail Systems 1800–1914,* ed. J. Benson and G. Shaw. London: Leicester University Press.

Sheon, A. 1981. "Octave Tassaert's *Le suicide:* Early Realism and the plight of women." *Arts Magazine* 55 (9): 142–51.

Sheon, A. 1984. "Parisian social statistics: Gavarni, *Le diable à Paris,* and early Realism." *Art Journal* 44 (2): 139–48.

Shōgo, Nomura. 1974. *Denki—Tanizaki Jun'ichirō.* Tokyo: Rokkō Shuppan.

Simmel, Georg. 1957 [1904]. "Fashion." *American Journal of Sociology* 62 (6): 541–58.

Simpson, Mark. 1994a. *Male impersonators: Gay men performing masculinity.* London: Routledge.

Simpson, Mark. 1994b. "Here come the mirror men." *The Independent* (November 15). Available online at: http://www.marksimpson.com/pages/journalism/mirror_men.html.

60 Minutes. 2003. "The look of Abercrombie & Fitch." *CBS News.* Available at: http://www.cbsnews.com/stories/2003/12/05/60minutes/main58799.shtml.

Slade, Toby. 2006. "Clothing Modern Japan." PhD thesis, University of Sydney, unpublished.

Smith, D. 2002. "Global Cinderella: Sabrina (1954), Hollywood and postwar internationalism." *Cinema Journal* 41 (4): 27–51.

Smith, T. 2005. "The rules of her game: A–Z at work and play." In *Andrea Zittel: Critical Space,* ed. P. Morsiani and T. Smith. New York: Prestel Verlag.

Springer, Claudia. 2005. "Playing it cool in The Matrix." In *The Matrix Trilogy: Cyberpunk Reloaded,* ed. Stacy Gillis. London: Wallflower.

Stacey, Jackie. 1994. *Stargazing: Hollywood cinema and female spectatorship.* London: Routledge.

Stafford, Andy, and Michael Carter, eds. 2006. *The Language of Fashion,* trans. A. Stafford. Power Publications/Berg.

Stam, R. 2004. "Introduction: The theory and practice of adaptation." In *Literature and film: A guide to the theory and practice of adaptation,* ed. A. Raengo and R. Stam. Malden, Mass.: Blackwell.

Steele, V. 1988. "The working woman as artist, aristocrat, and erotic fantasy." In *Paris fashion: A cultural history.* New York: Oxford University Press.

Steele, V. 1996. *Fetish: Fashion, sex and power.* Oxford, England: Oxford University Press.

Steele, V. 2006. *Paris fashion: A cultural history.* 2nd ed. Oxford, England: Berg.

Steinem, G. 1987. "A visit with Truman Capote." *Glamour* (April 1966). Reprinted in *Truman Capote conversations,* ed. M. Thomas Inge, 73–81. Jackson: University Press of Mississippi.

Stendhal. 1991 [1830]. *The red and the black,* trans. Catherine Slater. London: Penguin.

Stewart, D. 2007. "Incurably romantic." *Smithsonian* 37 (11): 86–94.

Stonewall. *Timeline of gay and lesbian history.* Available at: http://www.stonewall. org.uk/information_bank/history__lesbian__gay/89.asp. Accessed May 13, 2007.

Street, Sarah. 2001. *Costume and cinema: Dress codes in popular film.* London: Wallflower.

Structure 2000. *Back-to-school actual.* Columbus, Ohio: The Limited Corporation.

Sullivan, C. A. 2003. "Classification, containment, contamination, and the courtesan: The *grisette, lorette,* and *demi-mondaine* in nineteenth-century French fiction." Ph.D. dissertation, University of Texas at Austin.

Sylvia. 1876. *How to dress well on a shilling a day; a ladies' guide to home dressmaking and millinery.* London: Ward Lock.

Takehiko, Noguchi. 1963. *Tanizaki Jun'ichirō ron.* Tokyo: Chūō Kōronsha.

Tanizaki, Jun'ichirō. 1996 [1910]. "Shisei" (The tattooer). In *Seven Japanese Tales.* London: Vintage.

Tanizaki, Jun'ichirō. 1934. *The collected works.* Tokyo: Chuokoron-Sha.

Tanizaki, Jun'ichirō. 1977. *In praise of shadows,* trans. Thomas J. Harper and Edward G. Seidensticker. New Haven: Leete's Island Books.

Tanizaki, Jun'ichirō. 1985. *Naomi,* trans. Anthony H. Chambers. Boston: Tuttle.

Tasker, Yvvone. 1993. *Spectacular bodies: Gender, genre and action cinema.* London: Routledge.

Taylor, Charles. 1999. "Something in the way he moves: In defense of Keanu Reeves." Salon.com (April 29). Available at: www.salon.com/ent/movies/feature/ 1999/04/29/keanu/index.html.

Taylor, F. W. 1947. *The principles of scientific management.* New York: Norton.

Taylor, L. 2002. *The study of dress history.* Manchester, England: Manchester University Press.

Thackeray, William. 1999 [1850]. *Pendennis.* Oxford, England: World Classics.

Thackeray, William. n.d. [1860]. "Men & jackets." In *The Complete Works,* vol. 13. Oxford, England: Oxford University Press.

Thackeray, William. n.d. [1860]. *Roundabout papers.* In *The Complete Works.* Oxford, England: Oxford University Press.

Troy, N. J. 2003. *Couture culture. A study in modern art and fashion.* Cambridge, Mass.: MIT Press.

Van Leeuwen, T. 1983. "Roland Barthes' système de la mode." *Australian Journal of Cultural Studies* 1 (1): 18–35.

Venohr, Dagmar. 2002. "Die vestimentäre Metapher in Nietzsches 'Unzeitgemäße Betrachtungen II.'" Eine semiologische Analyse. Unpublished thesis, University of Hildesheim, Germany.

Vogue International. 1987 (January). Available at: http://www.vogue.co.uk/magazine/issue.aspx/Front-Cover/Year,1987/Month,January. Accessed May 22, 2007.

Walker, L. 2000. "Feminists in brideland." *Tulsa Studies in Women's Literature* 19 (2): 219–30.

Walker, L. 2001. *Looking like what you are: Sexual style, race and lesbian identity.* New York: New York University Press.

Warhol, A. 1975. *The philosophy of Andy Warhol (A–B and back again).* New York: Harcourt Brace Jovanovich.

Watson, J. 1999. *Literature and material culture from Balzac to Proust: The collection and consumption of curiosities,* Cambridge, England: Cambridge University Press Studies in French.

Weil, B. 1994. "Home is where the art is." *Art-Monthly* 181: 20–22.

Wilde, O. 2007 [1891]. *The picture of Dorian Gray.* New York: Norton.

Williamson, Judith. 2002. *Decoding advertisements: Ideology and meaning in advertising.* New York: Marion Boyars.

Wilson, E. 1928. "A short view of Proust." *New Republic* (March 21). Available at: http://www.readingproust.com/. Accessed April 17, 2007.

Wilson, E. 1993. "Audrey Hepburn: Fashion, film and the 50s." In *Women and film: A sight and sound reader,* ed. P. Cook and P. Dodds. London: Scarlet Press.

Wilson, Elizabeth. 2005a. *Adorned in dreams: Fashion and modernity.* 2nd edition. London: I. B. Tauris.

Wilson, Elizabeth. 2005b. "Fashion and modernity." In *Fashion and Modernity,* ed. Christopher Breward and Caroline Evans. Oxford: Berg.

Winge, T. M., and J. Eicher. 2003. "The American groom wore a Celtic kilt: Theme weddings as carnivalesque events." In *Wedding dress across cultures,* ed. H. Bradley Foster and D. Clay Johnson. Oxford, England: Berg.

Wittgenstein, Ludwig. 1963. *Tractatus logico-philosophicus.* Frankfurt am Main, Germany: Suhrkamp.

Wolf, N. 1994. "Brideland." In *To be real: Telling the truth and the changing face of feminism,* ed. R. Walker. New York: Anchor Books.

Wronsov a.k.a. von Busch, O. 2005. Textile Punctum. http://www.kulturservern.se/wronsov/selfpassage/textilePunctum/textPunctum.pdf.

Yasunari, Kawabata. 2005. *Asakusa kurenaidan (The Scarlet Gang of Asakusa),* trans. Alisa Freedman. Berkeley: University of California Press.

Yonge, C. M. 1879. *Magnum bonum or Mother Carey's brood.* London: MacMillan. Reprinted by Garland, 1976.

Young, A. 1999. *Culture, class and gender in the Victorian novel: Gentlemen, gents and working women.* London: St. Martin's Press.

Zelevansky, L. 1994. *Sense and sensibility: Women artists and Minimalism in the nineties* (exhibition catalogue). New York: Museum of Modern Art.

Zittel, A. 2002. "Diary: June 14–September 6, 2001." In *Andrea Zittel: Diary #01,* ed. S. Vendrame. Milan: Tema Celeste Editions.

Zittel, A. 2005. "Things I know for sure." In *Andrea Zittel: Critical Space,* ed. P. Morsiani and T. Smith. New York: Prestel Verlag.

Zittel, A. *Andrea Zittel's A-Z Smockshop.* http://www.zittel.org.

Film

Reeder, R., dir./prod. Galliano Autumn/Winter 1994/5 collection. *VideoFashion* 19, episode 5. New York.

Index